Psyche and the Arts

Psyche and the Arts challenges existing ideas about the relationship between Jung and art, and offers exciting new dimensions to key issues such as the role of image in popular culture, and the division of psyche and matter in art form.

Divided into three sections – getting into art, challenging the critical space and interpreting art in the world – the text shows how Jungian ideas can work with the arts to illuminate both psychological theory and aesthetic response. *Psyche and the Arts* offers new critical visions of literature, film, music, architecture and painting, as something alive in the experience of creators and audiences challenging previous Jungian criticism. This approach demonstrates Jung's own belief that art is a healing response to collective cultural norms.

This diverse yet focused collection from international contributors invites the reader to seek personal and cultural value in the arts, and will be essential reading for Jungian analysts, trainees and those more generally interested in the arts.

Susan Rowland is a Reader in English and Jungian Studies at the University of Greenwich, UK. She has published books on Jung, Literature and Gender including *Jung as a Writer* (Routledge 2005). She was chair of the International Association for Jungian Studies from 2003 to 2006.

Psyche and the Arts

Jungian approaches to music, architecture, literature, film and painting

Edited by Susan Rowland

Routledge
Taylor & Francis Group

LONDON AND NEW YORK

First published 2008 by Routledge
2 Park Square, Milton Park, Abingdon, Oxon OX14 4RN

Simultaneously published in the USA and Canada
by Routledge
711 Third Avenue, New York, NY 10017, USA

*Routledge is an imprint of the Taylor & Francis Group,
an informa business*

Typeset in Times by RefineCatch Limited, Bungay, Suffolk

Paperback cover design by Sandra Heath

British Library Cataloguing in Publication Data
A catalogue record for this book is available from the British Library

Library of Congress Cataloging-in-Publication Data
Psyche and the arts : Jungian approaches to music, architecture,
literature, film, and painting / edited by Susan Rowland.
       p. cm.
    Includes bibliographical references and index.
ISBN 978-0-415-43835-3 (hardback) – ISBN 978-0-415-43836-0
(pbk) 1. Psychoanalysis and the arts. 2. Arts – Psychology. 3. Jungian
psychology. I. Rowland, Susan, 1962–
    NX180.P7P79 2008
    700.1′9 – dc22   2007041762

ISBN: 978-0-415-43835-3 (hbk)
ISBN: 978-0-415-43836-0 (pbk)

For Edmund Cusick, poet
(1962–2007)

You, who knit the underworld to the overworld
With your shaman words.

Contents

Contributors

Byron Almén is Assistant Professor of Music Theory at the University of Texas at Austin. He has published several articles that explore the relationship between music and Jungian thought.

Paul Bishop is Professor of German at the University of Glasgow, where he teaches German language, German literature and comparative literature. He edited *Jung in Contexts: A Reader* (1999), and he is the author of various books on Jung and Jung-related themes, including *Jung's 'Answer to Job': A Commentary* (2002) and *Analytical Psychology and German Classical Aesthetics: Goethe, Schiller, and Jung* (2007).

Angela Connolly is a psychiatrist and Jungian analyst of the Centro Italiana di Psicologia Analitica, where she is a faculty member, training analyst and member of the training commission. She is the deputy editor (Europe) of the *Journal of Analytical Psychology*. She has published in Italian and English on gender, on bilingualism in analysis, on Jungian film studies and on her analytical work in Russia.

Edmund Cusick was a poet and Head of the Writing Department at Liverpool John Moores University. *Ice Maidens* was his second collection and it contains the poem that won the Keats–Shelley Memorial Prize, 2005. Edmund died in January 2007 aged 44 years.

Terence Dawson is an Associate Professor of English Literature at NTU, Singapore. He is the author of *The Effective Protagonist in the Nineteenth-Century British Novel: Scott, Brontë, Eliot, Wilde* (2004), and co-editor, with Polly Young-Eisendrath, of *The Cambridge Companion to Jung* (1997; 2nd edn. 2008) and, with Robert S. Dupree, of *Seventeenth-Century English Poetry: The Annotated Anthology* (1994).

Don Fredericksen is Director of Undergraduate Studies in Film at Cornell University and a Jungian psychotherapist. Recent publications include *Bergman's Persona* (2005).

Leslie Gardner is a literary agent, and also a doctoral candidate at the Centre for Psychoanalytic Studies, University of Essex, doing work on Jung and Vico's rhetoric.

Elenice Giosa is a teacher of English as a foreign language and a doctoral student in the Psychology Institute together with the Education Faculty of the Universidade de São Paulo, Brazil. Her research is centred on the Education of Sensibility.

Lucy Huskinson is Lecturer in Philosophy of Religion at the University of Wales, Bangor, and Visiting Fellow at the Centre for Comparative Literature and Cultural Studies, Monash University, Australia, and the Centre for Psychoanalytic Studies, University of Essex, UK. She is author of *Nietzsche and Jung: The Whole Self in the Union of Opposites*, and editor of *Dreaming the Myth Onwards: New Directions in Jungian Therapy and Thought*.

Inez Martinez is Professor Emerita of English and writes psychological literary criticism. She has published work on the value of Jungian concepts in revealing unconscious dimensions of literary texts.

David Parker is a painter with a special interest in art, psychology and psychotherapy. He is senior lecturer in fine art at the University of Northampton.

Claudio Paixao Anastacio De Paula is a clinical psychologist. He lives in Belo Horizonte, Minas Gerais, Brazil, where he shares his time between private practice as a psychotherapist of Jungian orientation, supervision of psychotherapists, work as a Professor of the Psychology course and Masters Programme at Faculty FEAD, and playing with his two children.

Bettina Reiber recently completed an MA in Art Theory and Aesthetics at Middlesex University. She has given conference papers on art, art theory and aesthetics. She works as an Associate Lecturer in Fine Art at Central St. Martins College of Art and Design, University of the Arts London, and as a practising artist and curator.

Lee Robbins is on the faculty of the Gallatin School at New York University where she teaches interdisciplinary courses in the history of depth psychology. She is working on a book contrasting Jung's 'Self' with the Buddhist notion of no-self.

Susan Rowland is Reader in English and Jungian Studies at the University of Greenwich, UK. She publishes on Jung, literature and gender and her books include, *Jung: A Feminist Revision* and *Jung as a Writer*. She was Chair of the International Association for Jungian Studies 2003–6. She has also published articles and a book on detective fiction.

Craig Stephenson is in private practice as a psychologist in Paris, France. He lectures for the Independent Group of Analytical Psychologists (IGAP, London) and the International School for Analytical Psychology (ISAP, Zürich). He translated Luigi Aurigemma's *Perspectives Jungiennes* from the French for the University of Scranton Press.

Lena Vasileva is currently a sessional lecturer, teaching Literature and Film Studies at further education institutions. She wrote her PhD at Kingston University, London on the influence of the Gothic Tradition on John Fowles's writing, and her current research is focused on Hollywood horror movies and chthonic archetypes in arts, film and literature.

Acknowledgements

Psyche and the Arts is one of several volumes marking a new departure in Jungian scholarship. It emerges from the unique collaboration of scholars, some of whom are Jungian analysts, some of whom are academics, or clinicians or students or artists, brought together by the formation of the International Association of Jungian Studies (IAJS) in 2003. The first independent conference of the IAJS, 'Psyche and Imagination', was held at Greenwich University, Greenwich, London in July 2006. As well as including poetry reading, the world premiere of the English version of *An Oedipus* by Armando Nascimento Rosa, and a major arts exhibition, the conference produced the remarkable essays of this volume and its companion collection, *Dreaming the Myth Onward*, edited by Lucy Huskinson. First of all, I would like to pay tribute to everyone who took part in the 'Psyche and Imagination' conference, with an especial thank you to Leslie Gardner who made the financial organisation possible, and to those of us who danced late into a warm starry night beside the river.

I would also like to acknowledge the immense imaginative and practical effort that went into the formation of IAJS, making the conference and this book possible. For all of those who were the first Executive Committee of 2003–6 (when I was Chair), thank you to: Kristine Connidis (Canada), Terence Dawson (Singapore), Don Fredericksen (USA), Leslie Gardner (UK), Ien Hazebroek-Buijs (The Netherlands), Luke Hockley (UK), Lucy Huskinson (UK), Raya Jones (UK), Alberto Lima (Brazil), Renos Papadopoulos (UK), J. Craig Peery (USA), David Rosen (USA), Lee Robbins (USA), Andrew Samuels (UK), Nick Stratton (UK), David Tacey (Australia).

We thank Al Ruban, Faces Distribution Corporation, for permission to reproduce two photographs from John Cassavetes' film, *Opening Night*.

Of course it is the contributors, with their splendid originality, who make this book. I end with a special mention of the poet Edmund Cusick, who died suddenly during the preparation. Few who heard him will forget his performance of his poetry of spirit and soul at 'Psyche and Imagination'. Here his paper begins a journey into art and psyche. He reminds us of the privilege of having such friends.

Introduction

Susan Rowland

BEGINNINGS

This book began at a conference by the River Thames in London, July 2006. In the hot summer air and green trees of the Old Royal Naval College in Greenwich, 'Psyche and Imagination' was held in conjunction with the University of Greenwich, and was the first independent conference of the International Association of Jungian Studies (www.jungianstudies.org). A ground-breaking venture of Jungian scholarship, the conference sought to expand the definition of academic endeavour by including at its heart, poetry readings, a visual arts exhibition and drama, in the marvellous shapes of the world premiere of the English version of Armando Nascimento Rosa's play, *An Oedipus* (2006).

By making the cultural division between aesthetic theory and practice liminal, the conference re-positioned Jungian ideas in relation to art, creativity and criticism. Two volumes of richly creative essays have emerged from this dynamic conjunction of international research, arts practice and alchemical refining of the soul. *Dreaming the Myth Onwards* (2008), edited by Lucy Huskinson, takes the potent Jungian treatment of myth into the twenty-first century. This book, *Psyche and the Arts*, explores the transforming energies of the Jungian psyche on the creative works of the cultural imagination. In architecture, film, music, literature and educational performing, these essays trace the intimate psychic interiority of art and offer a re-envisioning of theory and practice. In so doing, *Psyche and the Arts* offers a renewed and numinous space for the making, appreciation, and criticism of art in our time. So first of all, it is useful to begin by understanding Jung's own approach.

INTRODUCING JUNG AND ART

There is a certain 'doubleness' to C.G. Jung's approach to the psyche that is uniquely valuable in comparison to other theories that subsume art into their own categories. Jung says that 'his' psychology cannot replace the separate and valuable discipline of art criticism. Crucially, this means that art is 'other': it cannot be *reduced* by Jungian ideas (Jung 1922: paras. 99–100). On the other hand, and here comes the first doubleness, Jung's notion of the psyche is particularly attuned to artistic creation. His founding position is that the unconscious is by nature creative, in part unknowable, and that this undermines any other secure knowledge (Jung 1954: para. 358).

It follows therefore, that Jungian theory can be understood by arts criticism as both embedded and structural. For the founding principle of 'absence' in the unknowable unconscious, means that the concepts do not have anything 'outside' to stand upon. So Jung admits that his ideas are *embedded* in his own personality, history and twentieth-century European culture. By contrast, the structural approach to Jung has a certain classical beauty. All the concepts are arranged in oppositional pairs. It is the task of the psyche to convert psychic opposition into a dynamic living relationship: this Jung called 'individuation'. As well as the defining pair, conscious/unconscious, there is the moral opposition of ego versus shadow, where the shadow is the thing the conscious person has no wish to be, and the gender opposition of either ego versus anima (male), or ego versus animus (female). Moreover there is a transcendent opposition in the ego versus the self, an entity representing totality and a numinous connection to the world. Jung also introduced the notion of the 'persona' as the social mask we construct in order to operate in society. Please see the Glossary at the back of this book for more explanation of Jungian ideas.

The scheme of oppositional pairs forms a logical construct, a grid within which psychic events can be made comprehensible. It is a way of making Jungian ideas universally applicable. Yet, to shift perspective to look closely at the processes suggested by this structure is to see the binary pairs 'deconstructed' in the actual living of a life. Here, Jungian individuation as deconstruction of a binary system returns us to the notion of the theory as 'embedded' in actual historical conditions. In effect, Jungian theory is a means of *telling a story* about being; a story that is indivisible from historical and cultural context, yet never reducible to it. For the creative unconscious is always 'other' (because unknowable). Its unpredictable divine, demonic or even mundane aspects are affected by, but not controlled by, culture.

Here we see Jung's concepts as tools both for *shaping* and *interpreting* our sense of who we are. Jungian concepts help us to tell stories that shape ourselves. They may be stories about the other as gender in narratives of passion and betrayal, about good and evil in the shadow, about social complexity via the persona and about humans and gods or aliens in the self. So Jungian ideas offer an understanding of creativity, and, they provide a means of interpreting the results of that creativity. It is this dual property of Jungian thought, a third doubleness, to be both investigator of the maker, and also of what is made, that is at the heart of *Psyche and the Arts*.

CRITICAL FRAMES

The practice of arts criticism always contains the question of its own relation to the art object. To put it another way, all arts criticism contains an explicit or implicit 'theory' or 'argument' about the relation of criticism to art. Criticism 'frames' art. For example, even the term 'art object' contains the notion that art consists of separate objects (paintings, books, 'pieces' of music, films, buildings etc.), and that is itself the outcome of a theory that sets up an essential separation between world and art. In effect, the theory of art as discrete objects is a 'frame' that constitutes its thesis: that art is discrete objects upon which criticism can be 'applied'.

It follows that art-as-discrete-object is a transcendent theory of art. The work exists on its own. It requires nothing else from outside the frame of its objectness, such as historical context, to give it meaning or identity. Even the work of criticism is unnecessary to the essence of the art, such is the completeness of the object. No criticism will ever wholly penetrate the art object. Paradoxically, criticism framing art as transcendent object makes it transcendent of even its own attentions.

Of course, art need not be viewed as wholly transcendent of the world around it. The opposite of a transcendent work of art would be an immanent one. An immanent work of art would be barely visible since it would be absorbed into the surrounding culture. Moreover, it might be 'taken in' by a critical approach. It might be swallowed and digested by arts criticism until nothing was left. A fascinating illustration of transcendent and immanent art was performed on the London streets several hot summers ago. An artist left several huge snowballs in busy thoroughfares in August and allowed them to melt away over several days. One could argue that beginning as transcendent – snow in August is unheard of in London – so quite outside *nature*, transcendent of it, the snowballs gently submitted to nature's powers after all and declined to immanent *natural* puddles, soon evaporating.

One could also argue, however, that this delightful example also demonstrated that the wholly immanent and wholly transcendent are never possible. From the moment something transcendent arrived on the hot streets, the snowballs began to melt, were subject to nature, just as the most gloriously ethereal painting is still a material form, subject to natural forces of decay etc. On the other hand, the snowballs were never completely eaten up by the city. For those who witnessed their amazing presence, there was something marvellous, otherworldly in the memory of snowballs, two metres in diameter in the City of London.

So criticism discovers art as a *dialogical* relation of transcendent and immanent qualities in differing amounts. Some art works will invoke transcendent ideas and approaches while others will invite more immanent visions. Yet none will exist wholly without the other. Indeed immanent qualities will be understood in relation to the art's transcendent powers and vice versa. Criticism's critical *frame* will be liminal in that it is capable of tracing the presence of culture and history in the art, yet also able to mark art as 'other', as numinous.

JUNG, PSYCHE AND THE ARTS

So far I am suggesting that arts criticism exists in a spectrum between treating the art as a wholly separate object and as an immanent merging with, or entering into, the art to 'explain' or present it to the world from within. I am also suggesting that Jungian psychology is uniquely placed to energize this spectrum. If we wanted a portrait of a transcendent art criticism (impossible to do absolutely, of course), then a Jungian version would be the application of his pairs of binary concepts to a work. To return to the snowballs of August, they cry out to be considered as a delicate embodiment of opposi-tions. The oppressive heat and dirt of the city has a frozen white purity momentarily in its midst, like a dream from an unconscious of snow and ice. On the other hand, an immanent Jungian criticism will not allow rational concepts to dominate the *story* of encountering the melting snowballs in their particular positions framed by offices and riotous traffic. It is the *story* of something beautiful and natural (immanent) yet also supernatural (transcendent). Immanent criticism has to take place *inside* the experience of the art, or in the interior of the art itself. It needs to be partly ritual, an invocation to the power of the work, the effect of meeting that ever-changing union of natural and supernatural that is snowballs in August. The city workers stopped and smiled, and then went on.

So just as pure Jungian transcendent criticism would be a sterile meditation upon concepts, so absolute Jungian immanent criticism would collapse into vapid solipsism. Jungian theory is likewise dialogical between conceptual thinking transcendent of local conditions and immediate embodied psychic experience. The result is a theory that is more properly a *form of story telling* that weaves the contingent into meaning by reference to a scheme of ideas. This then offers a challenge to the possibility of Jungian criticism: can it too make use of a dialogical strategy, between imposing from 'outside' a set of concepts (transcendent Jung in transcendent criticism), and working from 'inside' in the particular and historically located creative processes of the work?

In effect, it is the dialogical nature of Jungian ideas that enables Jungian criticism to explore the contemporary problem of universals versus particu-lars. Are works of art universally relevant? Do they mean in the same way over long periods of time and to different peoples? Can art be transcendent of all local cultures and histories? Or, is art immanent and particular, wholly *grounded* in a particular culture and setting? Jung's answer to universals and particulars is his writing, which shows his 'universals', concepts, as emerging out of his particular life, culture etc., and as underpinned by his only absolutely transcendent universal, the creative unknowable unconscious. The result is the dialogical theory – between partially transcendent concepts and immanent story – and a dialogical arts criticism. Jungian arts criticism will weave in and out, at the same time constituting and dismantling the 'frame' of the work of art. In fact, Jungian arts criticism will create *and* undo the division between artwork and world, it will be both inside and outside the art.

The philosopher Jacques Derrida put it in a very similar way (Derrida 1977). Challenging transcendence, which he calls the metaphysical, he says that critical writing cannot stabilize the meaning of a text because it is always already 'inside' it. It is inside the work because the centre of a text, the stabilizing point, has to be 'outside' if it is to do its job. Only a metaphysical principle outside of the system of signs is capable of stabilizing the process by which words appear to acquire meaning. Of course, Derrida admits that we cannot completely discard our transcendent ideas or metaphysical notions. Yet he remains more sceptical of them than Jung.

It is worth noting the effect of this debate on notions of nature and myth. For example, we treat nature as both an immanent and a transcendent concept when we regard ourselves as both 'inside' and 'outside' the animate and inanimate Earth. By 'laws of nature', nature as cosmos, we recognize that we are wholly *in* nature, we inhabit her body, we are immanent to her. However, from our monotheisms we inherit nature as 'other'. Here humans, fashioned in the image of a father god, share 'his' transcendence of matter, of mater, Mother nature.

These notions of simultaneous existence in immanence and transcendence are deeply ingrained. Gazing at a vast snowball in August, I perceive the beauty of its oppositions, of its delicate challenge to its city backdrop. Yet accompanying eye and intellect is the bodily connection to the art. I inhabit its space, feeling the cold radiate out to me, raising the hairs on my arm. I do not need to touch it to feel the delicious cold on my skin. In this way the art snowball draws me into its physicality – I am taken inside the frame of the art and become, in body and soul, part of the work.

There is a story being enacted here. If we live in immanence and transcendence then we are dwelling in a profound intersection of creation myths. Our monotheisms bequeath a myth of transcendence, of a creator father who is separate from what he has made and of humans in 'his' image, separate from nature. On the other hand, the actual cultural expressions of this myth of transcendent paternity never seem to entirely lose sight of its 'other', the immanent mother. In the 'other' far older myth, the earth herself is sacred and gives birth to all life, including humans. We have our being within the body of the divine mother. Often the religious expression of this myth is animism, of the world as divinely inspirited in a multitude of sacred voices.

Of course, these creation myths, visible in our religions, philosophies and culture, are also shaping energies for the artist. Just as Jung the writer weaves these myths into a relationship in his psychology by wedding conceptual ideas to the many playful, less rational and animistic voices in his psyche, so does the artist create in a dialogue between the spiritual inspiration of a pure, ideal form, and the web of embodied, encultured living. Similarly the Jungian critic is invited to trace a living pattern between art of the father that appeals for its beauty and stability to transcendent or metaphysical ideas, and art of the mother, immanent, bodily, particular and immersed in the finally also unknowable, mysteries of time and body. The immanent pole of criticism becomes part of the art itself because it is characterized by Eros, connection, relationship and feeling. The Logos part of the mind supports the transcendent aspects of criticism in which ideas and spirit offer to 'frame' the work of art (see Glossary for Eros and Logos).

As one profoundly caught up in the creation myth of earth Mother, Derrida sees criticism as immanent. Its role as 'frame' (transcendent) is evanescent, as the inside and the outside of the work can never be securely marked (Derrida 1987). Yet in acknowledging that metaphysics and transcendence cannot simply be disregarded, Derrida too admits the need for a dialogical relation between the myths, which are, of course, our great stories forming consciousness. In any one human era, there needs to be a balance between the father creation myth of rational, abstract, spirit (that Jung called Logos), and the mother earth myth of connection, body and feeling consciousness (Jung's Eros). Both Jung and Derrida recognized that the dominance of sky father thinking in modernity desperately required the compensatory healing attention of the animistic earth mother. For art this means a change of orientation from art trying to please the transcendent sky father *entirely*, to one capable of bringing earth and sky into an erotic relationship. So the miraculous super-nature (father) of the snowball gradually melts into the erotic embrace of the hot city cradled by mother earth.

With these considerations, we can see the essays in this book as seeking to remedy modernity's neglect of the goddess in the art, while still cherishing the role of transcendence and universals in making meaning. For as I have argued, no artwork or critical essay is ever wholly immanent, for it would be unable to discern the art in the *text*ure of reality. Similarly, no art or criticism is ever wholly transcendent, for it is born of a body in the form of the soul that unites body and spirit in a creative union, *a union that is, itself, creativity*. True creativity like healthy consciousness depends on finding a union between the creation myths in a particular culture. The following essays bear witness to the marriage of strange gods.

PSYCHE AND THE ARTS

The book begins with the poet Edmund Cusick. Writing in the golden conjunction of artist and critic, he demonstrates with peculiar grace, the liminal space between practitioner and interpreter that characterizes the visionary imagination. The paper explores the poet's book, *Ice Maidens*. The collection's cover plate – John William Waterhouse's *Hylas and the Nymphs* – offers an archetypal image of the allure of the anima, and Cusick's poem 'Waterhouse', tracing the influence of images of the entrancing feminine over the male artist, offers an introduction to the wider themes of the work. In poems such as 'Vindolanda' and 'Nana', Cusick explores the association of spiritual forces within the landscape through feminine images. Other poems explore the glamour of the female image in the male psyche, and in particular, suggest points of confluence between the supernatural and the erotic, where the energy of fantasies, or of actual encounters, rises from both sexual and spiritual sources.

This immersion in the deeps of artistic creation is followed by Part I of the volume: 'Getting into art: Jungian (immanent) criticism'. We begin with Terence Dawson's thought-provoking paper, 'The discovery of the personal unconscious: Robinson Crusoe and modern identity'. This chapter re-examines Robinson Crusoe from a post-Jungian perspective. It asks why it is that the first modern English novel harbours a mythic intensity. The argument has three strands. (1) The literary-historical: the claim is that Defoe's novel illustrates the first extended intimation of the personal unconscious in English literature; the modern novel thus arose from a need to express specifically autobiographical material. (2) Jungian psychology: the objective is to propose tighter and more useful definitions of the persona and the ego. (3) Reader-response: the intention is to offer a fresh explanation for the novel's mythic resonance.

Dawson on the novel is followed by a fascinating contribution by Lucy Huskinson, 'Archetypal dwelling, building individuation'. She deftly incorporates C.G. Jung's metaphor of the psyche as a multi-storied house of different architectural styles, with Heidegger's notion that 'to be human is to dwell', in order to examine the idea that buildings can mediate between the human being and the world. It follows that in our relating to these buildings we have a means to substantiate and explore our very being and its relation to the world. We then move on to another paper in which artist and critic are mutually embedded and inspirational. 'On painting, substance and psyche' by David Parker is an exploration of the art of painting in relation to the art of alchemy. This essay argues for a revaluation of the intrinsic relationship between psyche and matter in the practice of both activities. The essay addresses the topic from a practitioner's point of view – closer consideration being given to how the physical as well as psychological relationship towards materials might guide imagination and symbol formation for both artist and alchemist.

We return to novels in 'Haruki Murakami's reimagining of Sophocles' *Oedipus*' by Inez Martinez. This is a timely return to the Oedipus myth by a formidable literary critic who demonstrates the value of closely connecting to the work of art. Haruki Murakami in his novel *Kafka on the Shore* reimagines the Oedipus myth as liberating initiation into being human. His novel renders physical incest transforming into symbolic healing love. Murakami further re-imagines the human dilemma of how to take responsibility for unconscious acts. He abjures Sophocles' Oedipus' responses of heroic guilt and victimization. Instead Murakami portrays responsibility for unconscious acts as collective. Murakami thus exemplifies par excellence Jung's concept of the artist as one who brings healing reimagination to collective psyche.

An arresting challenge to conventional criticism of visual art is provided by Bettina Reiber in 'Psyche, imagination and art'. In Jung's writing on art, psyche, imagination and art are intimately linked. By contrast, in contemporary mainstream art criticism, psyche and imagination hardly finds a mention. After examining both the Jungian and the current art critical position, an alternative to mainstream art theoretical thinking is presented, that of the aesthetic judgement according to Kant which recognizes that art cannot be defined and that responses to art are based on a very particular kind of feeling which is linked to our rational faculties.

A powerful essay follows by Craig Stephenson, 'How Myrtle Gordon addresses her suffering: Jung's concept of possession and John Cassavetes' *Opening Night*'. The raw impact of film is skilfully rendered less chaotic by considering how critics, baffled by the esoteric idiom of possession which Cassavetes employs to describe his protagonist's suffering in *Opening Night*, might employ Jung's concept of possession to appreciate better the film's scenario. Stephenson aligns Jung's concept with Cassavetes' imaginative critique of personhood as defined by consciousness, and considers how Gena Rowlands portrays Myrtle Gordon enacting a fluid and paradoxical notion of embodied selfhood.

A second treatment of film occurs in 'The father, the dark child and the mob that kills him: Tim Burton's representation of the creative artist' by Lena Vasileva. This paper is concerned with Burton's probably favourite tale – the myth of the Frankenstein monster, and the different guises it takes in his movies. Vasileva's insightful study shows the transformations of this myth throughout Burton's career as a director. In his films, as well as animation features, he artfully re-works the story of the sensitive, socially clumsy, creative nonconformist, who is striving for acceptance but is perceived by people as a 'monster'. He is rejected and ultimately destroyed by society.

There follows Part II of the volume, 'Challenging the critical space', that collects together writings offering a more experimental approach to the framing of critical practice. In 'Stripping bare the images' by Don Fredericksen, the Jungian critic is trenchantly warned against 'iconophilia'. In relation to the Jungian community's recent and growing fascination with the putative archetypal and/or symbolic register of popular film, Fredericksen gives a stunning extended critical reflection of the current Jungian iconophilia regarding film. The issues go beyond film and Jungian commentaries on film to the broader question of the nature and function of the imagination in our 'mage-clogged' culture.

A further critical exploration of Jung and the imagination is provided by the persuasive and excellent scholarship of 'Psyche and imagination in Goethe and Jung' by Paul Bishop. This paper uses Goethe's poem 'Dedication' to explore the parallels between Jung's theories and German aesthetics. Jung placed himself in the intellectual tradition emerging from Goethe; his writings are saturated with references to this iconic figure of German-speaking culture. Numerous historico-intellectual contexts inform Goethe's poem, but this paper argues it strikingly illustrates an approach to the feminine, to the imagination, and arguably even to art and aesthetics, that suggests a fundamental affinity between Jung and Weimar classicism.

We then come to a bold and innovative paper by Byron Almén on music, which takes on board the 'lack' of direction from Jung on this particular art. In 'Jung's function-attitudes in music composition and discourse', he notes that music occupies a tenuous position within Jungian studies, due in part to Jung's own ambivalence about music as a therapeutic modality. However, Jung's model of the differentiated conscious mind – his theory of psychological types – offers many productive insights into music and its relation to the psyche. In this article, early twentieth-century theories and discourses about music serve to illustrate distinct experiential and interpretive modalities that emerge from interplay between the musical work and the listener's preferred configuration of function-attitudes.

We then come to a remarkable chapter aiming to explore and provide for what is another perceived 'lack' in Jungian criticism. 'Jung in the twilight zone: the psychological functions of the horror film' by Angela Connolly notes that Jungian contributions to cultural studies have been vitiated by an incapacity to account for the cultural dimensions of human individuality. She argues that the concept of the cultural complex provides a theoretical basis for the study of the concrete manifestations of universals in different contexts. This concept and the Jungian Shadow, the most metaphorically evocative of all the archetypes, are utilized to suggest that horror can be divided into three sub-categories: uncanny horror; abject horror; and sublime terror where the encounter with the cultural shadow complex can lead to an expansion of consciousness.

Lastly in this section, in 'Writing about nothing', Leslie Gardner turns her attention to Jung's own art, the rhetoric of his writing. The result is a groundbreaking analysis of aspects of Jung and Lacan in their attempts to come to terms with a hoax or fiction. Lacan exploits the writing of 'nothing' (a fiction) to find the psychoanalytic relationship; Jung exploits another sample of hoax writing to reveal the basis of his analytic approach. Gardner demonstrates that Jung's historical approach has more artistic and therapeutic integrity. Furthermore, from these writings she structures a dialogue about the nature of psychological writing itself, in which Jung can be best illuminated by recourse to the rhetoric of Vico.

Part III, 'Making/interpreting art in the world', offers papers that are daringly experimental in showing criticism arising from the emergence of art as a collective act. Here as in the other papers, the art of writing is a supporting pillar for the artwork itself. Here however, the critics are also educators, and the art is more the collective product of the imagination than it is a material object. For these last three papers, art is a collective dance in which artist, critic and the substance to be worked upon, are all positions taken by different people at different times. Jung called such a work of the imagination, alchemy.

First of all we have the moving and illuminating account, 'The poetical word: towards an imaginal language' by Elenice Giosa. She argues profoundly against the dominance of education by the language of rationality, which is shorn of affect and poetry. Against it, in her paper, language is considered a symbolic mediator – a mode of accessing deep imaginative powers. Giosa speaks of the animic word, from anima or animus, fruit of the imaginal dialogical process established in the classroom. She analyses an experience with students in Brazil, which offers an attempt at making together an Education of Sensibility, a pedagogical expression that reunites the person with the nature of his or her surroundings – towards our individuation process.

In 'Healing with the alchemical imagination in the undergraduate classroom' by Lee Robbins, a wonderful act of erotic creation is performed in the writing, bringing together the alchemical work of students in the collective and material space of the classroom. The paper describes Jung's vision of the alchemical imagination as a tertiary space that is born between what is perceived as inner and outer reality. This place of alchemical transformation and healing came to life for a team of students enrolled in a course called Alchemy and the Transformation of Self. The non-ego real came to life and was embodied by the students in an experiential assignment called the Alchemy Project, based on Jung's model of the unconscious. Students worked with alchemical images of transformation in a wide variety of expressive media to give form to personal encounters with wounding and healing. Here there is no meaningful distinction between making art, writing criticism and healing.

A final paper, and the second one from Brazil, shows the rebirth of art, specifically folktales, in the modern collective, which believes itself far divorced from such traditional sources of creativity. In 'The serenity of the senex: using Brazilian folk tales as an alternative approach to "entrepreneurship" in university education', Claudio Paixao Anastacio de Paula, shows art enabling a psychic rebirth as sophisticated university students become reconnected to their depths in the unconscious. He argues that the 'entrepreneurship fashion trend' in Brazil has led young people to try to create their own history thereby denying and rejecting *senex*. An alternative approach to this trend, developed with students from a Brazilian university, is described. Based on an analysis of the Brazilian identity, the workshop used four folk tales collected in the nineteenth century to approach puerile elements of 'entrepreneurship' (from amorality to difficulty in establishing a fraternal relationship) leading the participants to a new perspective: transforming personal and cultural complexes into a source of generative energy.

Psyche and the Arts is offered in the spirit of Jungian criticism: to trouble the boundaries between criticism and the arts of healing and imagination, to make critical and independent yet also grounded, social commentary, and to promote the growth of the soul in all its domestic, public and cosmic spaces. It represents a hope for more such writing to open up a web of dialogue to span the transcendent and immanent spheres of being.

REFERENCES

Derrida, J. (1977) *Of Grammatology*, trans. Gayatri Chakravorty Spivak, Baltimore MD: Johns Hopkins University Press.

—— (1987) *The Truth in Painting*, trans. Geoff Bennington and Ian McLeod, Chicago: University of Chicago Press.

Jung, C. G. (1953–91) *The Collected Works of C. G. Jung, vols. 1–20, A and B*, ed. H. Read, M. Fordham and G. Adler, trans. R. F. C. Hull, Princeton: Princeton University Press and London: Routledge & Kegan Paul. Referred to throughout this volume as *CW*.

—— (1954) in *CW* 8, paras. 343–442.

—— (1922/1966) 'On the Relation of Analytical Psychology to Poetry', in *CW* 15, paras. 97–132.

Nascimento Rosa, Armando (2006) *An Oedipus: The Untold Story, A Ghostly Mythodrama in One Act*, trans. Luis Toledo, rev. and ed. Michael Mendis, New Orleans: Spring Journal Books.

Chapter I

Psyche and the artist: Jung and the poet

Edmund Cusick

ART, IMAGINATION AND PSYCHE: A JOURNEY BY WATER

I offer this paper in two guises, partly as a creative artist, partly as a Jungian critic. What I hope to do is to put some of my own work in the context of Jungian themes, and make some observations about how a Jungian understanding of the life of the psyche informs my own experience as an artist. It is by invoking the creative alchemy of artist and critic that my work introduces this volume of *Psyche and the Arts*.

I would like to begin by taking as starting point a work of art, and a myth, which resonates with meaning for me as an artist: the myth of Hylas. Hylas himself is not so much a mythic figure as a footnote in someone else's story: in particular, Jason's. He was, tradition tells us, one of the Argonauts, who was sent to get water, before the Argos departed from Mysia. Arriving at the pool Hylas was seduced by a nymph who dwelt there, and drawn into the water, never to be seen again.

The painting is by the pre-Raphaelite painter John William Waterhouse and is entitled *Hylas and the Nymphs*. The original hangs in the Manchester City Art Gallery, and a detail from it is reproduced to form the cover of my poetry collection *Ice Maidens* (Cusick 2006). From a Jungian perspective, the painting does not so much invite interpretation as plead desperately for it. Hylas is pictured on the brink of the pool, staring into the eyes of the nymph: pale, beautiful, adolescent. Below the waist her body dissolves from view into the water. It would be hard to find a better image of anima possession. The overwhelming nature of his experience, and his own helplessness before their siren call, is reinforced by the multiplicity of the image – six more nymphs surround Hylas, each with the same seductive gaze.

It is an image which, I believe, offers a wealth of meanings, and which has a particular resonance for the male artist. From the point of view of the Jungian critic it has a cautionary meaning. Hylas bears a striking resemblance to classical imagery of Aquarius – but this water bearer is never going to rise to pour out the waters of inspiration. He is rather about to be consumed by them. In this sense Hylas could be seen as standing as a type of the critic. The work of the psychological critic is based on the assumption that we can contain the unconscious within the grasp of rational understanding – but consciousness in fact is, of course, itself the contained, not the container.

For the artist, contact with the archetypes may be held – expressed or embodied – through the emergence of the work of art, but cannot by definition be brought under rational control. In one tradition it is said that as soon as Hylas touched the lip of his pitcher to the water's surface, the nymph rose from the pool, with one hand embracing his neck to kiss him, while with the other grasping his arm to pull him under. For me, it is a detail that I find enormously evocative. The first movement comes from consciousness, but once the water is invited to rush in, it will continue to the point of salvation or destruction. The surge of energy into the archetype is mesmerizing, and unstoppable.

Hylas' story has an appeal at another level. The mapping of narrative structures has become a preoccupation of the twentieth-century cultural industries – nowhere more so than in the world of screenwriting. At the heart of the commercial orthodoxy regarding the structuring of plot is the hero's journey, an idea derived from Christopher Vogler (1999), who is informed by Joseph Campbell (1949) who in turn, of course, is informed by Jung (1953–91). The hero's journey is a pattern of events discernible within any heroic plot – which is to say, any Hollywood film: the call to action, the refusal of the call, the meeting of a mentor, and so forth, which charts the rise to maturity of the hero. Hylas is on a hero's journey, but it founders at the first step.

There is, however, more to the complexities of life than the schematics of personal growth through endeavour. We may respond to the myth of quest, trial and achievement, but we sense the truths in other stories: Orpheus turning back at the gates of Hades, Narcissus unable to break from his reflection, Persephone succumbing to the taste of the underworld. They haunt us because their journeys were arrested.

To my mind there is a particular appeal to poets for such myths. Since the age of narrative poetry has passed, we have learned to value verse precisely for its capacity not to drive us forward, but to abandon outward progress – to stand still and explore for us, the readers, the depth of meaning in a single scene, a single image. For this we borrow a word from religious experience: *epiphany*. An image will come alive in poetry if it resonates with readers, and the greatest of poets find and evoke images whose meanings ripple outward to touch an entire generation: Wordsworth's daffodils, Eliot's wasteland, Larkin's empty church, Hughes' fox by night. Waterhouse's work bears the stamp of his own generation. His paintings are pregnant with images of women and water, their brooding and enigmatic presence shot through with a peculiarly fin de siècle blend of intense yearning and the sense of spiritual presence. *Ophelia* (in Tate London), and *Echo and Narcissus* (Walker Art Gallery, Liverpool) have both, at different points in history, passed into popular consciousness and been reproduced on a huge scale.

What I believe is remarkable about 'Hylas and the Nymphs' is that the artist has a physical presence inside the painting, rather than only the implied presence in the gaze which frames our own. Hylas, poised on the brink of immersion into rapture, offers us identification with the protagonist – we cannot help but feel the beauty of his seductress – but at the same time the picture contains and contextualizes Hylas, simultaneously placing us outside his experience.

ANIMA

Inasmuch as many of the poems in *Ice Maidens*[1] wrestle with engagement with the feminine they are, I hope, in the tradition of this painting – offering the reader to the chance to inhabit the perspective of the male artist, but also to stand outside it. One poem, 'Waterhouse', addresses this complex explicitly:

Waterhouse

Beneath the water's face he finds
in these green depths the soul refracts
like light, sees in his rippling eyes
the world within, self upon bright self
breaking to his sight.
So the artist turns from love
to the lure of water and illusion,
the gaze of painted creatures
meeting his own gaze.

The women he desires he bathes
in this same stream, flowing
from canvas to canvas, making
of them mermaids, sirens. They gleam
between tall reeds, milk-white naiads
playing among the waterlilies,
dragonflies. Imploring pools lap
at their child's breasts. Just once,

as Hylas, he came to the brink
of caressing these pink-nippled
girls, the nymphs he thirsted for.

Yet as their hands, cold as river
pearls, reached to draw him
down, he knew some colours
move only in water, are seen
only by those who drown.

In his discussion of visionary art Jung speaks of extraordinary poetry which may shatter the conventions of literature, and defy even the comprehension of its own author. The hallmark of such poetry is that it deals exclusively with content from the collective unconscious. I cannot claim to write visionary art, but I would suggest that any art which evokes an unconscious archetype will, while not being sucked into the maelstrom that is visionary experience, nonetheless feel the ominous pull of its undertow. For the individual artist, the image which triggers intercourse with the anima, may appear to be both accidental and mundane, but once triggered, the energy of the archetype may erupt in ways that are unpredictable and compelling. In the language of the poet, rather than that of the analytical psychologist, I would put it this way: there are poems which more or less do as they are told, and poems which leave you no choice but to do what you are told, refusing the neatness of logical progression or the closure of your intended conclusion. It may be that to get involved with nymphs in any situation, or any century, is always dangerous. My own experience is reflected in this poem.

At Vindolanda

floods spill through tarpaulin shrouds, burst
over lawns and paths. Oaks bend
before storm water's weight. Three girls run across the ruins,
feet sodden, their faces masked and glinting
in clear plastic macs, pearl eyed
with rain. Exhumed from these earthworks
the first letter between women, its cursive script
stripped from centuries of mud's discretion: *I offer*
prayers for you, Lavinia, at the temple of the nymphs.

All along the wall, each mile fort has its shrine,
each villa a sacred well: the legions surrendering
to the cold communion of the springs, drinking
in the lapping voices of outlandish spirits,
till every river's name invokes a Goddess.

The girls twirl in a swirling hail, hold up
cupped hands, squeeze under ropes, splash
in the open dig. Their plebeian feet
churn the quarters of centurions and priests.
The sky falls, whirling down to three wide open
mouths. Prised from fresh dredged graves,
the statues are paraded under hot museum lights:
Local Deities, Water Spirits, Nymphs of the Springs.
Between this water and the sculpted stones,

some living thing that we have lost. But here,
in Vindolanda among the nymphs,
I remember how on the frontier

of sleep you came to me, night by night, holding me
breathless, appearing then as you were, once,
in the azure glare of underwater lights: the crossed straps
scarring your pale shoulders; the wet veil of hair
slashed across one cheek; tight drops
scaling your tensed thighs, reptilian,
beautiful; the cup of shadow offered
at the hollow of your collar bone; you,
balanced, as herons balance on the brink

of killing. Or some discarnate thing,
which, as you dived, you yielded to,
till your blue nails tore the water's skin,
splayed across the tiles; and after them your face
rising, broken and baptised
in the mosaic flickering of light.

My clothes are a shell of water.
There is no one here, no-one but the three girls,
splashing, unafraid; above, the pregnant clouds,
piling and coiling, murmuring in the soft breath
of gods that is like the sound of boulders
falling. The tarpaulins stretch
to bulging pouches, growing.

MYTH AND THE IMAGINATION

Myth is the natural territory for the Jungian. A sequence of poems in *Ice Maidens* deals with the Arctic, which for me is the land of myth. In a historical sense, the far North quite literally is the unconscious – the great region of the unknown, of which enormous tracts were unexplored even into the last century. The archipelago of Spitzbergen, or Svalbard, is one such location. To stand at Ny Alesund, the world's most northerly permanent settlement, and rest your hand on the iron girders of the pylon from which Nobile's airship was moored before it disappeared in the arctic wastes, or to walk the desolate bank of shale at Smeerenburg, on which a hundred condemned men chose to face the hangman rather than to face the winter, is to enter the territory of myth. This sense of mythic is never stronger than at Ytrenorskoya, the island of the dead.

Ytrenorskoya

First we buried them
hacking holes in the frozen topsoil
but they came back to us, thrust up
by the rising ice, shouldering aside
our crosses, pushing plank
coffins through the mud.
Then we built cairns,
till in the long dark when the ice
thickens and the seals are few, the bears
came, scattering the stones
and after them the white foxes
and screaming gulls, bearing
scraps of winding sheet and skin.

Now in the spring we do as the Dutch do,
sailing to Ytrenorskoya
at the archipelago's edge,
our cargo, children,
white in their stiff shrouds.

Through the winter till the ice melts
they wait their laying out
the air too pure to rot them,
and on Ytrenorskoya, wreathed
in mist and incense, the priest
says the good words above the pit
and sailors with iron spars
lever boulders onto them.

Here we bring those
who have died of frostbite
those with lungs burnt
by thirty degrees of frost
those who ate polar bear liver
and the parasitic worm
that breeds there
those who drowned
when the Royal Navy
sank seven whalers
in the Sjorje fjord.

There is one point of landing
for our boats, one point
of departure. And once

each spring we see
between the clumps of stone
patches of brilliant moss, the red lichen
that grows now
only on this island.

In different ways the poems I have offered so far have been concerned with the element of water. If water is the unconscious, then those who are called to spend their life on that element, and to whom we, the voyagers, must submit ourselves, have for me an aura of the archetypal: of the ferrymen of legend, of Charon, of the psychopomp, the soul's guide in the uncharted realms. It was only as I came to prepare this paper that I saw this fascination linking two poems written years apart, each dealing with a helmsman.

Igor

shrugs, lifts a single finger, contemptuous.
Eskimos? In Russian there is one word
for snow, schoolteacher. This –
He jerks a thumb at the fields of drift ice,
its grey redeemed only by the distant yellow
excrement of walrus, the red-brown excrement
of seals; at pyramids, arches, thrown up
by chance collisions of floe on floe. On the port bow,
an aquamarine cathedral, glistening,
tortured into spires. *It is ice, yes?*
Why do you want more words?

On Igor's watch, while the crew sleeps
in endless light, between SatNav, radar,
radio, the log, he teaches me fragments
of latitude, depth charts, the sea.

Half my age, he commands
ice strengthened vessel *Akademic Kaplinsky,*
registered Murmansk, bends course to chase
whales for me, tells me
of the Naval Academy Planetarium:

They take you in there – it is dark.
They show you one constellation –
just one. They say, what is that star?
We have to learn one hundred stars.

Matt

Got him. Matt cuts the engines. As we drift
he climbs the cabin roof, balanced, easy,
in the lurch of swell. His eyes lift a single fin
from miles of sea we've tried to search.
He points. *There. He's diving. Six minutes.*
Propellers gurgle as we turn. He's stalking it,
forty metres down. We hold our breath.

A chain clinks on the mast. Five minutes.
We whisper, as though afraid our words
could sound down twenty fathoms
and then it blows, near enough to touch,
its skin as smooth as tight stretched silk.
An eye, a ragged scar along a fin.
Orca. Matt says. *Attack anything.*
Seals, porpoise. No discrimination.

At night they're diving in a green half light.
Matt checks them, man by man, buckled,
strapped, into depth gauge, air tank, knife.
As they ready for the jump he puts his hand
on each man's shoulder, once. The masks
they turn to him fill with his own image
then bow to darkness, silt. We wait.

On the deck where everything makes noise
he comes behind me, silent as the air.
Ashore he never seems to follow me
but always to be there. It's like a private game.

In one cold hour they're back; surface
in a swirl of bubbles, struggle at the ladder,
their own mass too burdensome to raise.
Matt lifts them with one hand, tears
their faces from rubber balaclavas.

Now leaning at the rail alone, we stare
into the slow half-trance of signal buoys
and beacons, hear the slap of the Atlantic,
watch stars dance above St Agnes.
There's questions I don't ask. He gives no regiment,
no dates. He talks of Wilfred Owen, of lost mates,
of getting off his face and waking on the beach,
watching the dawn. He mutters once, *The Army let me do*
what I was good at. But it's late, the whisky's

low, before he says, *I didn't have a problem*
killing people – It was other things,
that made me leave. His face is sealed,
remote and tight, when he says to the lights,
the sea, not me, *The Army*
made me do what I was good at.

For the men in these poems the region of water offers a place both of refuge
and of discovery. For myself as a poet, I find my own place on the shoreline.
The sea is the boundary of experience, but also a symbol of the boundless.
The last poem I wish to offer here is one which I hope expresses this.

Nana

A farm, pitched like a ship
against the hail of seaspray on cliffs
eaten year by year by the malicious tide.
Upstairs, one bedroom wall is window,
a slow hour glass filling with the sea.
And at this rising, sinking line
Nana, a hundred years dead
and nine years old, kneels to stare,
measuring endlessly time she cannot feel.

All who have come here, gazed
on this bleak shore have sensed it,
that line of ending, ebbing and drawing near.
Here, men dug with their own hands,
the bones of deer, raised stone slabs
above their dead, slanted to the setting sun.
The Celts called these bruised, weed-stained
reefs Caer Arionrhod, poised between life and life,
death and death. Here the knell of Christ
tolled to mark the road to the isle of pilgrims,
where the brown limbs of saints are laid,
thick as apple roots beneath the spade.

So at my own death, I may recall
these fields with their rusting fence,
this tattered swell that weeps and fills, these deeps
where time is held in store among the waves.
Once more then, perhaps, I'll see her, her image
flat against the patient light: Nana,
still watching, waiting, for that final bell
to wake her into freedom, into sleep.

NOTE

1 This and other poetry quoted here by Dr Edmund Cusick from *Ice Maidens* (Headland, 2006), is reproduced by permission of Headland Publications.

REFERENCES

Campbell, Joseph (1949) *The Hero with a Thousand Faces*, Princeton: Princeton University Press.

Cusick, Edmund (2006) *Ice Maidens*, West Kirby: Headland Publications.

Jung, C. G. (1953–91) *The Collected Works of C. G. Jung, vols. 1–20, A and B*, ed. H. Read, M. Fordham and G. Adler, trans. R. F. C. Hull, Princeton: Princeton University Press and London: Routledge & Kegan Paul.

Vogler, Christopher (1999) *The Writer's Journey: Mythic Structure for Writers*, New York: Pan Books.

Part I

Getting into art: Jungian (immanent) criticism

Chapter 2

The discovery of the personal unconscious

Robinson Crusoe and modern identity

Terence Dawson

> It is otherwise with a person in the second half of life who no longer needs
> to educate his conscious will, but who, to understand the meaning of his
> individual life, needs to experience his own inner being.
>
> C. G. Jung, 1931

INTRODUCTION

It is notoriously difficult to define the subjective implications of what each
individual experiences either of the *outer* world or of their *inner* world of
dreams and waking fantasies. In these pages, I want to take another look at
one of the most important changes that occurred in the way in which individuals respond to the images that come from the inner world, a seismic shift
so great that we are still wrestling with its implications three hundred years
later. A great many scholars agree that in the course of the eighteenth century
the aspect of the personality that *philosophers* call the 'self' began to assume
new characteristics. For example, Charles Taylor identifies three major new
developments: inwardness, the affirmation of ordinary life, and a belief in
nature as a moral source (Taylor 1989). And Roy Porter insists that the second
half of the century witnesses 'the creation of modern mentalities' (Porter
2000: 475). But in spite of the range and variety of evidence that they as well
as many other scholars have supplied, there is no consensus about how best to
define the *specific* change in identity brought about by this shift.

Although Jung's textual theory harbours an intriguing and persuasive theory of cultural history (Dawson 2008), his followers have contributed little to
the wider debate about the emergence of modern identity.

Daniel Defoe was approaching sixty when he wrote his first extended narrative fiction. He had begun his career as a businessman. Then he spent close
to thirty years working as a controversial and opinionated journalist, in the
course of which he spent three days in the pillory, followed by imprisonment.
He knew the world; he had suffered its uncertainties. It is no surprise that the
heroes of all his longer narrative fictions are *survivors* who have to struggle in

an indifferent, always fickle, and sometimes hostile world. All these narratives have a firm over-arching argument, their characters live in a credible social world, and the challenges facing them are vividly depicted. There are good reasons for regarding Defoe as the 'father of the English novel'.

The first and arguably the greatest of Defoe's novels is *Robinson Crusoe* (1719). Ironically, although a popular success in England, it was first recognized as a literary masterpiece in Germany (Novak and Fisher 2005: xiv), and it was the success of Rousseau's *Émile* (1761) that made it a classic of children's literature (Hunt 1995: 1, 12–14). Its epic intensity has long been recognized. The central episode, which traces the hero's experiences during his twenty-eight years on an uninhabited island, has engendered an astonishing number of spin-offs (Green 1990; Spaas and Simpson 1996). A great many writers have regarded it as an available narrative structure that each has developed in a very different way. As Ian Watt wrote almost half a century ago, '*Robinson Crusoe* cannot be refused the status of a myth. But the myth of what?' (Watt 1951: 96). The question has two aspects: (1) what kind of myth lies at the heart of the novel? And (2) how is it related to the subsequent history of the English novel?

In these pages, I want to illustrate how a post-Jungian reading of *Robinson Crusoe* provides an unexpected answer to both these questions. I have two objectives. The first is to propose new definitions of two of Jung's key terms: the persona and the ego. And the second is to define the central concern of *Robinson Crusoe* as the separation of the ego from the persona.

THE METAPHOR OF IMPRISONMENT

Crusoe's trajectory through the novel takes the form of repeated imprisonment and escape. In his family home, he feels imprisoned; he decides to '[break] loose' (Defoe 1994: 7). He is taken prisoner by pirates from Sallee; he escapes. Although he quickly becomes a successful plantation owner in Brazil, he continues to feel constrained, as he notes in a curiously prophetic image: 'I liv'd just like a Man cast away upon some desolate Island, that had no body there but himself' (ibid.: 27). He feels compelled to improve his fortune; he is shipwrecked. Washed up on an uninhabited island, it is not long before he likens his life to imprisonment: 'I was indeed at large in the Place, yet the Island was certainly a Prison to me, and that in the worst Sense in the World' (ibid.: 71). And the island continues to feel like a prison until he begins to read the Bible every day and turn his thoughts to God. Following the events of his rescue, however, when he finally returns to England a very wealthy man, there is no insistence on keeping his thoughts bent on God. It is not long before Crusoe, now aged sixty-one, grows restless again and sets off on his 'farther adventures'.

Restlessness is not something that Crusoe outgrows as he matures; it is an intrinsic aspect of the protagonist that Defoe imagined when *he* was approaching sixty years of age. The young hero does not '[break] loose' from his family because his family are unusually difficult. He leaves because he has a fatal 'Propension [= propensity] of Nature' that compels him to do so (ibid.: 4). Wherever Crusoe is, he soon feels constrained; whatever his situation, he soon becomes dissatisfied with it. A condition envisaged as constraining is represented by the metaphor of a prison; and escape from this constraint is represented by a feeling of being more at one with himself.

The initial choice facing Crusoe is either to accept an identity based on *the expectations of others* (his family, society) or to submit to his 'Propension of Nature' that leads him into a quest for *an identity which he has yet to establish*. He knows exactly what the former entails; but he has no precise idea of what exactly he is seeking. Crusoe's restlessness signals an instinctive rejection of the former together with an instinctive interest in discovering the latter, however uncertain it may be. In Jungian terms, his determination to '[break] loose' is an imaginal representation of both his reluctance to live solely within the *persona* and his determination to connect with his own *ego*.

The relevance of this pattern can be traced through the ensuing events. When Crusoe finds himself imprisoned in Sallee, he has to make a choice between accepting his condition and finding a way to recover his freedom. His experience of being a slave represents the danger of accepting a false identity (that of a merchant, i.e. part of his persona). And regaining his freedom reflects his need to continue searching for an authentic personal identity (i.e. his ego). In Brazil, although he establishes himself as a successful plantation owner, he sets off on a quest to buy himself some slaves, and he is shipwrecked. The shipwreck can be interpreted as implying that he is no more suited to be a plantation owner than he is to be a merchant and, moreover, that his conscious intentions are illegitimate. Nonetheless, he manages to survive and he reaches an uninhabited island.

THE ISLAND AS *TEMENOS*

The island is of course the single most resonant image in the novel – and it is far more ambivalent than is usually supposed. Children who read even the simplest retelling of the novel will invariably want to act out the hero's part, however cursorily. They will seal off a corner of a room or the garden and declare that this is their 'island'. In other words, the island is as much *a metaphor for keeping others out* as it is a 'do-it-yourself utopia' (Novak 1962: 45). It guarantees isolation in order to achieve something that requires solitude. And this, of course, reflects a crucial aspect of Jungian analysis.

The island on which Robinson Crusoe is shipwrecked is a *temenos* (a 'sacred precinct') in which he slowly rebuilds his identity. And in Jung's view, the imaginal experience of such a sacred space is 'a means of protecting the centre of the personality from being drawn out and being influenced from outside' (Jung 1935/1977: para. 410). It reassures those in analysis that they harbour *within themselves* both the key to their own psychic healing and the 'sacred space' necessary to achieve this. Crusoe's island is equivalent to the space of an analytical encounter.

The social world of the novel (as of all of Defoe's novels) represents a constant threat not necessarily to his person, but *always* to his identity. Young Robinson is anxious to get away from the pressure to conform. He soon finds himself in a world in which he is forever prey to storms and pirates. On the island, he gradually learns to rebuild a personal identity, until the day he discovers that the only visitors are cannibals who eat their vanquished foes. Once again he realizes that the social world is always ready either literally or metaphorically to swallow him up. The most obvious challenge facing all of Defoe's heroes is survival: as Maximillian Novak writes, 'Crusoe's mind is dominated by fear' (Novak 1963: 25).

Ian Watt argues that Crusoe is an example of the new species: *homo economicus* (Watt 1957: 69–82). But as Everett Zimmerman pertinently notes, 'The ubiquitous references to being devoured point to a generalized fear: of being dematerialized – the reversal of the desire to accumulate' (Zimmerman 1975: 32). Enjoying his wealth is *never* Crusoe's objective. It is the pressing *fear* of losing his identity – the fear of being metaphorically swallowed – that causes him to want to make money. In other words, money is only an obvious and available *metaphor* for self-worth. Indeed, one wonders whether the fear of being 'dematerialized' might not be the driving force behind entrepreneurial capitalism.

THE VOICE OF THE SELF

Perhaps surprisingly, Crusoe's elaborations on his 'Propension of Nature' recall *Jung*'s definition of the self. Following his first experience at sea, Crusoe reflects on his 'ill Fate' and concludes that 'the calm Reasonings and Perswasions of [his] most retired Thoughts' could only have been swept aside by 'a secret overruling Decree' (Defoe 1994: 12). Writing within a Puritan tradition, it is no surprise to note that his first impulse is to attribute this 'overruling Decree' to the 'secret intimations of Providence' (ibid.: 127). Revealingly, he soon abandons this insistence and begins to describe it in emphatically *psychological* terms. One such passage is worth quoting at length:

> when we are in (a *Quandary* as we call it), a Doubt or Hesitation, whether to go this Way, or that Way, a secret Hint shall direct us this Way, when we intended to go that Way: nay, when Sense, our own Inclination, and perhaps Business has call'd to go the other Way, yet a strange Impression

upon the Mind, from we know not what Springs, and by we know not what Power, shall over-rule us to go this Way; and it shall afterwards appear, that had we gone that Way which we should have gone, and even to our Imagination ought to have gone, we should have been ruin'd and lost. Upon these, and many like Reflections, I afterwards made it a certain Rule with me, That whenever I found those secret Hints, or pressings of my Mind, to doing, or not doing any Thing that presented; or to going this Way, or that Way, I never fail'd to obey the secret Dictate; though I knew no other Reason for it, than such a Pressure, or such a Hint hung upon my Mind.

(Defoe 1994: 127)

This is not a description of the workings of Fate, or Providence, or even intuition. Defoe does not emphasize the spiritual origin of this 'secret Dictate'. He emphasizes that it is a natural psychological occurrence that emerges 'from we know not what' source, which impresses by 'we know not what' power, and that can 'over-rule' *even our firmest intentions*. It evidently comes from what Jung would describe as the unconscious. Then Defoe adds something curious: with hindsight we realize that such a 'secret Dictate' often prevents us from doing something to our ruin or loss, which accords with Jung's view that the unconscious oversees our thoughts and behaviour, and anticipates their implications and consequences. In other words, the powerful, irresistible 'Dictate' that Defoe describes corresponds exactly with Jung's definition of the intimations that come from the *self* (see Jung 1950/1968: paras. 43–67).

THE INSISTENCE ON THE PERSONAL

Richetti notes that on the island Crusoe becomes 'a contemplative consciousness who can literally observe himself at work, resembling in that fruitful split the master in Hegel's formulation who interposes the slave between the thing and himself and thereby achieves freedom' (Richetti 1975: 35; Hegel 1979: 111–119). My objective here is to look at three different ways in which the novel breaks new *literary* ground.

In dreams that appear in earlier literature (e.g. Shakespeare's *Richard III* and *Macbeth*), a protagonist experiences a warning, but is powerless to avoid his fate: in other words, the collective entirely subsumes the personal. In contrast, Crusoe *engages* with the implications of his dreams; he *takes responsibility* for them. For example, he dreams of a situation that *exactly* anticipates his discovery of Friday. It is of course only a literary device (and not a real dream), but what is remarkable about it is that it is *not* a 'visionary' dream (Jung 1930/1966: para. 139); it has a self-evident relation to his *immediate* situation. Upon waking, Crusoe reflects:

> I made this Conclusion, that my only Way to go about an Attempt for an Escape, was, if possible, to get a Savage into my Possession: and if possible, it should be one of their Prisoners, who they had condemn'd to be eaten, and should bring thither to kill.
>
> (Defoe 1994: 144)

He realizes that his dream has presented him with a solution to the challenge implicitly facing him, and waits his opportunity. And one and a half years later, this is exactly how he rescues Friday.

The protagonists of earlier fictions (e.g. the Wife of Bath, Hamlet, or Milton's Satan) are engaged in struggles that have a predominantly collective significance; even Hamlet's dilemma has little or nothing to do with his *individual* identity. In contrast, Crusoe's dilemma on the island is emphatically personal: *it concerns no one but himself*. He engages in a succession of vividly described activities, in each of which he imagines a need, then he finds out how to meet it, and lastly he contemplates his success. For example, he has no vessel to hold liquid, so he sets out to find clay with which to make an earthenware pot. He ends: 'No Joy at a Thing of so mean a Nature was ever equal to mine, when I found I had made an Earthen Pot that would bear the fire' (ibid.: 89). He gets no joy from possessions as such; but he gets a deep-rooted satisfaction from successfully resolving the difficulties that face him. His identity consists in what he can *do*, which in turn is a vivid metaphor for accepting himself as the specific individual that he is, and neither pretending nor aspiring to be more.

One of Crusoe's most interesting characteristics is his ability to recognize that the collective is only a *cultural* norm. Although he manifests a worrying need to play 'master' (Richetti 1975), he also learns not to judge others through his own cultural spectacles. For example, after pondering about his desire to kill as many savages as he can, he comes to a startling conclusion, and renounces his intention:

> I was perfectly out of my Duty, when I was laying all my bloody Schemes for the Destruction of innocent Creatures, I mean innocent as to me: As to the Crimes they were guilty of towards one another, I had nothing to do with them; they were National, and I ought to leave them to the Justice of God.
>
> (Defoe 1994: 125)

By 'National', he means that the crimes in question belonged to the entire nation and thus not to any specific individual. The recognition that the 'National' is conditioned by culture *implies* that the collective is relative, and thus can be imprisoning; and by extension, the individual has a right to seek his own moral certainties.

In each of these examples, there is an insistence on the personal rather than the collective. And in each, Crusoe as *narrator* observes Crusoe as *object of reflection* and learns from the experience. John Allen Stevenson reminds us that 'a distinction must be drawn between the psychology of the character and the psychology of the kind of heroism [he] represents' (Stevenson 1990: 14). Crusoe as character changes remarkably little in the course of the events that he describes. At the end, he is still a curiously flat character; he has not learned anything; he is not a better man. And Defoe does not appear to have changed from the writing of his fiction. And yet the novel portrays a very specific kind of heroism. Crusoe's struggle to survive reflects the heroism implicit in an unwavering determination to discover his own *individual* identity.

REDEFINING THE PERSONA AND THE EGO

It has long been recognized that Jung's most frequently cited definition of the ego as 'the centre of [the field of] consciousness' (e.g. Jung 1950/1968: para. 1) is problematic. Can consciousness be envisaged in spatial terms (centre/field)? Can one really use the same term to refer to a response to an *outer* stimulant (e.g. an approaching rain-cloud, verbal information, irony, or a painting) as to a new awareness about the nature and implications of an *inner* experience (e.g. a powerful emotion, a vivid fantasy image, an autonomous intuition, or a compulsive thought)? In similar fashion, it might also be doubted whether consciousness pertains only to the ego. In Jungian terminology, appropriate responses to the outer world are *usually* governed by the *persona*, just as one's thoughts about inner experiences can *also* be dictated by the *shadow*. Envisaging the ego in terms of consciousness and of space (a 'centre' that can be 'expanded') is an invitation both to individual psychological inflation and to a collective cult-like smugness.

Jung was often infuriatingly vague and contradictory in his definitions. For example, in the same paragraph in which he defines the *ego* as 'a sort of complex', he also describes it as 'the absolutely indispensable centre of consciousness' (Jung 1935/1977: para. 19). And he then proceeds to contrast two aspects of the ego: one that is turned toward the outside world; another that lies in 'the shadow-world' of unconsciousness, where 'the ego is somewhat dark, we do not see into it, we are an enigma to ourselves' (ibid.: para. 38). It is impossible to make clear sense of this, for a *complex* indicates an *aspect* of either consciousness or unconsciousness, but *never* the centre of the former. Moreover, it is not easy to understand how the 'centre of consciousness' can *also* be partly unconscious.

Jung's distinction between the *persona* and the *ego* is invaluable, but flawed. He was too ready to ascribe to the *ego* attributes that properly belong to the *persona*. The confusion, of course, comes from Jung's choice of terms: *persona* (mask) *suggests* 'inauthenticity', while *das Ich* = 'the I' (usually translated as the *ego*) *suggests* 'consciousness'.

As a result, the persona has always been the poor relative of Jungian psychology, treated carelessly because envisaged as inauthentic. This is mistaken. The persona, determined by archetypal factors, is just as authentic as the ego, but for different reasons. The persona is related to social and therefore *collective* identity; the ego, to individual and therefore *personal* identity. The persona is the carrier of consciousness that is directed toward the outer world. The persona not only helps the individual to navigate the outer world of society, but also shapes the course of relationships and even intellectual ideas. It is the persona that allows individuals to imagine the *necessary fiction* that their identity is continuous. In all these ways, the persona corresponds to that aspect of identity that philosophers call the 'self'. It is *only* when coloured by the *shadow* that the persona becomes inauthentic. Thus the phrase 'inflated ego' is a misnomer, for *inflation* is always relative to something explicitly or implicitly connected with the outer world. Inflation comes not from the ego, but from the *persona*, which is easily contaminated by the *shadow*.

In contrast, the ego is *not* related to the kind of consciousness that is turned toward the outer world. Nor can it be defined in spatial terms, for it has no location, and it cannot expand. The ego is a virtual complex that crystallizes whenever an individual turns *inward* in order to explore the *personal significance* of an inner experience; i.e. when the individual begins to ask how inner experience impacts on their *personal* identity. It describes a *tendency*, an *inclination*, or a *lens*. As soon as what it reveals reaches consciousness, the insight is immediately coloured and absorbed by those aspects of the personality that turn naturally toward the *outer* world.

This reading of *Robinson Crusoe* suggests that the ego can be defined as two inseparable aspects of the tendency to turn inwards: a *perceiving* aspect (Crusoe as *narrator*) that is always in process of transformation as a result of its own attitudes toward, and responses to a *perceived* aspect of itself (Crusoe as *object of reflection*, i.e. as dream-ego). Because it is forever flipping between *actuality* and *latency*, the ego is intrinsically unstable. As long as the perceiving aspect is connected with an inner image, the ego can be described as actual. But as soon as the individual looks outward again, the persona resumes control and the ego becomes only a latency. This is why, alone of all Jung's terms for the various aspects of the personality, it cannot be represented in a dream. It describes a specific kind of *self-awareness* that comes from being connected to one's inner world – in other words, the kind of self-awareness that begins to be explored in *literature* in the early eighteenth century.

ROBINSON CRUSOE AND THE MODERN NOVEL

Defoe appears to have regarded *Robinson Crusoe* as an allegory of the events of his own life (Defoe 1994: 240). Although it is uncertain what *he* meant by this, this reading offers one way of understanding his assertion.

Readings of *Robinson Crusoe* tend to emphasize the characteristics pertinent to the cultural ideology of the early eighteenth century (trade, landed property, the puritan tradition of spiritual autobiography, etc.). In these pages I have tried to demonstrate that the novel *also* gives expression to a new psychological dilemma: the separation of *the domain of the personal* (mediated by the ego) from the much larger and anterior *domain of collective values* (mediated by the persona). The novel's central theme of *survival* is a metaphor indicative of an unconscious desire not to allow the ego to be absorbed entirely by the persona. The motif of survival (rather than discovery) suggests that the ego has always been latent, but it has no energy of its own. It requires the 'secret Hints' that come from the *self* in order to stir it to a sense of the threat posed to it by conformity to the collective. For the first time in literary history, the collective (family expectations, society) is imagined as *imprisoning*, and the domain of the individual, as *liberating*. *Robinson Crusoe* is not just about middle-class resourcefulness. Although set in a fast-moving modern world imagined as hostile to individuality, it also offers a vivid mythic representation of the struggle required by individuals if they are to differentiate their ego from their persona.

Prior to the eighteenth century, literary texts were almost solely concerned with the *collective* unconscious. It would never have occurred to Homer, Chaucer, Shakespeare, or Milton to write about their *personal* dilemmas. Obviously, they had personal concerns, but they have left us little or no record of these in their literary works. *Robinson Crusoe* is perhaps the first major work in English literature in which the text suggests that its author was wrestling with the problem of *individual* identity. From the time of its publication, it became more and more common for individuals to imagine that living solely within the bounds of collective expectations was a form of imprisonment. They became increasingly aware of their need to discover their own individual, i.e. *personal* identity. And inevitably, this new need required a new 'vehicle' and so a new genre was born: *the modern novel* arose in order to meet the desire to explore an authentic personal identity that is *distinct* from any of the various facets of the social or collective persona.

REFERENCES

Dawson, T. (2008) 'Literary Criticism and Analytical Psychology', in Polly Young-Eisendrath and T. Dawson (eds) *The Cambridge Companion to Jung*, 2nd ed. Cambridge: Cambridge University Press.

Defoe, D. (1994) *Robinson Crusoe*, ed. Michael Shinagel, 2nd ed., New York: Norton.

Green, M. (1990) *The Robinson Crusoe Story*, University Park: Pennsylvania University Press.

Hegel, G. W. F. (1979) 'Independence and Dependence of Self-consciousness: Lordship and Bondage', in J. V. Findlay (ed.) *Hegel's Phenomenology of Spirit*, trans. A. V. Miller, New York: Oxford University Press, pp. 111–119.

Hunt, P. (ed.) (1995) *Children's Literature: An Illustrated History*, Oxford: Oxford University Press.

Jung, C. G. (1935/1977) 'The Tavistock Lectures', in *The Collected Works of C. G. Jung (CW)*, ed. H. Read, M. Fordham, and G. Adler, 20 vols, London: Routledge & Kegan Paul, 1953–83, *CW* 18, paras. 1–415.

—— (1930/1966) 'Psychology and Literature', in *CW* 15, paras. 133–162.

—— (1931) 'The Aims of Psychotherapy', *CW* 16, para. 110.

—— (1950/1968) *Aion: Researches into the Phenomenology of the Self*, 2nd ed., *CW* 9.ii.

Novak, M. E. (1962) *Economics and the Fiction of Daniel Defoe*, Berkeley: University of California Press.

—— (1963) *Defoe and the Nature of Man*, London: Oxford University Press.

—— (2001) *Daniel Defoe: Master of Fictions*, Oxford: Oxford University Press.

Novak, M. E. and Carl Fisher (eds) (2005) *Approaches to Teaching Defoe's* Robinson Crusoe, New York: Modern Language Association of America.

Porter, R. (2000) *Enlightenment: Britain and the Creation of the Modern World*, London: Allen Lane/Penguin.

Richetti, J. (1975) '*Robinson Crusoe*: the Self as Master', *Defoe's Narratives: Situations and Structures*, Oxford: Clarendon Press, pp. 21–62.

Rousseau, J.-J. (1761) *Émile*; trans. Allan Bloom (1979) *Emile, or On Education*, New York: Basic Books.

Spaas, L. and B. Simpson (eds) (1996) *Robinson Crusoe: Myths and Metamorphoses*, Houndmills, Basingstoke: Macmillan Press.

Stevenson, J. A. (1990) '*Robinson Crusoe*: The Eccentric Everyman', *The British Novel: Defoe to Austen*, Boston: Twayne, pp. 5–20.

Taylor, C. (1989) *Sources of the Self: The Making of the Modern Identity*, Cambridge, Mass.: Harvard University Press.

Watt, I. (1951) '*Robinson Crusoe* as Myth', *Essays in Criticism* 1, pp. 95–119.

—— (1957) *The Rise of the Novel: Studies in Defoe, Richardson and Fielding*, London: Chatto & Windus.

Zimmerman, E. (1975) *Defoe and the Novel*, Berkeley: University of California Press.

Chapter 3

Archetypal dwelling, building individuation

Lucy Huskinson

INTRODUCTION

Buildings can be regarded as living beings. This is clearly exemplified in the natural forms of Art Nouveau, which curl and unfurl in organic movement, and in the buildings of the architect Frank Lloyd Wright with their interplay of concrete and nature. In this essay, however, I want to bring the building to life in a more fundamental way, beyond its visual attributes. Far from being a mere created end product, I regard the building as active participant in the creative process of human beings.

Some buildings seem more alive than others, because they hold more personal meaning for us. The building we call home, for example, is charged with meaning, because it is closely involved with the most intimate aspects of our lives. As one writer puts it, 'It has witnessed our indignities and embarrassments, as well as the face we want to show to the outside world. The home has seen us at our worst, and still shelters us and protects us' (Ballantyne 2002: 17). But it is not just the building we live in that is infused with personal meaning; any inhabited space or dwelling place is integral to our psychological wellbeing. In this paper I am concerned principally with the archetype-in-itself of building as dwelling – of the transcendental possibility of building – rather than its archetypal image: its finite properties as they may appear to the individual. Bachelard, in *The Poetics of Space* (1958), expresses the point well:

> [I]t is not a question of describing houses, or enumerating their picturesque features and analyzing for which reasons they are comfortable. On the contrary, we must go beyond the problems of description . . . in order to attain to the primary virtues, those that reveal an attachment that is native in some way to the primary function of inhabiting.
>
> (Bachelard 1958: 4)

Heidegger attributes archetypal status to dwelling. According to Heidegger, the place of dwelling designates the fundamental character of our being.

Dwelling, he tells us, is 'the manner in which we humans *are* on the earth . . . To be a human being means to be on the earth as a mortal. It means to dwell' (1954: 147). Heidegger defines the nature of our dwelling as a means to affirm and explore the identity of our being, and its relation to the world. For Heidegger, the constituent parameters of our being and dwelling are the 'fourfold' of earth, sky, gods and mortals. Buildings, he tells us, are edifices of the fourfold that 'preserve' and 'gather' our being (ibid.: 151, 158). In Heideggerian terms, buildings are thus not simply structures that provide shelter and project our personas to the outside world; they also serve a role of mediation, through which we enter into dialogue with ourselves, with our fellow beings, with nature, and with the world beyond. Buildings, as places of dwelling, involve the totality of our existence: our whole selves always in relation to the Other. Through the building you are united with your whole self.

From the time of the Renaissance, the Vitruvian principles, as we now know them, of function, technology, and form, have been regarded as the fundamental conceptual components that not only constitute the ideal building, but also have come to stand for a definition of 'architecture' in general. Heidegger, however, calls for a new definition. He instils life or 'being' into architecture, replacing the more functional components of Vitruvius with his own categories of earth, sky, gods, and mortals. Through Heidegger we see that architectural design is not the mere assembly of building components according to abstract geometric principles, it is also a learning process, a process of exploration, discovery, and understanding; it is a process of individuation. Architectural design questions our being or dwelling in the world; it is inherently an ontological process – indeed, an alchemical process of spirit infused with stone.

JUNG: BUILDING THE PSYCHE

I believe that Jung intuited this profound relationship between the building and our very being. He does not explicate it in detail, but does offer many instances of it. Perhaps the most striking is his assertion that a building is 'a structural diagram of the human psyche' (Jung 1961: 185). Jung makes this point in reference to a dream of a house he had in 1909 on his voyage to America with Freud and Ferenczi, but it could quite as easily have referred to his self-designed and self-built house at Bollingen, constructed decades after Jung had this dream, and described by him as the 'concretisation of the individuation process' (ibid.: 252). Indeed, the topographical model of psyche as a building is, I believe, implicit throughout Jung's work and life, developing alchemically within him, from dream-image to physical embodiment in concrete. Certainly Jung himself acknowledges that the dream-house of 1909, 'became for me a *guiding image* which in the days to come was to be corroborated to an extent I could not at first suspect' (ibid.: 185; italics mine).

Jung came to recognize the significance of the building for his psychological model and for his personal development, but he did so only implicitly, focusing on its powerful effects rather than its inherent value. Thus, Jung extolled the virtue of his dream-house because, as he says, 'it led me for the first time to the concept of the "collective unconscious" (ibid.: 182). In Heideggerian terms we might then say that Jung was not aware that it is the building or dwelling place within him that enabled the mediation between himself and the creative realm of the gods. Jung is, rather, simply interested in whatever message the gods wish to convey to him.

There are many occasions in Jung's dream-life where we find a building that constitutes dwelling place. These dream-buildings literally house the creative and purposive energy that directs Jung's conceptual work, and the subsequent affirmation of his very being. Although Jung is aware of the creative process at work within him, he does not allude to the building-image as integral to it. For example, Jung tells us he had a series of dreams of an unknown building, an annex or wing, built on the side of his house, which contained the unconscious anticipations of his theoretical work. Jung suggests that the problems of the *coniunctio* and of Christ were found within rooms of this large wing, within a laboratory of fish and a vast hall or reception room for spirits (ibid.: 240–1). On another occasion Jung tells us that this dream-annex to his house anticipated his discovery of alchemy; this time Jung found himself exploring the dream-building to discover a library of obscure books on symbolism (ibid.: 228). However, it was another dream of a building, this time of a seventeenth-century manor house of grand proportions, with many annexes and out buildings, that Jung described as '*the crucial* dream anticipating my encounter with alchemy' (ibid.; italics mine).

At best these dream accounts of Jung provide *evidence* of the archetypal 'transformative' energy of the building as 'dwelling', for Jung tells us that each of these dreams immediately precede an inspirational insight into the development of his theories or personality. That is, there would seem to be a superficial causal link between Jung having a dream in which a building as 'dwelling place' predominates, and his conscious realization of new creative aspects to his work. Had Jung explored 'dwelling' more deeply, he might have found in his dreams what he would have considered 'empirical evidence' of the archetypal reality of building.

Dream-house

But, let us turn back to Jung's dream-house of 1909, which contributes to a striking topographical model of building as psyche. Jung offers two slightly different descriptions of it, in *Memories, Dreams, Reflections* (1961) and in his essay 'Mind and Earth' (1927/1931). Although the latter does not allude to the house as having been dreamt, it is evident that Jung is referring to the same dream house of 1909. In this dream Jung explores a multi-storey house of different architectural styles, which appear progressively older as Jung descends stone stairs from upper storey to basement. Each storey of the house represents a different layer of the psyche; so when Jung explores and walks through the different floors of the house, he is effectively exploring the different realms of the psyche, and traversing its boundaries of consciousness, personal unconsciousness and collective unconsciousness.

Jung tells us, on more than one occasion, that the upper storey of a house represents consciousness. In this dream-house it is depicted as a 'salon furnished with fine old pieces in rococo style' that exhibits an 'inhabited atmosphere' (1961: 184). He continues in 'Mind and Earth' to note that 'we live on the upper storey . . . [J]ust as the building rises freely above the earth, so our consciousness stands as if above the earth in space, with a wide prospect before it' (1927/1931: para. 55). This is paralleled by his house at Bollingen, the final addition of the upper storey of which was described by Jung as 'my ego personality' and 'an extension of consciousness' (1961: 251–2).

The ground floor of a building represents the 'first level of the unconscious': the personal unconscious (ibid.: 184). In the dream we see this aspect of the psyche represented by rooms of the fifteenth or sixteenth century, with medieval floors of red brick (ibid.: 182), 'and careful examination of the masonry reveals that [this floor] was reconstructed from a tower built in the eleventh century' (1927/1931: para. 54).

The floors beneath ground level correspond to 'deeper', 'darker' levels of the unconscious – the collective unconscious – which is visualized in the dream-house as an ancient vaulted room, deduced by Jung to be Roman, and by an even older room, situated at the lowest level of the house, which appears as a 'low cave cut into the rock', thick with dust, bones and broken pottery (1961: 182–3), and with 'neolithic tools in the upper layer and remnants of fauna from the same period in the lower layers' (1927/1931: para. 54). Jung tells us that in this basement room he discovered 'the world of the primitive man within myself' (1961: 184).[1]

It is important to note that the significance of the building as psyche is not reduced to its topography; the building itself is a dynamic, affective being. It would be a category mistake for this paper to concern itself with the visual structure of the building, of what a dwelling place actually looks like. A dwelling place is not a special kind of building; rather, the building is the most common expression of dwelling.[2] It is irrelevant to my principal concern to ask which architectural style is most appropriate for the depiction of dwelling place, or, indeed, whether we should be talking about houses at all. However, there is value in examining different images of dwellings in order to appreciate different responses to human existence that are initiated by the archetype of dwelling.

As I mentioned at the start of this essay, there is a difference between archetype-in-itself and the archetypal image. The archetype-in-itself can never be known, but its meaning and effects can be communicated to us through its symbolic imagery: its archetypal image. When the archetype of dwelling manifests itself, it does so in a particular image; it becomes schematized, or filtered through the subjective disposition of the recipient. The meaning of the archetype of dwelling is concerned with human existence, with being. As soon as the archetype of dwelling becomes conscious – that is to say, has been filtered through the subjectivity of the conscious recipient – the archetype takes on a particular archetypal content, and is now concerned with human existence and being for and from the perspective of the recipient. Thus, when one dreams of a particular dwelling (such as a house), the archetype of dwelling activates, through its image, a concern with human existence in terms appropriate to the dreamer (just as the design of a building portrays the particular concerns of the architect).

To examine Jung's particular dream-house of 1909, for example, is to examine his particular concern with existence or being. We note that his house is structured into different floor levels, rooms, and architectural styles; and this, I argue, is because Jung understands being (or, in Jungian terms, 'psyche') as itself structured with differentiated aspects. We also find stairways connecting the different levels of the house, which suggests that his conception of being entails movement and communication between its parts, so that no part is to be experienced in isolation.

Another interesting example – that 'builds' upon this previous example of Jung – is in Chris Hauke's *Jung and the Postmodern* (2000). Hauke upholds the view that the Jungian model of the psyche is *not* structured, and he subsequently maintains that Jung's image of a structured house is not an appropriate representation of the Jungian model of the psyche. Significantly, Hauke does not dispute the validity of the house-image as representative of the Jungian psyche; he simply argues that the configuration of the house-image, as portrayed in Jung's 1909 dream, is inappropriate. Indeed, Hauke retains the image of house as psyche, and takes it upon himself to redesign Jung's house-image into a more accurate representation of Jung's theoretical model. Hauke attempts some radical 'home improvements' to Jung's 1909 dream-house, according to postmodern precepts of plurality where lack of structure and hierarchy predominate. Hauke wishes to replace verticality with horizontality, placing all layers of the house on view at once, dismantling the notion of structure in favour of accessibility, in an amalgamation or 'mixture' of all aspects of the psyche – of 'past, present and future' (Hauke 2000: 108). Different architectural styles are played off against one another so that none is privileged. Hauke transforms Jung's 1909 dream-house into something like a one-storey bungalow, with the basement rooms of unconsciousness merged with the upper storey rooms of consciousness. The particular concerns for human existence or being are similarly transformed, so that the redesigned house of Hauke is now 'dealing with contradictions, a pluralistic coexistence and an overlapping of values rather than any simplistic periodising

of "movements" or positions [that concerned Jung's 1909 dream-house]'
(ibid.: 87).

Self-building

Let us return to the archetype-in-itself of building as dwelling, and reiterate
that the building is not just a clever metaphor that reduces the psyche to
an abstract image or diagram. It is archetypal, a Self-image no less. Jung
regarded the designing and construction of his house at Bollingen as a process of individuation, and its end product as a symbol of the Self. 'Only after
[it was built]', Jung says, 'did I see how all the parts fitted together and that a
meaningful form had resulted: a symbol of psychic wholeness' (1961: 252).
I would argue, however, that the Self is identified with the *process* of its own
realization, so that the Self was present in the very construction of the
house, and that it was Jung's dwelling place – in the proper Heideggerian
sense – even before the first stone had been laid.

Jung recognized the affective power of the Self in other buildings, including the Taj Mahal, to which he attributes an animated life, as if it were 'more
like a plant that could thrive and flower in the rich Indian earth'. In this
'supreme flower' Jung found 'an instrument of self-realization' (ibid.). The
stupa at Sanchi is another example. To walk meditatively in circumambula-
tion around the stupa, is to take part in the process of becoming whole – of
connecting with the Self. When Jung took this walk he felt overwhelming
emotion that led him to understand 'the life of the Buddha as the reality
of the Self which had broken through and laid claim to a personal life'
(ibid.: 309). Although Jung identifies these buildings with the Self, he seems
to regard them as isolated examples; he does not consider the underlying,
universal archetype of dwelling, in which these buildings partake.

My argument for buildings as archetypally representative of psyche, or
as Self-symbol, is not dependent on Heideggarian or Jungian thought, far
from it. It is an argument that finds support throughout the history of intellectual thought in both eastern and western traditions. I could have presented
my argument through the thought of Bachelard, or even Saint Teresa of
Àvila (also known as Saint Teresa of Jesus), to name just two very different
authors, who offer topographies of house as fundamental to our very being.[3]

And we don't even need to turn to theoretical expositions to substantiate
the tenets of the argument: a cursory inspection of the English language, for
instance, reveals the prevalence of the notion of the building as a representation of the psyche in the common references to such turns of phrase as the
'recesses' or 'corridors' of the mind, and of 'being at home with oneself'. Yet,
the important point is that the archetype of building as dwelling incites
real transformation of personality; it is thus a matter for experience rather
than intellectual elucidation. No philosopher can adequately encapsulate
its affective nature. Although Jung's structural diagram of the psyche may

appear superficial, a deeper process of individuation is at work, re-situating the ego-personality within a place of dwelling, within Self-hood. However, I would like to end my paper with the elucidation of one further example in support of my argument, which I have chosen to illustrate the psychic significance of the building in terms of its visual appeal. This is the ancient art of memory, which was a method that utilized the images of buildings in order to unify the memory, increase its capacity, and impart universal, cosmic knowledge to the individual.

MEMORY-BUILDING

Before I talk about the buildings of the art of memory, I shall briefly outline the significance of memory to the ancients in terms of its active role in the development of personality and its relation to the cosmos. Indeed, I believe that upon the dynamics of their conception of memory a process of individuation can be determined.

For Aristotle, the role of memory is as intermediary between perception and thought; it is integral to the process of translating the *perception* of particulars to *knowledge* of universals – *epagôgē* – which enables us to have both general principles and the insight to discern how these are applied to particular situations. Memory is therefore essential for the attainment of practical wisdom, which is itself an intellectual virtue necessary for *eudaimonia*, or 'human flourishing', which is, I maintain, Aristotle's version of the individuation process. Unlike Aristotle, Plato argued that there is knowledge derived independently of sense-impressions. For Plato, memory was divine. He argued that latent in our memories are the Forms of Ideas that the soul knew before it was embodied at birth. We could argue that these different conceptions of memory inform the two major traditions of the art of memory: the Aristotelian conception underlies the art as it was first conceived, in its classical form, and that of the Platonic underlies the art as it was redeveloped in occult form in the Renaissance. Moreover, these different formulations place different emphasis on the art of memory as a process of individuation.

The purpose of the art of memory in its classical form was to train and order the memory in the absence of the printed word. The ancient Greeks conceived it as a mnemonic, a device of rhetoric to enable the orator to deliver his long speech from memory with unfailing accuracy. The purpose of the mnemonic was to imprint on the memory a series of places, and the most common type of place-system was the building. The Roman rhetorician Quintilian tells us that in order to form a series of places in the memory, one must imagine a building as spacious and varied as possible, divided into different rooms, including a forecourt, living rooms, bedrooms, and parlours. The images by which the speech is to be remembered are then placed within these rooms. Each image correlates with points to be remembered in the speech, so that when making his speech, the orator would move in his imagination through his memory-building, experiencing the images he has placed in each room. This method ensures that the points of the speech are remembered in the right order, since the order is fixed by the sequence of rooms in the building. If the orator wishes to remember much material he must equip himself with a large number of buildings – perhaps a whole street of houses, arches and colonnades, and ramparts of a city (Quintilian 1922: XI, ii, 17–22).

Later, in the Renaissance, the art of memory was conceived as a technique to acquire knowledge of eternal reality. Although its purpose had changed, its expression and utilization was still firmly attached to architectural imagery. The orator of the classical tradition was transformed into the magician of the Renaissance, who spoke from a memory shaped by divine principles; and, consequently, the somewhat 'mundane' memory-building of the classical tradition was reconstructed according to principles of sacred geometry. This, which, together with the talismanic imagery of mythology and astrology that often adorned the interior, instilled the building with numinous effect.

These memory-buildings were sometimes built literally; examples include Camillo's Memory Theatre built in Venice in the sixteenth century, Palladio's *Teatro Olimpico* in Vicenza, built in the 1580s, and the original Globe Theatre of London, built in 1599. Each of these buildings was built according to Vitruvius's architectural plans of the perfectly proportioned amphitheatre, which comprised the sacred geometric shapes of double square and circle. The elaborate imagery that adorned these buildings was considered to have talismanic power or astral *spiritus*, which imparted to the spectator eternal knowledge and the unification of the contents of his memory – all of this achieved in one brief glance of them. Furthermore, these images magically animated the speeches that the orator remembered by them, infusing them with planetary virtue, and entrancing those who listened. If Jung's tower at Bollingen represents, in Jung's words, 'a concretized psyche', then these buildings represent the psyche with greater focus on the collective unconscious.

In both traditions of the art, the building is a mechanism or motivation for the integration of memory within the wider development of personality. In its classical form, the building functions as an ordering of conscious and pre-conscious material – of preventing material from being forgotten and recovering it if it is – and in the Renaissance art, it mediates between the individual and eternal reality, enabling dialogue with the collective unconscious.

Whenever the ego encounters the archetype of building as dwelling, it is transformed and directed towards Self-hood. As we have seen in the examples of Jung's dream-houses and the concrete-house at Bollingen, the building-archetype is encountered in both psychic image and physical object. It is internal, within us and external to us. It is both artist and artwork. Just as we inform the design of the building, the building informs the design of us – of our personality, of our very being – in a shared process of individuation.

NOTES

1 Jung's description of his 1909 dream-house reminds me of the nineteenth-century French historian Jules Michelet's description of his childhood visits to the Musée des Monuments Français, 'Even now I can recall the feeling, still just the same and still stirring, that made my heart beat when, as a small child, I would enter beneath those dark vaults . . . and look, room after room, epoch after epoch. What was I looking for? I hardly know – the life of the time, no doubt, and the spirit of the ages. I was not altogether certain that they were not alive, all those marble sleepers, stretched out on their tombs. And when I moved from the sumptuous monuments of the sixteenth century, glowing with alabaster, to the low room of the Merovingians, in which was to be found the sword of Dagobert, I felt it possible that I would suddenly see Chilpéric and Fredégonde raise themselves and sit up' (*Histoire de la Révolution Français* 1952, vol. II: 538–9; translated and cited in Haskell 1993: 252). Both Jung and Michelet are aware of the living, affective character of the building. Furthermore, Jung's dream-building of 1909, and Michelet's museum (indeed, museums in general), are buildings of 'living memory', and exemplify the 'memory-building' of the art of memory that I discuss near the end of this paper.
2 Heidegger refers to a bridge as an illustration of dwelling (Heidegger 1954: 152).
3 According to Bachelard, 'With the house image we are in possession of a veritable principle of psychological integration . . . On whatever theoretical horizon we examine it, the house image would appear to have become the topography of our intimate being' (1958: xxxvi). Three centuries earlier, St. Teresa imagined the soul 'as if it were a castle . . . in which there are many rooms . . . at the centre, in the midst of these, is the principal room, where much secret intercourse is held between God and the soul' (1577: 7). 'The inmost Mansion [is] where God *dwells* in our soul' (ibid.: 113; italics mine).

REFERENCES

Bachelard, Gaston (1958) *The Poetics of Space*, trans. M. Jolas, Boston: Beacon Press, 1969.

Ballantyne, Andrew (2002) *Architecture: A Very Short Introduction*, Oxford: Oxford University Press.

Haskell, Francis (1993) *History and its Images: Art and the Interpretation of the Past*, New Haven: Yale University Press.

Hauke, Chris (2000) *Jung and the Postmodern: The Interpretation of Realities*, London: Routledge.

Heidegger, Martin (1954) 'Building, Dwelling, Thinking' in *Poetry, Language, Thought*, trans. A. Holstadter, New York: Harper, 1975.

Jung, C. G. (1953–1983) *The Collected Works of C. G. Jung* (*CW*), ed. H. Read, M. Fordham, and G. Adler, 20 vols, London: Routledge & Kegan Paul.

—— (1927/1931) 'Mind and Earth', *CW* 10: paras. 49–103.

—— (1961) *Memories, Dreams, Reflections*, trans. Richard and Clara Winston, London: Fontana Press, 1995.

Quintilian, Marcus Fabius (1922) *Institutio Oratoria* (*circa* A.D. 93), trans. H. E. Butler, Bks. X–XII, vol. 4, The Loeb Classical Library, London: William Heinemann Ltd.; Cambridge, Massachusetts: Harvard University Press.

Saint Teresa of Jesus (1577) *The Interior Castle: or The Mansions* (trans. 'A Discalced Carmelite'), Catholic Publishing Co. Ltd., South Ascot; The Pittman Press, Bath, 1944.

Chapter 4

On painting, substance and psyche

David Parker

INTRODUCTION

Given that the practice of painting concerns, at its most basic level, familiarization with the material and structural properties of the medium and its methods of application, any attempt to fully understand how psyche and imagination are engaged in the activity of painting demands a close reading of the phenomena involved. In this essay I would like to attend to some of these factors, using Jung's ideas on alchemy and the process of individuation, and Elkins' ideas on the importance of material substance to the creative process within both alchemy and painting.

I chose to tackle this theme after reading James Elkins' refreshingly original examination of the practice of painting in which he explores painting in relation to alchemy. As a painter, with a deep interest in the underlying psychotherapeutic aspects of the activity, I was particularly struck by Elkins' scepticism of both Jung's psychology in general and Jung's reading of alchemy in particular (Elkins 2000: 4). That said, the book held my attention in its deep understanding of the material and physical nature of painting and the desire to both literally and metaphorically 'get under the skin' of painting. In this sense, Elkins' ideas seemed to connect quite strongly with my experiences as a painter – though I felt that his disregard for Jung's particular psychological approach to alchemy failed to address important questions regarding the psychological lining to painting. Artist, writer and art therapist David Maclagan discusses such issues in considerable depth (Maclagan 2001). My intention here is to try to connect some of these ideas (from a practitioner point of view) to speculations on the practical aspects of alchemy.

Although Jung's interest in alchemy is primarily concerned with understanding the symbolic nature of the unconscious in psyche, and not the pragmatic day-to-day concerns of the alchemist and his substances, his psychological work has long been recognized as pertinent to how modern artists have negotiated meaningful forms of expression in an age of doubt and uncertainty.[1] This is not to claim that artists have always knowingly drawn on

Jungian ideas as sources of expression, though clearly there are many that have (e.g. Jackson Pollock), but rather to note that Jung's interpretation of the symbolic language of the unconscious appears to have been mirrored by many of the experiments in modern art.[2]

Questions therefore arose. Can we discuss the highly particular activities of both painting and alchemy, with their underlying psychological foundations, from the viewpoints of both Jung and Elkins and gain insight into the intimate relationship between mind and matter in both activities? Also, in the process, can we find a fruitful connection between Jung's aim to understand unconscious symbols and Elkins' aim to attend to the important part played by physical and material substances in painting? I believe so, for my intuition and experience tells me that both aspects are deeply interconnected in painting, and, for this enquiry, perhaps also alchemy. To ignore one at the expense of the other would be to do a disservice towards any attempt to understand how both painting and alchemy appear to create a unique and special bond between material substances and psychological processes. Without such a bond, it is probable that neither painting nor alchemy would hold such intense meaning and fascination for their practitioners. Where perception and imagination are seen as necessary components to a successful negotiation between art and life, then both will require a *symbolic structure*, and for the painter, a *material basis* on which to hang an essentially creative approach to lived experience.

From my reading of Elkins, it is clear that for him Jung appears to privilege the philosophical aspects of alchemy over the alchemist's practical and hence physical relationship towards the substances under transformation. What therefore is missing, and what perhaps all painters know intuitively, concerns the way in which transformative experiences – and thereby a measure of psychological stability – involves *aesthetic* considerations, in the sense that Maclagan uses this term and that these are embedded and informed by responses to physical engagement with the materials of their craft (Maclagan 2001: 23). In other words, the body of the practitioner knows instinctively, through physical sensation and empathy for material and substance, when what is happening is revealing a psychologically significant meaning – even though this meaning may not be wholly consciously assimilated. Surely this is what James Hillman is getting at when he states 'the fingers have an eye in them' (Hillman and Eshleman 1985). As Maclagan suggests, this is such an important point when trying to discuss how psyche and imagination traffic meaning in an activity like painting (and presumably alchemy) that to ignore this aspect in favour of a mainly secondary symbolic reading based solely on a figurative or representational interpretation of imagination, seems misguided (Maclagan 2001: 48–51).

JUNG AND THE FIGURATIVE SYMBOLIC

Jung's work on alchemy seems largely (though not entirely) to demonstrate a psychological interpretation that uses imagery which is essentially figurative and/or representational. It seems as if, for Jung, the imagination, prompted by the internal conflicts between conscious and unconscious processes, only presents meaning when attached to figurative or representational forms of symbolic expression.[3] This perhaps is misguided when talking about painting – and for the sake of this comparison perhaps also alchemy. Such a view of the symbolic psyche does not fully address how the actual *process* of each activity might in fact be negotiating a psychologically transformative meaning. This being the case, perhaps the symbolic is carried and expressed by qualities which are other than the purely figurative or representational and yet are essentially aesthetically, and therefore psychologically, transformative in potential (Maclagan 2001).

It is perhaps within the material and temporal process – as an intuitive negotiation between mind and matter and heightened states of awareness and insight – that psychological meaning and transformation takes place. In other words, the materials and substances under transformation are affecting a psychological change in the painter/alchemist. This being so, the symbolic structure as such is not just figurative or representational but rather *presentational* – a revealed insight disclosed by a *felt* rather than *thought* relationship to the material as a substance.[4] Such an approach to psychological meaning is of course notoriously difficult to articulate with any clarity precisely because, intellectually, we are forced to use words in order to communicate and clarify what we mean beyond the phenomenal visual and tactile experience itself.

As Maclagan shows us, words, in such a context, are perhaps really secondary abstractions to an essentially felt meaning (Maclagan 2001: 111–28). The closest we can get with words to actual felt experiences, is to use adjectives that resonate with the feeling of a given sensate experience, and this places meaning in the realm of the poetic. This then is a line of thinking that echoes Hillman's *Thought of the Heart and the Soul of the World*, by bringing back into play a perspective on psychological experience that encourages us to reconsider the root meaning of the word 'material' as the matrix or mother of experience (Hillman 1997). With regard to the roots of alchemy, we can also turn to the work of Mircea Eliade, professor of the history of religions, for some interesting comparisons on this observation (Eliade 1978: 42).

THE STUDIO AND THE LABORATORY

So, what particular factors are common to the activities of both painting and alchemy? In each case we can begin with the void – the blank canvas or the crucible – and the desire to introduce the chaotic, unstructured material – the prima materia. What follows is, in effect, a process of becoming for the active psyche. This process carries with it the potential for success and/or failure determined by the degree to which, psychologically, the artist/alchemist achieves a balancing of opposing elements in the work itself and a level of stability between these. In each case (painting or alchemy) such material must be manipulated, processed and shaped towards a desired goal which may or may not be understood in terms of a prescribed, ideal outcome. Either way, what is desired by the artist/alchemist is always changed by the materials and the process – a point addressed at some length from a phenomenological point of view by Nigel Wentworth in his study on *The Phenomenology of Painting* (Wentworth 2004: 25–52). In the end, as every painter knows, a rigid and inflexible approach that does not remain open to changes in the work leads to a dull uninspiring result – also, crucially and fundamentally, this is not a one-way process.

In the lived experience of each activity, both the material itself and the manipulator affect each other in a two-way process. Psychologically, the material under structural transformation appears almost to become an extension of the creator. Such a point, as Elkins highlights, is also characterized by popular perceptions of the artist, where the skills and knowledge of the artist/practitioner appear to become embedded in the very identity and personality of the individual (Elkins 2000: 147–8). With the flow of energy between psyche and matter, notional boundaries between artist/alchemist and their materials become undifferentiated or rather 'de-differentiated', to import a term from Anton Ehrenzweig (1971: 19).

Through the process of painting, marks, shapes, colours etc. and their structural organization record bodily actions as well as mental processes. However, these effects are also determined by the material qualities of the medium in its various states – dry, wet, sticky, thin, thick, lumpy etc. and their attached tonal and chromatic qualities. What happens and what appears in the process is therefore conditioned by the medium as much as it is conditioned by the artist/alchemist. Both activities steer a course of development with no absolute prescribed or even repeatable outcomes – each is a unique process and a unique product. Implicit to both are aesthetic considerations, embracing all the nuances and particulars of changes of state within both the psyche of the practitioner and the substance under transformation – a negotiation between psyche and matter or spirit and matter. Such psychological states can appear as strangely 'altered states' of consciousness, states intimately connected to perceptual experiences of matter and its condition in the structural matrix of the developing work. Within such states, perception and imagination, stimulated by the material and structural properties under transformation, mediate and blur boundaries between conscious and unconscious activity, crucially exposing the extraordinary daemonic forces of unconscious drives.

Perhaps this then is the symbolic alchemical fire, the living phoenix created by the friction between matter and psyche? Any figurative or representational fantasies that may or may not attach themselves to the outcome throughout the process, or after the work is completed, may attenuate the psychological meaning but are not in themselves the sole index of aesthetic or psychological value. From a painter's position, and presumably also an alchemist's, the work evolves in each case as a unique entity. It effectively grows from an undifferentiated state (chaos) through various stages of development, to its final mature stage when what is left consolidates, both physically and metaphorically, thereby mirroring the internal aesthetic sensibilities of both painter and alchemist.

THE THERAPEUTIC IN PAINTING AND ALCHEMY

In the process of this creative transformation, both alchemy and painting are perhaps, by their very nature, essentially therapeutic activities – therapeutic, in the sense that they both mediate and manifest through matter, an imaginative interchange between conscious and unconscious processes – the therapeutic process being *the activity itself*. Such a process involves a constitutional need to act out, through flux and change, the dynamic relationship between primary, intuitive, unconscious drives (operating essentially outside textual language) and conscious secondary elaborations. For painters, exposing their imagining psyche by engaging others in aesthetic appreciation of the work also activates a cultural dimension – thus moving the therapeutic theatre from the individual to the collective and bringing into sharp relief Hillman's thinking on the need to effectively instigate a therapy of culture itself (Hillman and Ventura 1993).

Following this line of thinking, it is not unreasonable to conjecture that most of the experiments of avant-garde art throughout modernism have really, in essence, been strategic and (in an expanded sense of the word) therapeutic, creative reactions to a perceived emptiness and loss of meaning. Such a loss of meaning was perhaps brought about by an overemphasis on the value of scientific rationalism developing from the Enlightenment, where the 'glue' of faith through religious belief was challenged, and non-rational (Otto 1923) modes of being were denigrated and dismissed as experiences without concrete foundations. The ensuing one-sided sickness of a developing modern culture demanded a spiritual counterpoint by those who felt such a loss of meaning, echoing in collective terms Jung's dynamic model of the individual psyche – the experiments of modern art being one expression of such a need.

THE FIGURATIVE AND THE NON-FIGURATIVE IMAGINATION

I started this essay by stating that I wished to balance Jung's thinking on alchemy with that of Elkins in relation to the art of painting. I have throughout tried to think through and articulate my understanding of the meaning of both writers from the point of view of a painter. My feeling is that Jung, like the alchemists before him, needed to express the inherent psychological meaning of the alchemical process through a secondary and largely (though not entirely) rationalized figurative use of imagery. It almost seems as if, for the alchemist, the actual experiencing psyche, once it had left the laboratory or studio, lost contact with the sensate and innately concrete nature of the transformative aesthetics implicit in the 'stuff' of matter, and because of this a secondary figurative elaboration through symbolic representation was called upon. Rich though that language might be in its use of poetic metaphor and obscure, hermetic figurative symbolism, the fact remains that the original and primary source for practical alchemists must have involved an imaginative engagement with matter and substance *for its own sake.*

This being the case, any symbolic meaning would be taking place directly within this engagement, without necessarily having recourse to figurative symbolism as such. In other words, I am suggesting that the symbolic constitutes something innately meaningful and constructive to the experiencing subject and that this 'something' is not necessarily fully consciously or intellectually known or assimilated by figurative imagery alone, neither is it necessarily rational in its psychological meaning. This experience, as Maclagan argues, is essentially an aesthetic experience, i.e. a 'breathing in', an experience which contributes to our inner imaginative life as we 'inhabit works of art imaginatively' (Maclagan 2001: 10)

Regardless of Elkins' views on Jung's psychology, and their relevance or not to an understanding of painting, I believe his deep reflections on the practice of painting and alchemy (and bearing in mind the limitations of language when discussing such practices) do go some way towards bridging a gap between what we might call the art of psychology and the psychology of art. I am also convinced that Jung's deep research into the significance of alchemical symbols for an understanding of psyche also provides a useful and rewarding theoretical framework in which to discuss aspects of painting. However, I say this with the proviso that painting, like alchemy, is of course a different order of experience to language. It is an experience that generates symbolic meaning through aesthetic engagement with the visual and haptic within substances – where imagination, as Maclagan shows us, is not necessarily tied to its expression through figuration and its relationship to language but can, and does, embrace it.

Following Elkins' lead, I hope I have managed to convincingly argue a case for the crucial symbolic nature of matter and substance in both painting and

alchemy. I am more comfortable as a painter than a writer, and I know intuitively that how paintings evolve, and the psychological meaning underscoring
them, remains deeply connected to what one is able to consciously assimilate
within the medium and structure and what one is unable to consciously
assimilate. Also, that it is within this strange dynamic that any meaning and
value they may carry as aesthetic objects helps to guide the imagination
towards deeper, more meaningful levels of experience. For a painter, the question then, of course, is whether such essentially personal meaning and value is
rich enough to carry over beyond individual value and into collective value as
an aesthetic and psychologically valuable cultural experience.

JUNG AND THE AESTHETIC DIMENSION

At this point a brief discussion of my perception of Jung's attitude towards
aesthetics in relation to psychology seems apposite given that this attempt to
conflate the two terms remains fundamental to my argument. On this point
then it is intriguing to note the extent to which Jung seemed unable (or at least
unwilling) to embrace the aesthetic response as a valid index of psychological
content in his few forays into modern art. His insightful attempt to understand
the psychology of Picasso's art clearly indicates this: 'I have nothing to say on
the question of Picasso's "art" but only on its psychology. I shall therefore
leave the aesthetic problem to the art critics, and shall restrict myself to the
psychology underlying this kind of artistic creativeness' (Jung 1978: 135).

Now, this could simply be indicative of Jung's desire to keep his psychology within the scientific frame in order to preserve its validity – any mention of the aesthetic in this respect being problematic – there are, as always, so
many paradoxes with Jung. However, his psychology of Picasso's art rightly
engages with the perceived structural and spatial fragmentation indicative of
an artist working with powerful internal imaginative sources. Such sources
involve the free play of memory and imagination via the discrete activity of
painting, perhaps largely independent of directly observed, external sources.
Jung then states in his essay on Picasso: 'the main characteristic is one of
fragmentation, which expresses itself in the so-called "lines of fracture" –
that is, a series of psychic "faults" (in the geological sense) which run right
through the picture' (Jung 1978: 137).

Jung continues: 'The picture leaves one cold, or disturbs one by its paradoxical, unfeeling, and grotesque unconcern for the beholder' (ibid.: 137). This
he refers to as 'non-objective art' (ibid.: 136), presumably meaning without
concern for an external objective reality or those forms and structures perceived through a Euclidian-based geometry and a pictorial space developed
from it. What Jung seemed to fail to recognize, or be able to tolerate as an art,
was the modern artist's move towards a need to reconfigure space and form
as aesthetic device. Such a move was perhaps made in order to better express

the changing relationship developing between a perceived external reality and a felt internal psychological condition. Modern artists were effectively reinvesting art with content and meaning (essentially psychological) that, of necessity, involved a spatial shift in the relationship between the viewer and the viewed. This was a shift that effectively dismantled the pictorial conventions of representation in order to direct aesthetic experience, and hence regain depth of meaning, by de-objectifying representational content in order to place the viewer psychologically 'within the image' rather than separate and detached without. In effect, a perceptual shift took place – one that broke away from pictorial conventions rooted in a mainly object-based view of the external world.

By intuitively grasping the limitations of a dualistic view concerning object and subject, painters were attempting to express the psychological disturbance or insecurity brought about by the new 'Modern' human condition. In this respect, what Jung aimed to address with his scientific psychology modern artists aimed intuitively to address with their art – both were perhaps symptomatic responses to a modern industrialized civilization and its shadow effect on psyche. The differences between Jung and his psychology and modern artists and their art, in relation to the aesthetic response, were perhaps differences of temperament and constitution – paradoxically exemplified by Jung in his study on *Psychological Types* (Jung 1923).

Perhaps constitutionally Jung the scientist saw wholeness or completeness as only being demonstrable within art when such art measured up rationally to an idealized representation of external reality: an aesthetic pleasure based on a consensus reality and a sense of beauty constructed from an optimistic and confident attitude towards the world. Maybe Jung saw modern art as a neurotic and schizoid expression – one which failed to reintegrate emotionally, aesthetically and optimistically – and in this sense perhaps he was right. However if this was so, modern artists such as Picasso might also have been constitutionally driven to work through their problematic relationship to consensus reality by imaginatively re-configuring their emotional experiences in order to better mediate and balance psychological conflicts. Such a re-configuring demanded an introverted engagement with internal sources of imagery – sources indicative of a withdrawal from an increasingly alienating and emotionally sterile industrialized social order.

A turning inward then, towards a desire to work with unconscious content, within both psychology and art, has the ability to change our perceptual apparatus, providing us with a means to make structural changes to consciousness, both on an individual and a collective level. What is perhaps astonishing is that Jung understood the psychotherapeutic importance of art making personally as well as professionally – the periods of creative play discussed in *Memories, Dreams, Reflections* (Jung and Jaffe 1963: 168–9) during a period of intense inner disturbance, demonstrates a clear acknowledgement of this. It does seem however that he was unable or unwilling to accept the possibility that what modern artists were creating were significant expressions of value to the collective psyche, and in this sense their art was perhaps effectively a culturally validated psychotherapeutic aesthetic. It is also significant that Jung the scientist/psychologist clearly felt driven to engage his personal unconscious through playful involvement with objects and materials and related methods of handling and application. In this sense, surely the body and its sensual and tactile faculties were vital and necessary to his imaginative process, in his need to negotiate a way through quite traumatic and painful psychological experiences.

CONCLUSION

Both Freud and Jung demonstrated the value of imagination and free association in the development of their respective psychotherapies – and Jung in particular, showed the value of visual activities such as drawing and painting as vehicles for negotiating psychological conditions. However, it seems that within both psychologies, aesthetic responses were considered the domain of culture and irrelevant to psychology as such. Also, that psychology and related therapeutic concerns demanded figurative and/or narrative representations to express the latent meaning underlying what might be presented.

As a painter, and following Elkins and Maclagan in this respect, I feel drawn to say that, regardless of the particular circumstances under which a painting or drawing might be produced, what is presented as an imaginative response to the materials and substances under transformation contains and reveals a psychological meaning through its specific handling and application. Also, this meaning is determined as much by the medium itself as by the practitioner. It is therefore perhaps as well to consider that what has been explored and presented culturally in painting, via the various manifestations of abstraction, indicates an emerging aesthetic value rooted in its material condition and psychological and imaginative responses to this – regardless of any figurative or representational considerations. Also, in my view, such psychological responses mirror those of the alchemists in their efforts to discover, through matter, the aesthetically transformative potential of physical processes. Such fundamentally aesthetic responses can act as gateways to the unconscious in psyche and are perhaps the prime movers in the development of emotional and spiritual intelligence within both painting and alchemy.

NOTES

1 I am referring here to how artistic sensibilities after the Enlightenment appear to have been focused on a subjective need to re-engage with the deeper 'spiritual'

dimensions of life in order to counterbalance an overemphasis on rationalist and materialist paradigms. In painting within the developing industrialized societies, this can be traced through Romanticism to Modernism. In terms of the particular forms that painting began to employ in order to effect a re-engagement, non-figurative abstractions were perhaps an inevitable outcome. Such an outcome indicated the psychological insecurity felt by a loss of meaning regarding man's place in a universe without the divine purpose taken as beyond question before the Enlightenment. Wilhelm Worringers' pioneering book *Abstraction and Empathy* (1908) discusses these issues as perhaps the first study on the psychology of representation and abstraction as stylistic predispositions in art. Worringer argues from the premise that man's unease with the material world promotes a tendency towards abstraction and spiritual concerns.

2 My use of the word 'symbol' is determined by Jung's use of it, i.e. symbols are 'natural and spontaneous products' 'a symbol (that) hints at something not yet known' (quoted from Jung and Von Franz 1978: 41). In this sense, I understand the symbolic to function as a means by which the opposites or conflicting aspects within psyche are brought into balance in order to synthesize from the conflict. This can be 'acted out' in creative work and thus point towards a deeper sense of self, one which encompasses non-ego states – a more complete state of being. This way of thinking about the symbolic is not concerned with the restricted use of the word as applied to cultural symbols per se, where any symbolic meaning that may be attributed to an image is predetermined by its expression as a consciously assimilated, culturally defined image. In this sense, such a 'symbol' effectively reverts back to a sign, having as its referent a culturally defined meaning that is frozen or reified, thereby moving meaning away from creative imagination.

3 Clearly Jung does discuss substances such as salt, sulphur, mercury etc. as having symbolic meaning in alchemy. However, my point is that his desire to elucidate psychological meaning when discussing such substances results in a tendency to neglect or overlook how these substances actually promote aesthetic/transformative responses in the alchemist *directly* within their physical and visual transformation – without recourse to re-presentation.

4 I wish to emphasize at this point that this is definitely not a plea for a solely materialist basis for meaning and value as such. It is simply to re-establish and re-balance a tendency in intellectual speculative thought to overlook the important part played by our physical relationship with matter to any spiritual and psychological transformations.

REFERENCES

Ehrenzweig, A. (1967/1971) *The Hidden Order of Art*, Los Angeles: University of California Press.

Eliade, M. (1962/1978) *The Forge and the Crucible: The Origins and Structures of Alchemy*, Chicago: University of Chicago Press.

Elkins, J. (2000) *What Painting Is*, London: Routledge.

Hillman, J. (1997) *Thought of the Heart and the Soul of the World*, Woodstock, Conn.: Spring Publishing.

—— and C. Eshleman (1985) *Part One of a Discussion on Psychology and Poetry*, Publishing on the Internet, Sulphur Online. Available at: http://www.webdelsol.com/Sulfur/hillman_text.html (accessed 4 October 2007).

—— and M. Ventura (1993) *We've Had a Hundred Years of Psychotherapy and the World's Getting Worse*, San Francisco: Harper.

Jung, C.G. (1923/1971) *Psychological Types*, in CW 6, London: Routledge & Kegan Paul.

—— (1966/1978) *The Spirit in Man, Art, and Literature, CW* 15, Bollingen Series XX, Princeton University Press.

—— and A. Jaffe (ed.) (1963) *Memories, Dreams, Reflections*, London: Routledge.

—— and M. L. Von Franz (eds) (1964/1978) *Man and His Symbols*, London: Picador.

Maclagan, D. (2001) *Psychological Aesthetics: Painting, Feeling and Making Sense*, London: Jessica Kingsley.

Otto, R. (1923/1958) *The Idea of the Holy*, London: Oxford University Press.

Wentworth, N. (2004) *The Phenomenology of Painting*, London: Cambridge University Press.

Worringer, W. (1908/1997) *Abstraction and Empathy*, Chicago: Ivan R. Dee.

Chapter 5

Haruki Murakami's reimagining of Sophocles' Oedipus

Inez Martinez

If there is a contemporary writer who fulfills Jung's vision of the artist as a 'vehicle and moulder of the unconscious psychic life of mankind' (Jung 1930/ 1950: para.157), it is the Japanese author, Haruki Murakami. Particularly in his novel, *Kafka on the Shore,* Murakami imaginatively reshapes basic cultural frameworks such as real and imaginary, and taboo and initiation (Murakami 2002). He portrays the world of psyche as an objectively real place where psychological transformation may occur; and he depicts the taboo aspects of the Oedipus tale as a liberating initiation.

Sophocles' contrasting dramatic presentations of Oedipus pose a question we struggle with yet. Are we responsible for our unconscious acts or not? If so, how? Sophocles' Oedipus in *Oedipus Rex* responds to discovering that he murdered his father and then married his mother with heroic guilt: he furiously punishes himself with blindness and ostracism for being the man who did the deeds (406 BC). Later, Sophocles' Oedipus in *Oedipus at Colonus* no longer believes it was he who committed those acts, but the gods through him. He says:

> The bloody deaths, the incest, the calamities
> . . . I suffered them,
> By fate, against my will! It was God's pleasure.
> (Sophocles 406 BC: 133)

Heroic guilt has transmuted to heroic victimization.

These alternative responses to discovering we are subject to unconscious forces, the responses of heroic guilt or victimization, are the psychological legacy left by the Sophoclean Oedipus to succeeding generations – and not just those of Western civilization. Murakami's reimagination of the Oedipal dilemma bears witness to the spreading globalization of literary cultures.

Freud brought the sexual aspects of the Sophoclean legacy to general consciousness by asserting that every man experiences Oedipal desires. Jung expanded the idea of human subjection to unconscious forces to include every aspect of human life influenced by archetypes and complexes. Still, the challenge of how to respond to one's unconscious acts has remained framed by individualism. The ostracism and scapegoating of Oedipus depended upon his being unique. Oedipus is in the inflated position of thinking the gods singled him out for an especially unfree life. His heroic guilt and his sense of victimization are the outcome of an exclusively *individualistic* way of perceiving human subjection to unconsciousness. James Hillman resisted this individualistic emphasis on identity. He accused psychoanalysis, both Freudian and Jungian, of being caught in the Oedipal story not as content, but as method. He ascribes Oedipus's blindness to his search: 'Oedipus's blinding at the end . . . is the outcome of his method of proceeding – pursuit, questioning . . . self-discovery' (Kerényi and Hillman 1987: 137).[1] Hillman's solution anticipates Murakami's vision in emphasizing love (Kerényi and Hillman 1987: 153–4). In *Kafka on the Shore*, Murakami intertwines the realization of self and love.

Perhaps because Murakami is an offspring of a culture that privileges community more than Western cultures tend to, he renders the issue of identity and thus of responsibility for unconsciousness as not just an individual matter. Rather, he portrays psyche even on the level of identity as shared and responsibility for unconsciousness as collective, thus transcending both heroic guilt and victimization as responses.

Kafka on the Shore portrays the transformation of Kafka Tamura, a fifteen-year-old runaway enacting the Oedipal drama. The novel recounts the journeys of Kafka and of a parallel character, Nakata, journeys that take them both into the world of psyche where transformation occurs.

Murakami re-envisions the Oedipal search for self by depicting many forces and persons in the formation and acting out of Kafka's unconscious. One force is World War II, and one character is the elderly Nakata. Nakata, when he was seven, was visited with an experience of the world of psyche through the effects of the war on his second grade teacher. Another force is sexuality. Briefly, with her husband at the front, Nakata's teacher has a sexual dream of him, resulting in masturbation and, the following day, unexpected menstruation during a field trip with her class. Nakata finds the blood-stained cloths she has buried and presents them to her. Horrified, she strikes him. He goes unconscious and enters the world of psyche. When he revives, he has lost his ability to remember and his ability to read. He becomes a character with the strengths and limitations of a scarcely developed ego, a condition reflected in his speaking of himself in the third person. He lives totally immersed in the present, ever open to the unfolding of events. Among his gifts is the ability to talk with cats and stones.

Nakata is the character Kafka's father (the newly imagined Laïos) chooses as his executioner. Given his ability to speak with cats, Nakata searches for missing cats. In his search, Nakata eventually finds himself in the home of a man dressed as, and calling himself, Johnnie Walker.[2] This man the plot later identifies as the famous sculptor father of Kafka, Toichi Tamura.

Johnnie Walker is a killer of cats. He sadistically demonstrates to the heretofore innocent Nakata his gruesome procedure of slicing cats open and eating their hearts. Johnnie Walker demands that Nakata kill him, or he will continue to kill and eat the hearts of the writhing cats. Finally, Nakata can take no more. He knifes Johnnie Walker twice, and is covered with his blood (Murakami 2002: 137). He later awakens in a lot with no blood on him as simultaneously the runaway Kafka, by a shrine in the distant city of Takamatsu, awakens inexplicably drenched in blood (ibid.: 64–5).[3] It's as if the murder has occurred both in the world of ordinary reality and in the alternate world of psyche. It's a version of synchronicity in space as much as in time.

Unconscious murder and patricide is thus not committed literally by the son, nor only by the son. Nakata, too, is under the influence of unconscious forces. Right before he stabs Johnnie Walker, Nakata says, 'I don't feel like myself'[4] (ibid.: 136). Murakami thus renders patricide as an act of *shared* subjection to unconscious forces. Nakata comes to realize he has committed the murder in the place of Kafka (ibid.: 363), and Kafka soon thinks he has killed his father through a dream (ibid.: 188).

Note, too, that Kafka's father not only desires his death but also plots the consummation of his murder. In a later conversation, Kafka offers his understanding of his father's motives. Speaking to the woman he thinks is his mother, he says:

> My father was in love with you, but ... from the very beginning he couldn't really make you *his* .... that's why he wanted to die. And that's also why he wanted his son – *your* son, too – to murder him. *Me*.... He wanted me to sleep with you.... [italics in text]
>
> (ibid.: 271)

The murder of the father is thus imagined not as a result of father–son competition. Rather it is perceived as a fulfillment of the father's unrealized sexual desires to possess – through his son's erotic knowing of – the unpossessable beloved. This perspective frames the father's death both as virtual suicide and as parasitic extension of his identity through his son. Again, the shared nature of psyche is implied.

At this point, Kafka evades responsibility by claiming that his father 'programmed all this inside' him (ibid.: 271). In contrast, Nakata immediately reports his murder to the police, saying both 'I didn't plan to kill him' and 'Nakata just murdered somebody' (ibid.: 152–3). Nakata takes responsibility for the murder even though he did not intend it. Ignored by the police, Nakata resolves to set right whatever killing Johnnie Walker meant, and begins a journey to he-knows-not-where to do so, trusting in the world of psyche to reveal itself to him. On the journey he meets a young truck driver, Hoshino, who helps him.

The tale of Nakata and Hoshino parallels the initiation tale of Kafka.

Hoshino from the beginning associates Nakata with his grandfather who loved him. He comes to revere Nakata and fulfills Nakata's mission to restore 'things to the way they should be' (ibid.: 363) through imitating Nakata's pattern of taking responsibility and trusting in the unfolding world of psyche. Through Hoshino, as well as other characters, Murakami renders accepting responsibility for bringing the Oedipal drama to its transformative conclusion as a collective task.

Kafka's initiation begins with his father's curse. His father has prophesied that Kafka will kill him and will sleep with his mother and sister. Having the curse issue from the father and not from the gods makes the psyche of the father, a power-mad artist, the source of the Oedipal drama. The parallel filial relationship of Nakata and Hoshino, filled with love, reinforces the idea that *character* rather than fate influences whether patricide will occur.

Throughout the book, Kafka intermittently dialogues with and sometimes becomes a figure called 'the boy named Crow'.[5] Murakami thus pictures not only the collective, but also the personal world of psyche as shared. Crow functions dramatically like a chorus and psychologically like a Self. He helps Kafka anticipate, reflect upon, and understand his experiences. At the beginning of the novel, as Kafka prepares to run away from home to escape his father's curse, Crow counsels Kafka to imagine his fate as an inner pulverizing sandstorm. Kafka grasps that going through this storm will change him. He starts his journey with this augury of transformation.

As the novel unfolds, it is suggested that the world of psyche was once opened by Kafka's mother, Miss Saeki, the character analogous to Iocaste. She was blessed – or cursed – with perfect romantic love when she was a teenager. She wanted to protect that perfect state from intrusions from the world, and somehow came upon the entrance stone to the world of psyche, a world of timelessness where she discovered the chords that make her song about her love, 'Kafka on the Shore', so moving. Her efforts to make an impenetrable cocoon for her lover and herself fail. Her lover is viciously and pointlessly beaten to death in a case of mistaken identity. Devastated, she, herself, continues to live in both worlds, frozen in memories in what Kafka calls the world of 'real time' living the rest of her life wreaking havoc on the lives of others because of her emotional unavailability and her evasion of responsibility (ibid.: 206).

Through the image of the entrance stone, Murakami presents the world of psyche as physically accessible. The entrance stone functions like the omphalos, the stone upon which the oracle at Delphi was erected, connecting the under and over worlds. Murakami renders this connection as horizontal rather than vertical, a change suggesting that the world of psyche is as real as the 'real' world. In order to make the consequences of unconsciousness in Kafka's and Nakata's stories transformative, the entrance stone must be recovered, opened again, and then closed. These tasks fall to Nakata and his disciple, Hoshino.

Nakata's realization that he must open the entrance comes only as he follows a series of intuitions. Finally, he grasps that he must deal with the stone because he is the one who has been to the other world during his childhood trauma and returned (ibid.: 285). Hoshino locates the stone, and after Nakata has learned to communicate with it, accomplishes the Herculean task of turning it over. The two characters thereby function in the world of psyche to assist Kafka's initiation.

Opening the entrance makes possible the development of the relationship between Kafka and Miss Saeki. Young Kafka meets Miss Saeki in the elegant memorial library that she heads, is immediately charmed by her and wishes she might be the mother who abandoned him and for whom he is looking. Oshima, her assistant, a Teiresias-like character in that he is a wise young man who is physically a woman, is moved to mentor and help the runaway. He arranges for Kafka to work in the library and stay in a spare room there. Kafka thus lives with the painting that inspired Miss Saeki's song. It portrays Miss Saeki's young lover idyllically sitting on a beach. Miss Saeki in her fifteen-year-old form visits that room nightly to gaze upon the painting, a portrait of her timeless love. Kafka grasps that he and she are living in two different worlds, 'divided by an invisible boundary' (ibid.: 222). Kafka falls in love with this youthful apparition. Then, Oedipus-like, he pursues the fifty-something Miss Saeki with questions designed to discover if she is the mother who abandoned him. The result is that Miss Saeki appears in his room in a sleep-trance and makes love to him (ibid.: 260–1). The next day, Kafka presents her with his theory that she is the mother who abandoned him, and also with his love and desire for her. Again, she comes to him, this time awake (ibid.: 276–8). She seems enabled to become his lover through identifying him with her lost love and by entering a kind of waking dream state.

The contrast with the Sophoclean Oedipus could not be more complete. Not only is Kafka not overcome with horror at intercourse with his mother; he consciously wants to have it. He seeks to resolve his abandonment by her through romantic love and sexual fulfillment.

Murakami offers little explanation of Miss Saeki's motives for this incest. He simply has her continue a lifelong pattern of abandoning responsibility for her dreams.

Murakami has introduced the idea of being responsible for one's dreams early in the novel. At the end of a book exploring Adolph Eichmann's responsibility for the Holocaust, Kafka finds a note by Oshima. It reads: *'It's all a question of imagination. Our responsibility begins with the power to imagine. It's just like Yeats said*: In dreams begin responsibilities' [italics in text] (ibid.: 122).

This passage moves Kafka to fantasize that he is defending himself at a trial for his father's murder. He protests, 'you can't be held responsible for something you can't remember', but is answered, 'It doesn't matter whose dream it started out as, you have the same dream. So you're responsible for whatever happens in the dream' (ibid.: 122). This dialogue succinctly articulates the idea of collective responsibility for unconscious behavior.

The morning after Kafka and Miss Saeki have consciously made love in real time, Oshima rushes him off to a cabin in the woods to evade the police who are looking for Kafka in connection with his father's murder. While there, Kafka, in a dream, deliberately rapes a woman he thinks of as his sister, Sakura. He is attempting to escape the curse by fulfilling it. This purposeful participation in the fulfilling of the curse fails to free him. He admits this failure during his initiatory journey into the deep forest. Oshima has warned Kafka not to venture beyond the path in the woods because people who have done so have become permanently lost. Nevertheless, after Oshima leaves, Kafka feels compelled to discover what is in the forest's depths because he is driven to discover what lies in his own. He thinks, 'This forest is basically a part of me, isn't it? . . . The journey I'm taking is *inside me*' [italics in text] (ibid.: 370).

As he pushes ever deeper into the forest, he admits in a conversation with Crow that his effort to get control through raping Sakura failed:

> **You killed . . . your father, violated your mother, and now your sister. You thought that would put an end to the curse your father laid on you. But nothing's really over . . . Your fear, anger, unease – nothing's disappeared. They're all still inside you, still torturing you** [bold in text].
>
> (ibid.: 359)

The causes of Kafka's torture, his fear and anger, result from his having been abandoned by his mother when he was four. Crow counsels him to empathize with the fear and anger that motivated his mother and to forgive her in order to save himself (ibid.: 372). Murakami, in his re-envisioning of the Oedipus story, focuses on the pain his mother's abandonment causes the son. This is the wound his novel proposes to portray as capable of being healed in its conclusion when Kafka finds and enters the world of psyche, and encounters Miss Saeki in both her fifteen-year-old and fifty-something forms.

The young Miss Saeki has no idea who he is nor why he's there. In answer to his questions, she describes this world, a place where time and memories do not exist, where one feels part of, absorbed into all things, a world, in other words, where the ego does not exist, and where change does not occur to its nameless inhabitants.

Yet, for Kafka's abandonment to be healed, the mature Miss Saeki must enter this world and cause change. First, she must change her own pattern of not taking responsibility. So she comes to him in her fifty-something form fresh from death. With difficulty, she has reached Kafka in the world of psyche before she has lost her memories. She has come to persuade a reluctant Kafka to return to the world of real time. She does so by putting her will behind his life. She says, 'It's what *I* want. For you to be there' [italics in text] (ibid.: 409). As he continues to hesitate, she thinks to give him his heart's desire. She bestows the identity of her lover upon him. She says, 'I want you to take that painting with you' (ibid.: 410). She tells him, 'You were there. And I was there beside you, watching you. On the shore, a long time ago . . . and it was always summer.'

Kafka takes in the identity of being her beloved:

> I close my eyes. I'm at the beach and it's summer. Nearby, someone is painting a picture of me. And beside him sits a young girl . . . A natural-looking smile plays at her lips. I'm in love with her. And she's in love with me.
>
> (ibid.: 410)

Through the painting, Miss Saeki confers the timelessness of art on Kafka's experience of himself as her ideal beloved. She says: 'I want you to have that painting with you forever' (ibid.: 410).

At this moment, incest ceases to be literal, and instead becomes metaphorical and psychological. This climactic scene suggests the fluidity of identity in shared psyche, and the transformative power of identifying with a character imaginatively. In Kafka's case the identification moves him to return to life. His mother's gift enables him finally, as he hugs Miss Saeki goodbye, to ask if she is his mother. In response, she not only owns her anger and her fear of loss; she takes responsibility for having abandoned him. She accepts guilt, but not narcissistically or heroically. Instead she bears her guilt in a related way. She asks Kafka's forgiveness. Her transformation enables Kafka's as he thinks, '**Mother . . . I forgive you**' [bold in text] (ibid.: 411). Kafka lets go of being a victim. This moment is ripe with transformational possibilities also for the reader and for culture. The Sophoclean alternatives of heroic guilt and victimization have been transcended.

Murakami's vision portrays being subject to unconscious inner curses as initiation into being human. He thus removes the grounds for seeing oneself as specially chosen to be either uniquely monstrous or especially victimized. Kafka's understanding that his mother, like himself, has suffered inner curses makes him capable of having empathy for her, the one whose love most failed him. This empathy, together with his mother's remorse and offer of love, enable him to forgive her and free himself to receive love. Both of them thus participate on the unconscious level (in the world of psyche) in transformation of their respective entrapments in victimization, guilt, fear, and anger. Their choices enable Kafka to bring this new state of relative freedom into conscious life in the 'real' world.

Before he leaves, Miss Saeki takes a hairpin from her hair, a decoration comparable to Iocaste's brooch with which Oedipus blinded himself, plunges it into the underskin of her left arm, and squeezes out blood, inviting Kafka to suck. This blood literally enables him to complete his return to the 'real' world.

On his return journey, Kafka is warned not to look back. Predictably, he does. At that moment, he is paralyzed between two worlds, caught in the sandstorm of fate prophesied in the first chapter. Remembering his mother/lover's affirmation of his life frees him to choose life in the real world of time and change. In his words, 'The spell is broken . . . Warm blood returns to my body. The blood she gave me, the last drops of blood she had' (ibid.: 413). The blinding in *Oedipus Rex* has become nurturing in *Kafka on the Shore*, literally a turning point. Kafka reports, 'The next instant . . . I turn a corner and the little world in the hills vanishes, swallowed up in dreams' (ibid.: 413).

When Kafka first saw the hamlet where people live in timeless psyche, he called it a brand new world. The last line of the novel speaks of his return to Tokyo to undertake the rest of his life as an entry into a 'brand new world' (ibid.: 387, 436). Murakami presents the two worlds as a kind of palimpsest. Kafka's psychological journey back and forth between the two was made possible by Nakata's and Hoshino's opening of the entrance stone, that is, by collective participation in the synchronicity of the forces of psyche. Kafka's initiation is complete.

Murakami's reimagining of Oedipus unintentionally answers Hillman's objections to Oedipus's pursuit of self-knowledge. As Hillman presumably would wish, Murakami's Oedipus character, Kafka, is driven less by the desire for consciousness than by the desire for love.[6] These desires result in a connecting of the worlds of consciousness and unconsciousness. Further, as Hillman noted approvingly of Antigone (Kerényi and Hillman 1987: 158), Kafka concludes by returning to the city, to the continuity of life. Murakami's novel also reflects Hillman's linking of the child and imagination (Downing 2006: 77). *Kafka on the Shore* honors imagination as the realm of – and the Oedipal plot as the initiatory means for – healing and saving the child. Murakami thus offers readers metaphorical experience of patricide and incest as a healing initiation through imagination.

Might Murakami's re-visioning of the Oedipal journey transform our entrenched understandings of the meaning of the Oedipus story? Has Murakami, as Jung affirms of artists, 'plunged into the healing . . . depths of the collective psyche' (Jung 1930/1950: para.161)?

I have to think that Murakami is aware that he is presenting us with an opportunity for cultural transformation. After Kafka reflects on the idea that 'in dreams begin responsibilities', he thinks, 'What I imagine is perhaps very important. For the entire world' (ibid.: 123). Read: what *Murakami* is imagining is 'perhaps very important. For the entire world'.

Murakami's re-imagining of the Oedipus story presents the world of psyche as shared and life-transforming. Kafka's identity is composite. He exists as the strong young boy with his feelings, thoughts, and responses; as the inner figure Crow; and as the boy who has internalized his father's curse, unconsciously committed murder with Nakata, and psychically become one with his mother's beloved. Sharing patricide and incest has led him to empathy and forgiveness, has healed the wounds of childhood abandonment, and has initiated him into a 'brand new world'.

Further, Murakami reframes responsibility for unconscious acts by enlarging our understanding of psychological interconnectedness. Sophocles portrays Oedipus's state of unconsciousness as causing *consequences* to the collective: death ruled in Thebes. Murakami portrays unconscious psychological connections as *causal* as well. Nakata unconsciously helps cause the patricide; Kafka's mother first performs incest while asleep. Responsibility for the unconscious acts of patricide and incest is shared, rendering mere self-reflexive angst over whether one is guilty or a victim as too individualistic a perspective. Murakami sheds hope on the human condition by portraying taking responsibility for unconscious acts as a group task that, if conscientiously and lovingly undertaken, leads to life-generating transformation. Instead of living as a blinded, ostracized beggar, Kafka, the cursed son, becomes a life-embracing, initiated young man.

Rendering the psyche as shared, Murakami's reimagining of the Oedipus drama may indeed be important – for the entire world.

NOTES

1 Hillman's reading ignores that 'Oedipus's blinding at the end' was self-inflicted, a hero's response to discovering that unconsciousness informed who he was. It was an ego-act of *resisting* consciousness, not a result of *seeking* consciousness. The moments of dawning consciousness are the moments ripe with the possibility of exercising our limited capacity for freedom.
2 Having an international icon of intoxicants as an alter-ego implies that Tamura is an artist whose use of the imagination is intoxicated.
3 The blood appears in a butterfly shape on Kafka's shirt (Murakami 2002: 65). The butterfly, one of many repeated and resonant images in the book, links the blood of the murdered father with the connotation of metamorphosis. This link is later connected to the world of psyche. When Kafka first glimpses that world, he experiences himself as a butterfly (ibid.: 387).
4 From KAFKA ON THE SHORE by Haruki Murakami, translated by Philip Gabriel, © 2005 by Haruki Murakami. Used by permission of Alfred A. Knopf, a division of Random House, Inc. and Harvill Press, reprinted by permission of The Random House Group Ltd.
5 The novel explains that 'Kafka' means 'crow' in Czech (ibid.: 293). The novel also makes specific reference to Franz Kafka's 'In the Penal Colony' (ibid.: 54). Young Kafka identifies with that story, thus emphasizing his experience of himself as a victim.
6 Hillman rescues psychoanalysis from what he sees as its entrapment in the Oedipal method of seeking self-knowledge through his reading of *Oedipus at Colonus*. There he sees the aged, blind Oedipus as entering the world of anima and being able to love. He sees Antigone as soul and her return to the city as emblematic of soul freed from character to engage the 'agon of life' (Kerényi and Hillman 1987: 158).

REFERENCES

The final dates in the citations refer either to the year of publication in English or to the year of publication of the edition being used.

Downing, C. (2006) 'Another Oedipus' in *An Oedipus – The Untold Story: A Ghostly Mythodrama in One Act*, trans. L. Toledo, New Orleans: Spring Journal Books.

Jung, C. G. (1930/1950) 'Psychology and Literature' in *The Spirit in Man, Art, and Literature*, trans. R. F. C. Hull, *CW* 15, paras. 133–62, Bollingen Series XX, Rutgers: University of Princeton Press, 1966.

Kerényi, K. and J. Hillman (1987) *Oedipus Variations*, Dallas: Spring Publications, 1991.

Murakami, H. (2002) *Kafka on the Shore*, trans. P. Gabriel, New York: a Borzoi Book, Alfred A. Knopf, 2005.

Sophocles (406 BC) *The Oedipus Cycle*, trans. D. Fitts and R. Fitzgerald, New York: A Harvest Book, Harcourt, Brace, and World, 1939.

Chapter 6

Psyche, imagination and art

Bettina Reiber

INTRODUCTION

What is the relationship between psyche and imagination on the one hand and art on the other? The average person presupposes some sort of connection, she considers art as an expression of creativity, and creativity to be informed by the psyche and nourished by the imagination. For Jung also psyche, imagination and art are linked. In various articles published in *The Spirit in Man, Art and Literature* he discusses a range of those connections (Jung 2003). However, psyche and imagination play virtually no role in contemporary art criticism. Neither are they addressed in exhibition texts, catalogues, magazine articles, books on art criticism, or in art education at college.

Why is this? What are the possible consequences for art audiences and society at large? Is there an alternative approach? How could a different kind of art criticism connect to Jung's writings on art? What would art audiences and society gain from a new approach?

These are the questions I address in this paper where my focus will be on the visual arts.

CURRENT MAINSTREAM ART CRITICISM

Current mainstream art criticism manages to exclude any discussion of psyche and imagination in relation to art, by using a purely formalistic approach to establishing what is, and what is not, art that does not leave room for any feeling response to art to be recognized. Mainstream criticism operates with two strategies. The first is simply to presuppose the 'art' character of an object without further explanation. The 'art' object is then discussed within another established discourse.

Let us, for instance, look at the Tate Gallery's website on Simon Starling's piece *Shedboatshed*. Starling won the Turner prize in 2005.

Starling dismantled a shed and turned it into a boat; loaded with the remains of the shed, the boat was paddled down the Rhine to a museum in Basel, dismantled and re-made into a shed.

(Tate 2005)

This work is contextualized within 'modernity, mass production and global capitalism' (Tate 2005). There is, however, no mention of how and why it is art.

Similarly, Michael Landy's *Break Down* of 2001 consists of an inventory of every single thing he owned which he subsequently destroyed in an installation at the C&A store in Oxford Street, London. The brief online synopsis of his book documenting *Break Down* claims that Landy is an 'artist' and that he 'explores different aspects of contemporary consumerism' (Artangel 2002) without substantiating *Break Down*'s art status.

Consumerism, globalism, ethnicity, feminism, gay culture, post-colonialism, identity: these are some of the contexts in which art is evaluated within art criticism. Universities validate this approach in 'critical theory' departments and in practical art courses under names such as 'Critical Fine Art Practice'. What is left unexplained within critical theory is why the object in question is art. What, for instance, is the qualitative difference between Landy's project and an economic evaluation of the income that London households spent on consumer goods in 2001? Further, critical theory does not address whether 'art' in general can be thought to be an appropriate means by which to investigate social contexts.

Without the ability convincingly to claim their status as 'art' objects, there is no reason why scholarship about these objects should not be accom-modated exclusively within the remit and methodology of social sciences, be they sociology, economy, ecology or gender studies etc. The legitimation of critical theory as an academic discipline in its own right depends on it provid-ing a legitimation that the works it discusses are 'art' works. It is not sufficient to leave this question unaddressed.

The other approach to identifying an art object does give an answer to the problem of defining art. It derives from conceptual art theory of the late 1960s and says that something is a work of art if, and only if, it satisfies three criteria: first, it has to make the viewer ask the question, 'Is this art?'; secondly, the artist has to declare it to be a work of art; and thirdly, it has to be shown in an art space.[1]

The first piece to be recognized as modern art by this approach is Duchamp's *Fountain* from 1917. Duchamp submitted a porcelain urinal as an art object to an open exhibition. He did nothing to the object itself, it was a ready-made. He did, however, declare it to be a work of art by submitting it to an art exhibition, and it certainly did challenge everyone to ask the question: 'Is this art?'[2]

The 'Is this art?' approach complements the critical theory approach. If someone asks the critic, 'Before you give us the economic criticism inherent in this reconstituted shed, let us know first how it is a piece of art', the answer can easily be supplied: 'Well, the piece was said by the artist to be a piece of art, it was shown in an art space and you have just asked the question "Is this art?"' Thus simply by posing the question whether or not something is art the enquirer establishes the art status of an object. A substantive discussion does not and cannot take place. Any enquiry into or challenge to the art status of an object or event automatically establishes the piece as a piece of art.

WHAT IS THE ATTRACTION OF THE MAINSTREAM APPROACH?

At face value the mainstream approach supports the political and social demand for inclusiveness within the field of art. Boundaries between low art and high art, between traditional and new media, between media altogether, between art and craft, etc. can be broken down.

Yet, what seems to be inclusive in this way shows itself to be excluding in another: any substantive debate on what constitutes art is prevented. While any type of product may be included in the art canon, rational discussion on whether something is art has been cancelled wholesale.

This affects the position of the curator and art critic. Their choices become unassailable. Any challenge to the critic's or curator's choice necessarily legitimizes their choice since any enquiry into or challenge to the critic's or curator's collection of art works simultaneously qualifies the work in question as a work of art. There is no need and no scope for the curator or critic substantially to answer the query.

As a result the viewer is disempowered with regard to publicly expressing her views as to whether or not something presented in an art context is art. There is no public space for her in which to make up her own mind instead of following authority.

The problem stretches further to value judgements about art, that is questions of 'good' and 'bad' art. Anyone claiming that something is bad art will not find a forum where this kind of debate is permissible. There is only art, with no space for the distinction between good and bad. This is hailed as a victory over elitism and so-called bourgeois notions of good taste. Historic privileges of class appear to have been cancelled, and art reception becomes inclusive. But if there is no forum in which to discuss the quality of those works, is not any audience frustrated?

If the price for the mainstream approach is that viewers are excluded from the debate on what is, and is not, art and from the discussion of its quality, why is there this widespread, general acceptance of the mainstream approach? The root lies deeply within society itself.

Our society, postmodern society, has lost the belief that a value system that everyone could subscribe to can ever be found (Lyotard 2004: 37). And most people assume that such a shared value system has to be established in order to make a rational, substantive engagement with art meaningful. Since the general public wants art and art criticism to continue, and they believe a substantive discussion on art is not possible without shared values, the mainstream approach provides a vehicle with which to circumvent an actual debate on art while still enabling art practice and exhibition practice to occur.

The purely formal nature of this approach and precisely the fact that it does close off the debate on whether something is art, makes the mainstream approach attractive to the general public and the expert alike.

JUNG AND THE MAINSTREAM APPROACH

Jung is keen to distinguish his psychological work on art from the work of the aesthetician (Jung 2003a: 76; 2003c: 100; 2003b: 160). For him the psychologist addresses the psychology of the art work and the artist (Jung 2003c: 100, 101, 103, 117), or the psychic content of visual expressions in general (Jung 2003b: 160). The aesthetician's task, on the other hand, consists in providing answers to the question of what qualifies an art work as such. In Jung's understanding this depends on addressing the question of 'what art is in itself' (Jung 2003a: 76). For Jung it is a given that the academic discipline which has art as its subject does engage substantially with the question of the art status.

His writings predate the origins of the current mainstream art critical approach. He did not and could not conceive of the idea that a purely formalistic procedure would replace a substantive debate on the nature and quality of art works.[3]

WHAT ARE THE PROBLEMS WITH THE MAINSTREAM APPROACH?

For the individual

What is perceived as the advantage of the mainstream refusal to discuss the nature of art is, in truth, its problem: the mainstream approach prevents any substantive discussion on whether or not something is art and on its quality.

Yet such a discussion is a deeply felt human need. Do we not feel passionately about an art work and want others to agree with us? Do we not want to argue our case? Do we not want to find out why another has chosen a piece of work and called it art when we cannot understand her choice? Are these not the reasons why we are interested in art in the first place? Do we not want an answer to our question instead of having our question turned into an answer by virtue of a formal trick?

And is it not only after a strong emotional response has taken place that we wish to discuss – find words to understand – how such a reaction could be triggered?[4] Is it not only in response to our initial emotion that we begin to think of underlying mechanisms which may have informed the production of the art work and its reception? We wonder how such a deep and moving communication could have taken place on the basis of this physical object when so many other objects leave us cold and unmoved. We wonder how it is that something seemingly useless can have such a strong effect on us. What does our ability to respond in this way tell us about ourselves and about human nature? How is it that one object triggers this response and not another? How is it that one person has this response to a particular object and another person does not share it on that occasion? How is it that what moved me once no longer has this particular emotional effect on me?

However, the emotional response that lies at the root of these questions is implicitly or explicitly declared worthless by mainstream art criticism. In turn, viewers who insist on the value of their emotional response feel alienated from the official art critical debate and a society that supports it. Their approach to art – and potentially their sense of self – is undermined by mainstream art criticism which does not accommodate their kind of response to and interest in art.

On the academic level

Equally, just as there is no debate about different individual responses to art works, no debate can take place between different theoretical approaches to establishing the art status.

With regard to art's social function in Jung's terms

For Jung 'art represents a process of self-regulation in the life of nations and epochs' (Jung 2003a: 97). Art is of 'social significance' (Jung 2003a: 96) and art cannot be substituted by any other form of human expression. It is only in great works of art that the 'healing and redeeming depth of the collective unconscious' (Jung 2003c: 123) can be reached. In the art work we meet 'the psychic needs of the society in which he [the artist] lives' (Jung 2003c: 123).

The collective unconscious appears 'only in the shaped material of art as the regulative principles that shape it; that is to say, only by inference drawn from the finished work can we reconstruct the age-old original of the primordial image' (Jung 2003a: 94). It is the art work which allows the viewer a 're-immersion in the state of the *participation mystique*' (Jung 2003c: 123).

If we accept that art offers this healing function for the collective we need to engage in a debate about which works are art works and which works are true art or great art works in order to facilitate conscious access to the manifestations of the collective unconscious.

It is obvious that such claims cannot be made for just any object a gate-keeper sees fit to exhibit in a dedicated art space and which the artist calls an art work. The effects Jung describes presuppose a specific emotional response to an object by the audience.

If we allow the centrality of the emotional response to be excluded from the discussion on art, the social healing and rebalancing function that art can uniquely offer to society is publicly denied instead of being embraced and brought to the forefront of public consciousness by art criticism. Equally, the role analytical psychology can play in bringing the unconscious responses to consciousness becomes void.

VALIDATING THE FEELING RESPONSE: AESTHETICS

Traditional aesthetics does take the feeling response as its starting point. Not surprisingly, this academic discipline has been replaced by critical theory over the same period within which the significance of the feeling response has been replaced by the formalistic mainstream art critical approach. Aesthetics clearly offers an alternative to the current mainstream approach in that it does engage with art as art and seeks to identify what happens when we encounter art.

A most significant contribution to aesthetics is provided by the German philosopher Immanuel Kant in his Third Critique, the *Critique of the Power of Judgement* (2001). He goes into much detail in order to differentiate the aesthetic response from other feeling responses that human beings have and seeks to show that this feeling is unique in being connected with reason. Equally, he explains in detail how aesthetic judgement differs from rational judgements of knowledge.

Kant's explanation of aesthetic judgement is difficult for us to understand because we have become used to thinking that a statement is either an object-ive knowledge statement which we can scientifically prove, or it is simply a private matter. Yet for Kant aesthetic judgement constitutes a third kind of judgement which is neither a knowledge statement nor the expression of a purely private preference. According to him, aesthetic judgement is based on reason and this does entitle us to demand everyone's assent yet without our having the power to force that assent by way of proof.

It is immediately obvious that an art criticism which takes this thinking seriously will allow a public debate on art, namely on the aesthetic feeling that is being occasioned in different viewers potentially by different objects. The aim of such a debate would not and could not be to settle the debate about who is right in their feeling and who is wrong. Such a determinate outcome is not possible when it comes to art. But the aesthetic judgement justifies a rational debate about whether or not something is an art work on the basis of our feeling response and indicates that such a debate is necessary to cater for a human capability and need.

Kant's thoughts on aesthetic judgement complement Jung's own work on art. They provide a rigorous argument which supports Jung's writing systematically since they endorse the possibility and the necessity of rationally discussing art as art, as an antecedent to further specialist discourses in which to contextualize art works, be those discourses psychological, or of another discipline. Further, Kant's work on aesthetic judgement supports Jungian thinking in a more general sense in that it shows that certain forms of thought can be considered rational outside the narrow confines of scientific rationality.[5]

Because of his significance to Jungian studies – on art and in general – I will show in some more detail how Kant arrives at his position.

AESTHETIC JUDGEMENT ACCORDING TO KANT

Kant thinks that art cannot be defined. Art is not a series of specific qualities that we find in an object (2001).[6] Instead, Kant is interested in the statement: 'This is art'.[7] He focuses on this very particular statement. Since it cannot be understood by examining the objects, the art works themselves, he investigates what exactly is meant by this statement. To do this Kant seeks to determine the difference of aesthetic statement from any other.

First, aesthetic judgement is not a statement of knowledge such as 'This leaf is green' because we cannot know what is and what is not art.[8] On the other hand, aesthetic judgement is not simply a statement of personal preference such as 'This cake is delicious'. No one, according to Kant, expects another to agree with a statement of merely subjective preference. If I like this cake I am well aware that others might not like it and I have no interest in convincing them that really, if only they tried hard enough, they would realize that they like this cake too. This is fundamentally different from aesthetic judgement. When I say 'this is art' I want everyone else to agree and I feel invested in such a particular way in my feeling about the object, that I want to discuss my response to the object with others and wish to convince them. I feel that they must agree with me. Although I am well aware that many will not share my views, I still feel they ought to agree.

Kant then considers whether we are reasonable in demanding that others assent to our view on art, since clearly in reality many will not agree and since we lack objective proof that would 'force' another to agree with us. Such objective proof is only available in knowledge statements (such as 'this leaf is green').

Kant concludes that the statement 'this is art' originates in a feeling of pleasure which I derive from a particular interplay of my rational faculties of the imagination and understanding. It has to be emphasized that Kant's term 'imagination' is a technical term. It is not equivalent to the common use of the word which refers to creativity, visualization and fantasy. Kant uses the term exclusively in connection with sense perception. Imagination is that rational faculty which allows us to synthesize the manifold given in sense perception into a representation. In aesthetic judgement we do not process the representation into a concept; rather the imagination enters into a harmonious free play with the understanding. We think about the representation, wonder about it without exhausting it; we oscillate between the representation of the sense perception and our thoughts about it. This harmonious free play between imagination and understanding leads to the feeling of pleasure particular to aesthetic judgement. An object that stimulates this interplay between imagination and understanding will be called art by the person so stimulated. In this way Kant shows that and how the aesthetic judgement arises from our rational faculties. Everyone is capable of having her rational faculties triggered in that way albeit potentially by different objects.

The pleasure particular to aesthetic judgement is disinterested; I do not wish to have or to own the object, I simply enjoy what it does to me via my rational faculties.[9] This constitutes a difference from merely subjective statements where, by contrast, I do want to own or to have the object: I want to *eat* the cake.

Because aesthetic judgement is based on our rational faculties it can be regarded as rooted in 'the supersensible substratum of humanity' (Kant 2001: B 237). And because this substratum is universally and necessarily valid for all rational human beings I am entitled to demand everyone's assent to my judgement. I am rationally legitimized to make the demand that everyone must agree with me, my judgement can claim subjective validity but, since it is not a knowledge statement, I cannot make a claim to objective validity. That is, I can reasonably and legitimately demand that others must agree with me, but I cannot force them to agree by means of argument.

MINORITY VOICES

Some contemporary art theorists do seek to reintroduce the aesthetic into the current art debate. Thierry de Duve's main thrust in *Kant after Duchamp* is to replace the sufficiency of the formalistic mainstream 'Is this art?' question with the need to commit to a 'This is art' statement (de Duve 1999). Once such positive commitments are being made and can be demanded of others, questions on art can be substantially addressed again. Since no objective criteria for establishing the art status can be given, the feeling response, the aesthetic response to art works will by necessity have to be recognized and integrated in the discussions.

Michael Tucker in *Dreaming with Open Eyes* is deeply critical of mainstream art criticism (1992). His alternative approach to art operates within a Jungian framework. He presents works that move him aesthetically, which he considers to be art. He reintroduces psyche and imagination as key factors in his examination of art as art. For this reason, he promotes art works that have been ignored by mainstream art criticism and shows how some well-known artists' works make sense in his context of meaning. Tucker is one of the very few contemporary critics to emphasize the social function of art as art. Art for him has the potential of providing a vision for the collective, and so he insists that art must be recognized as art via the specific aesthetic feeling response in order for its potential for healing society to take effect.

WHAT DO WE GAIN IF THE FEELING RESPONSE FINDS A PLACE IN MAINSTREAM ART CRITICAL THINKING?

All importantly, validating the feeling response recognizes that our reaction to art as art is based on feeling and that this feeling is unlike any other. Indeed, it is precisely because of this unique type of feeling that art is also unlike any other form of human expression, be it scientific discourse or a verbal exchange regarding mere personal preferences.

Only if art is recognized as a phenomenon unlike any other can questions specific to art arise. What is it that makes some people attempt to produce such works? What is the drive behind creativity? How do creativity and imagination operate? Does it require a connection with a force which is not accessible in sense perception? Is such a connection that which we call genius? Is that force the collective unconscious? How is it that some viewers are able to experience an aesthetic response to objects which were produced in a different culture, at a different time? Is there some common ground that makes works resonate aesthetically across the ages and locations? Does this resonance, the aesthetic feeling, arise because we encounter the collective unconscious, because we respond to perceived archetypes?

Aesthetic experience touches us deeply; it engages our psyche, our mind and our body. If art is considered in its relationship to aesthetic experience, it is lifted from its role as part of the entertainment industry. It becomes an opportunity that invites us to open up emotionally and to exercise our sensibility, instead of replacing that sensibility with an apparent intellectualism.

Once we recognize art as connected to the aesthetic feeling response we can move forward with Jung and address the potential of art to 'restore the psychic balance . . . of the epoch' (Jung 2003c: 122). We are then able to use analytic psychology not to explain art works but to 'provide comparative material and a terminology for its discussion' (Jung 2003c: 114). Jung's writings on psyche and the imagination can help clarify which 'psychic needs of the society in which he lives' (Jung 2003c: 123) the artist has addressed in her work. If we restore aesthetic feeling to its rightful place, then we are able to engage with art as that which 'makes it possible for us to find our way back to the deepest springs of life' (Jung 2003a: 96).

NOTES

1 A key text is Kosuth 2003, originally published 1969.
2 The urinal was not shown in the exhibition, a fact usually ignored in its appraisal. Apart from this historic exception the need for a piece to be exhibited in a dedicated art space is upheld as key to its achieving art status.
3 Jung's writings are predominately directed at literature and poetry, but his statements are so general that they can be considered equally relevant for a visual art context. Indeed, Jung makes no substantive shift when he discusses Picasso's visual art (in Jung 2003b).
4 This view is shared by Jung. See Jung 2003a: 90, where he considers art as a 'living mystery' which is subsequently 'secreted into something by an intellect hungry for meaning'; art is an 'immediate experience' which is followed by a need for 'interpretation'.
5 On this point see Jung's analysis of analytical psychology against the standards of science (Jung 2003c: 101, 102).
6 Jung endorses this view when he says: 'the meaning and individual quality of a work of art inhere within it and not in its extrinsic determinants' (Jung 2003a: 83).
7 Kant addresses primarily natural rather than artistic beauty. However, he regards them as structurally interchangeable. Further, for Kant the aesthetic judgement consists in my saying: 'This is beautiful'. Thierry de Duve has convincingly argued that Kant's 'This is beautiful' can be equated in our time with the statement 'This is art'.
8 Jung endorses this distinction between 'cognitive understanding' and the 'sphere of art' (for instance Jung 2003a: 90).
9 See Jung's comparable statement that an art work is a product that 'can be regarded as existing in and for itself' (Jung 2003c: 102).

REFERENCES

Artangel (2002) http://www.artangel.org.uk/pages/publishing/pub_landy.htm (accessed 2 July 2006).

de Duve, T. (1999) *Kant after Duchamp*, Cambridge, Mass.: MIT Press.

Jung, C. G. (2003a) 'On the Relation of Analytical Psychology to Poetry', in *The Spirit in Man, Art and Literature*, trans. R. F. C. Hull, London: Routledge, paras. 97–132.

—— (2003b) 'Picasso', in *The Spirit in Man, Art and Literature*, trans. R. F. C. Hull, London: Routledge, paras. 204–214.

—— (2003c) 'Psychology and Literature', in *The Spirit in Man, Art and Literature*, trans. R. F. C. Hull, London: Routledge, paras. 133–62.

Kant, I. (2001) *Critique of the Power of Judgement*, P. Guyer (ed.), trans. P. Guyer and E. Matthews, Cambridge: Cambridge University Press. Pagination quoted according to the second Akademie Ausgabe: B edition.

Kosuth, J. (2003) 'Art after Philosophy', in C. Harrison and P. Wood (eds), *Art in Theory 1900–2000*, Malden, Oxford: Blackwell.

Lyotard, J.-F. (2004) 'Answering the Question: What is Postmodernism?' in J.-F. Lyotard, *The Postmodern Condition: A Report on Knowledge*, trans. R. Durand, Manchester: Manchester University Press.

Reiber, B. (2006) 'Art Theory's Legitimation – Whence Come We? Where Are We? Whither Do We Go?' in H. van Koten (ed.) *Proceeds of Reflections on Creativity*, Dundee: Duncan of Jordanstone College. Online. Available at: http://imaging.dundee.ac.uk/reflections/pdfs/BettinaReiber.pdf (accessed 10 December 2007).

Tate (2005) http://www.tate.org.uk/britain/turnerprize/2005/simonstarling.htm (accessed 2 July 2006).

Tucker, M. (1992) *Dreaming with Open Eyes, The Shamanic Spirit in Twentieth Century Art and Culture*, San Francisco: Aquarian/Harper.

Chapter 7

How Myrtle Gordon addresses her suffering

Jung's concept of possession and John Cassavetes' *Opening Night*

Craig Stephenson

In a book review published in *Harvest*, Terence Dawson challenges us not to be satisfied with employing post-Jungian criticism merely to reiterate interpretations offered by other schools of thought. He writes:

> Jungian criticism . . . is too often content with imposing a Jungian slant and terminology onto otherwise standard readings of the works it tackles. For example, one does not need to call upon Jung to offer 'a feminist revision of the hero's journey' in *Jane Eyre*; almost all criticism of this novel written in the last half century has been engaged in just such a revision! . . . It must be seen to deliver fundamentally different readings to other approaches. If it can't, or doesn't, it loses its *raison d'être*. And consequently it loses any right to expect to regain its place within academic debate. In other words, Jungian criticism needs to produce readings that could not be generated by any other approach; readings that stand alone on their own intrinsic coherence and yet also promote an interest in their methodology; and perhaps above all, readings that surprise by their unexpected claims.
>
> (Dawson 2005: 193)

In this paper, I will try to meet Terence Dawson's challenge and, at the same time, breathe a little life back into a Jungian commonplace: the notion of possession by a complex. First, I will briefly outline the epistemological and ontological significance of Jung's concept of possession, and then I will place it in service of John Cassavetes' *Opening Night* in order to generate a 'fundamentally different' critical reading of the film.

JUNG'S CONCEPT OF POSSESSION

Possession is the linchpin of Jung's analytical psychology and provides a throughline for Jung's *Collected Works*, from his inaugural dissertation for his medical degree (Jung 1902) to an essay completed shortly before his death in 1961, in which he recommends to psychologists the practice of placing classical case histories of possession in a parallel and analogous relationship to contemporary secularized cases of psychopathology (Jung 1961: para. 522). Within Jung's discourse, 'possession' is the ubiquitous concept with which he formulates ideas concerning the dynamic between an ego consciousness and an autonomous unconscious, which allows him, in turn, to convey phenomenologically the power of neurotic and psychotic symptoms.

Isaiah Berlin describes the space between the perspective of the actor and the observer as 'the deepest chasm which divides historical from scientific studies' (Berlin 1998: 53). I propose to locate Jung with his concept of possession as poised over just such an epistemological chasm. Elsewhere, I have written about how Jung errs when he essentializes or primitivizes possession and how readers of his analytical psychology easily slip from his theory of complexes into esoterics. At the same time, I have defended Jung's concept of possession from academic and clinical prejudices which denigrate it as a system of belief. In all this, I think it essentially important to reconnect Jung's concept of possession to its etymology: to the forceful image of selfhood in its own seat, and of the suffering inherent when selfhood experiences itself as unseated by something Other (Stephenson 2006).

In order to defend the value of Jung's concept of possession, I would like to introduce an analogy from the field of anthropology. Edward Schieffelin, as a contemporary Western anthropologist writing about possession in a non-Western culture, places himself in a precarious position similar to Jung's: how can ethnographic reporting honour the ontological weight which, for example, the Kaluli people of New Guinea give to spirits?

Schieffelin chooses to report a diagnostic moment in a Kaluli séance in two different ways. This is what happens: a child has fallen ill, and the family requests a séance to identify the cause. Two singers invoke spirits to address the problem. First, Schieffelin describes one singer failing in his performance to engage his audience convincingly. But secondly he also describes the spirits offering two diagnoses and, through the interplay of the two singers, demonstrating the inadequacy of the differential diagnosis. That is to say, Schieffelin positions himself as a practising anthropologist by articulating a contradiction: he describes the psychosociological dynamic played out between the human singers and their audience, and he describes the strategy in the lyrical singing of the two possessing spirits (Schieffelin 1996a). Schieffelin emphatically criticizes ethnological reporting which would employ performance theory to describe the phenomena of Kaluli séance, since this Western discourse of 'theatricalization' or 'dramatization' skews the reportage, loading the human actor-singers with more reality, more ontological weight than the spirits (Schieffelin 1996b).

Schieffelin's ethnographic reporting of the Kaluli ontology resembles Jung's reporting of the delusions of the patient who said that she lived on the moon where she was possessed by a vampirish male spirit. Jung gives the unconscious image of living on the moon the same ontological weight as that of the objective reality that she resided in the Swiss sanatorium (Jung 1962: 128–130). Like Schieffelin, Jung positions himself, in his predicament as practising psychotherapist, at the apex of a double perspective with regard to Western consciousness: he assigns an ontological reality to split-off autonomous complexes as unembodied spirits, as unconscious Other, equal to the reality of the suffering, possessed ego-identity. Jung locates his concept of possession in a Western theoretical or discursive vocabulary of the psychological 'complex' and, at the same time, he rehabilitates an imagistic or mythopoeic vocabulary of 'spirit' – without privileging, it should be emphasized, that second vocabulary to the extent of rendering his concept part of a system of belief. And, just as anthropological performance theory is betrayed by the Western cultural bias that disparages 'theatricalization' as 'shamming', Jung's concept of possession is betrayed by the cultural bias that denigrates it as 'esoteric'. In as much as Jung characterizes his practice of psychotherapy as compensating for a Western conceptual impoverishment, he attempts, within the psychotherapeutic context, to work towards psychological containment, re-orienting ego consciousness towards the presence of unconscious factors – personifying, embodying and thereby incorporating images of Otherness within the transferential context of therapy into the experience of selfhood. For Jung, the idiom of possession guards the valuable precariousness of that place described by Berlin between the actor and the observer. Embodying an unconscious image paradoxically both acknowledges and depotentiates the complex. It honours and yet limits its ontological claim. It expresses and yet confines it to time and space, rendering its archetypal or collective dimension as individualized, but also, rendering the individual suffering as collectively meaningful. Jung's therapeutic practice of personifying a complex or spirit through active imagination promotes, not so much a mimetic identification with the Other, as a differentiation from and relationship to the Other. Jung locates synthetic possibilities for healing in the act of giving a compensatory ontological status to the autonomous complex/spirit and enduring the ensuing contradictions and conscious suffering within the vessel of the transference and counter-transference relationship.

JUNG'S CONCEPT OF POSSESSION AND CASSAVETES' *OPENING NIGHT*

In 1977, Cassavetes released in Europe his film, *Opening Night*, ignored in America until after his death. In the film, Myrtle Gordon (played by Gena Rowlands), a celebrated stage actress, rehearses a new play within a familiar circle of professional colleagues: Manny Victor the director (Ben Gazzara), Maurice Aarons the male lead and her former lover (John Cassavetes), and David Samuels her producer (Paul Stewart). But Myrtle finds herself resisting the character she is playing and resenting the drama entitled *The Second Woman*, written by the sixty-five-year-old playwright Sarah Goode (Joan Blondell). After witnessing the death of a young fan, struck by a car outside the theatre, Myrtle rebels against what she perceives as the complacency of both the play and her peers. She sabotages the New Haven tryouts and dangerously teeters close to alienation, depression, and madness.

With regard to the protagonist of *Opening Night*, Cassavetes, as screenwriter and director, had this to say:

> I picked a woman who has a career, a job. She's not interested in children, she's not interested in men, even if she still is capable of romantic feelings. Myrtle has a job to do, a career, and that's the most important thing for her. Her whole life is acting, being an actress . . . [And] Myrtle is alone and in desperate fear of losing the vulnerability she feels she needs as an actress . . . You never see her as a stupendous actress . . . She didn't want to expose herself in certain areas. So when she faints and screams on the stage, it's because it's so impossible to be told you are this boring character, you are aging and you are just like her . . . When you have a problem as an actor people want to know why your feelings are different from theirs. And if you can't explain it to them, they attack you. And this woman can't resist the attacks – attacks coming not from her enemies but her friends. They are more threatening because they can destroy her image of herself . . . It's very brave on her part to try, then, to follow her idea of herself. She is special in that she's completely honest with herself, very stubborn and very alone.
>
> (Cassavetes 2001: 412–413)

Opening Night can be viewed as Cassavetes' subversive version of a backstage melodrama about theatre and midlife, about acting and being, about illusion and reality explored in the context of aging. Cassavetes schematizes the problem in the film in terms of three generations or three ages of women:

> Here's an old lady, Joan Blondell, who still has all her life and sexual feelings, which you can see though we don't go into them; and Gena, who's a few decades down from Joan; and the young girl, who is really seventeen years old.
>
> (Cassavetes 2001: 407)

And Cassavetes encapsulates the midlife predicament of his protagonist in the film's brief prologue. We see Myrtle enter the stage, playing the role of Virginia. Myrtle's former lover Maurice is playing Virginia's partner Marty, a photographer. Myrtle, the protagonist, and her character Virginia stand in between two of Marty's blown-up images on the living-room wall, one of a young girl's face which Marty describes as cruel and the other of an old woman's face which he sees as worldly wise. Myrtle's future predicament is thus depicted physically: to find herself trapped between the cruel but vibrantly hungry needs of the ghost-teenager Nancy and the hopeless defeatist vision of the resigned older woman Sarah Goode.

But, as much as Cassavetes encourages an interpretation of *Opening Night* as a reworking of the famous film *All About Eve*, starring Bette Davis (1950), having originally written the part of the playwright Sarah Goode for Bette Davis, he also admits to deliberately undermining the conventions of such theatrical melodrama with the formality of his camerawork:

> I don't want [people] to identify with the performers, with backstage theatricality, to the point where they become just as mundane as everybody else. So we didn't use those strengths that we know can create loneliness: long shot, then tight shot, key lighting and everything else. We shot it much more conventionally. Everything was normally lit and nothing was really explained. She came in drunk, we didn't know quite why she'd decided to drink, we didn't know quite why she smoked a lot of cigarettes, we didn't know quite why she didn't like the play.
>
> (Cassavetes 2001: 419–420)

In other words, both as screenwriter and director, Cassavetes works technically to prevent his audience from empathizing too much with Myrtle.

With great subtlety, at the same time that Cassavetes formally distances his audience from the performers and the melodrama, he introduces the idiom of possession to describe the suffering of his protagonist. In response to the professional and personal crises in which she finds herself, Myrtle seeks consolation in a seventeen-year-old self, the ghostly figure of the autograph-seeker Nancy struck by a car outside the theatre. Unfortunately, Myrtle discovers during increasingly violent episodes that the ghost Nancy is as much in rebellious opposition to her as she is to the cast and crew of the play. Cassavetes confesses: 'Here's a theatrical story, and suddenly this apparition appears – and I start giggling. Everybody knows I hate that spooky-dooky stuff and they said, "Are you going to leave that in?" ' (Cassavetes 2001: 410).

'I'm not acting', Myrtle insists when her director Manny finds her bruised and exhausted after having wrestled with the ghost during the night. On the one hand, horrified to witness Myrtle sabotaging the play in rehearsal and performance, her colleagues indulge her by taking her to a spiritualist, but Myrtle leaves the séance and rejects the esoteric solution of exorcising Nancy. On the other hand, when Sarah Goode witnesses the divided Myrtle pummelling her own head against a bedroom doorframe, she concludes that the actress is self-harming and certifiably insane. In this sense, *Village Voice* critic Dennis Lim describes Cassavetes as gleefully tipping his theatrical melodrama into a 'supernatural thriller' (Lim 2005). Cassavetes introduces possession as the idiom within which Myrtle experiences her distress, but he explicitly rejects any esoteric outcome that would legitimize Nancy's ghost – as well as any psychiatric reading of Myrtle's behaviours which would suggest a treatment model for a Dissociative Identity Disorder.

I believe, however, that Cassavetes doesn't know how to talk about the answer he discovers in Myrtle's predicament. I say this because he writes in the press-kit for *Opening Night* that Myrtle has to kill the ghost:

> Although she resists facing them, Myrtle must finally accept and resolve the dilemmas which lie not only at the core of the play she is doing but which reflect the basic realities of her own existence, from which she has heretofore fled, aided by alcohol, men, professional indulgences – and fantasy! The character is left in conflict, but she fights the terrifying battle to recapture hope. And wins! In and out of life, the theme of the play haunts the actress until *she kills the young girl in herself*.
>
> (Cassavetes 2001: 424–425)

This is not what his protagonist Myrtle embodies in his film.

To come back to Terence Dawson's challenge, I would argue that standard critical readings of *Opening Night* do not address adequately the significance of the idiom of possession in the film. Cassavetes expert Ray Carney, who consistently emphasizes autobiographical interpretations of Cassavetes' films (Cassavetes 2001: 409), aligns his comments about *Opening Night* with the director's stated intentions. Denis Lim also follows Cassavetes' press-pack lead: 'Nancy is savagely exorcised [and] a euphoric Myrtle turns up at Maurice's apartment with a new approach to the play' (Lim 2005). Of course, we do witness Myrtle attempting to overpower and kill off Nancy, but if this esoteric strategy addresses successfully Myrtle's suffering, then why does she continue to sabotage the play, arriving late for the opening night too drunk to walk?

Freud's only commentary on a case of possession emphasizes a similar situation. Freud analyzes medieval Viennese documents concerning a possessed man from Bavaria, an artist who, after nine years of suffering, sought help to exorcise a persecutory devil. According to Freud, the exorcisms and a subsequent commitment to enter a monastic order constituted more a neurotic evasion than a cure since, as the case history attests, once cloistered, the man succumbed to drinking (Freud 1923). As in Freud's case of demonological neurosis, Cassavetes portrays his possessed protagonist wrestling her demon to the floor, and yet still finding herself victimized and overpowered by spirit. And rather than protect her, her peers throw her out onto the opening-night stage in her drunken state, sacrificing her, one might argue, to their own needs or, perhaps a little more optimistically, to the Dionysian.

Australian film critic Adrian Martin opens a fundamentally different reading of the film when he emphasizes the setting of *Opening Night* as 'some vertiginous inner space where acting and reality have long ago lost their differentiating, ritual borders', which invites 'not a vulgar, but a very sophisticated psychoanalysis, drawing on many interpretative possibilities' (Martin 2001). A classical psychoanalytic argument would begin by emphasizing the task of becoming conscious, of integrating into ego consciousness what has been repressed, realizing what has been rendered 'unreal'. In addition, I suggest that Jung's concept of possession would emphasize discerning and, as much as possible, incarnating what has been expressed as disembodied spirit. That is to say, Jung personifies unconscious complexes – images and highly charged affects clustering around an archetypal core – as spirits or gods because he can thereby convey not only their affective power over the suffering individual ego but also their precarious quality as unlived potentialities of the personality. These, Jung suggests, manifest teleologically as impulses towards concrete embodiment in time and space.

I would argue that Cassavetes sets up a triad of inter-related questions which Myrtle must suffer and embody. First, there is the accidental death of Nancy: of what does Myrtle become conscious through witnessing the death of Nancy and the complacent responses of her professional peers? Second, there is the prison of the script: to what extent is Myrtle just as tyrannized by an older woman's vision of the feminine in which there is no hope, no redemption, no life, as by the grandiose but ghostly unlived potential of the seventeen-year-old girl? Third, there is the problem of the masculine: Myrtle feels abandoned by her costar Maurice who, at the beginning of the film, chastises her, 'You're not a woman to me anymore. You're a professional'. Also, she feels manipulated by her director Manny who tries to meet her suffering by sharing anecdotes about how he mismanaged his own midlife crisis. Myrtle rejects the men's advice as well as the older woman's insistence that she capitulate. She rejects the esoteric solution of exorcising her seventeen-year-old antagonist as well as the psychiatric judgment that she is mad. Instead, she puts all her suffering into the vessel of the theatre production and fights for the integrity of her character within the play.

During the film, we witness several scenes from the play, *The Second Woman*. In one of them, we see Marty slap Virginia. The scene is enacted in three different ways. First, Myrtle, as Virginia, screams, falls to the floor and refuses to stand up again. Second, Myrtle breaks the vessel of the play by coming out of character and saying to her leading man in front of the audience: 'You're a wonderful actor, Maurice'. Finally, at the end of the film, Myrtle abandons the script and subverts the moment of the slap, forcing Maurice (as Marty) to search for a new way to meet her in front of the opening-night audience. Like that seventeen-year-old with whom she has been wrestling, Myrtle declares a kind of war-game with Maurice: should either actor fail in the improvisation which she imposes, then all will be lost for both of them. What they find is a simple 'leg-shake' gesture, what American theatre director Joseph Chaikin would call an 'emblem', a new attitude incarnated between them in a rarefied spontaneous symbolic gesture

Figure 7.1 Myrtle Gordon (Gena Rowlands) embraced by the autograph seeker Nancy (Laura Johnson) who will shortly be struck by a car and rendered ghost.

Printed with permission of Al Ruban, Faces Distribution Corporation.

Figure 7.2 After the improvized opening night performance, Myrtle Gordon (Gena Rowlands) and Dorothy (Zohra Lampert), actor and observer, embracing over an epistemological chasm.

Printed with permission of Al Ruban, Faces Distribution Corporation.

(Chaikin 1987) which also offers a meeting place between the actors and the spectators (Chaikin quoted in Blumenthal 1984).

Actress Joan Blondell said that Cassavetes left her on her own to ponder how her character Sarah Goode, the playwright, felt about this final improvisation. It was up to her to decide if it was a triumph or a failure. On the one hand, Cassavetes' press-kit describes Myrtle as 'winning'. On the other hand, Gena Rowlands talks about the play within the film as a 'disaster' and a 'flop', and describes the improvised ending as figuring its 'ruination' (Cassavetes 2001: 424). After all, the play has been completely jettisoned, and the audience has felt moved without really knowing what it has witnessed.

I've referred to Isaiah Berlin's epistemological chasm between the actor and the observer, as well as the Western bias against performativity as shamming. I've located both Schieffelin the anthropologist of possession and Jung the psychotherapist with his concept of possession as deliberately positioning themselves over that chasm. And now I will conclude by locating Cassavetes' possessed protagonist precisely in that same place. At the beginning of the film, Nancy embraces Myrtle at the stage door, just before she is struck by the car and becomes a ghost. By the end of the film, Cassavetes has shifted his focus from the three women to include explicitly a fourth, Dorothy, the director's wife (played by Zohra Lampert) applauding Myrtle's performance and coming backstage to embrace her. Throughout the film, Dorothy has been the mostly silent, sometimes jealous but increasingly appreciative observer of Myrtle's active struggle. If there is a victory (and Cassavetes says there is one), it has little to do with exorcising Nancy and less to do with a successful opening night on Broadway. The victory has to do with the final image of the film, Myrtle and Dorothy embracing, actor and observer balanced precariously for a moment of self-possession in a seat of embodied selfhood.

REFERENCES

Berlin, Isaiah (1998) 'The Concept of Scientific History', in *The Proper Study of Mankind*, ed. H. Hardy and R. Hausheer, London: Pimlico, 17–58.

Blumenthal, Eileen (1984) *Joseph Chaikin: Exploring at the Boundaries of Theatre*, Cambridge: Cambridge University Press.

Cassavetes, John (2001) *Cassavetes on Cassavetes*, ed. Ray Carney, London: Faber & Faber.

Chaikin, Joseph (1987) *The Presence of the Actor*, New York: Atheneum.

Dawson, Terence (2005) 'Review', *Post-Jungian Criticism: Theory and Practice*, in *Harvest*, Vol. 51, No. 2, 190–193.

Freud, Sigmund (1923) 'A Seventeenth-Century Demonological Neurosis', in *Pelican Freud Library: Art and Literature*, vol. 14. London: Penguin Books, 1985, 377–423.

Jung, C. G. (1902) 'On the Psychology and Pathology of So-Called Occult Phenomena', in *Psychiatric Studies, CW* 1. Princeton: Princeton University Press, 3–88.

—— (1961) 'Symbols and the Interpretations of Dreams', in *The Symbolic Life, CW* 18, Princeton: Princeton University Press, 183–264.

—— (1962) *Memories, Dreams, Reflections*, New York: Random House.

Lim, Dennis (2005) 'The Play's the Thing', in *John Cassavetes: Five Films* [DVD], New York: Optimum Releasing Ltd., http://www.criterion.com/asp/release.asp? (accessed 2 February 2007).

Martin, Adrian (2001) 'John Cassavetes: Inventor of Forms', *Senses of Cinema*. No. 16, September–October 2001, http://web.archive.org/web/20011126192639/www.sensesofcinema.com/contents/01/16/cassavetes_forms.html (accessed 3 March 2007).

Schieffelin, Edward (1996a) 'On Failure and Performance: Throwing the Medium Out of the Séance', in Carol Laderman and Marina Roseman (eds), *The Performance of Healing*, London: Routledge.

—— (1996b) 'Evil Spirit Sickness, The Christian Disease: The Innovation of a New Syndrome of Mental Derangement and Redemption in Papua New Guinea', in *Culture, Medicine and Psychiatry*, Vol. 20, No. 1, March 1996, 1–39.

Stephenson, Craig (2006) 'Jung's Concept of Possession: Its Historical and Anthropological Bases; Its Implications for Psychiatric and Psychotherapeutic Practice', Ph.D. dissertation, University of Essex.

Chapter 8

The father, the dark child and the mob that kills him

Tim Burton's representation of the creative artist

Lena Vasileva

INTRODUCTION

Analytical Psychology has always had a very special relationship with image: it has believed in its power. Indeed, throughout the entire postmodern era of simulacra, when images are said to have lost their potency, Jungian psychologies kept stubbornly insisting that there was more to image than high recyclability and bone-rattling immediacy. Risking appearing old-fashioned, post-Jungians have been looking for depth and meaning in what was commonly seen as just a sum of 'emptinesses' and ghost reflections – popular culture.

Cinema is one of the most vivid and graphic communication channels through which popular culture articulates itself. A combination of word and image, cinema is a very powerful tool of cultural and self-expression. It tends to connect the personal with the collective in an attempt to illuminate the human condition; and in doing so, film inevitably translates the eternal pain of being human into today's cultural situation.

Tim Burton's camera zooms in for a close-up of the heart of human darkness. I argue that his works inscribe the contemporary human psyche into a fabric of mythology, thus reviving and celebrating the healing power of image.

Journalists tend to use similar words to portray Tim Burton. With his habit of gesticulation when words fail him, Burton looks both likeable and embarrassingly asocial. He has an abundance of disordered black curls that look touching and grotesque. He is mad, naïve and very sensitive. He writes introverted dark poetry about diffident creatures. He likes dogs more than people, wears impossible clothes that seem to be at least two sizes too big for him, and has occasional bouts of depression during which he avoids communication with the outside world. When he is having a bad day, Burton ignores everyone, even his best friends. As reviewer, Simon Garfield wrote, 'Burton *knows* scary, *knows* evil. You can bet he knows ghoulish. Why, he confronts these demons each time he peers in the mirror' (Garfield 2002: 34).

As a child, Tim did not have many friends but loved monsters and monster movies. He grew up watching the great veterans of the horror genre, such as Lon Chaney, Boris Karloff and Vincent Price. Little Tim would rip the heads off his toy soldiers and then tell the kid next door that it was the work of aliens (ibid.: 5). He was anything but what people call a 'normal' child. In one of the interviews he recalls that he has always kept questioning 'the norm': 'When you are a kid, you think everything is strange, and you think it is *because* you're a kid, everything is strange. Then when you get older, you realize everything really *is* strange' (ibid.: 66).

VINCENT

Like Burton himself, his characters are dark, introverted children misunder-stood by their parents who fail to make them normal. This is certainly true of one of Burton's first on-screen creations, a little boy called Vincent Malloy from a short animation feature entitled *Vincent* (1982). Vincent is a big fan of Edgar Allan Poe and wants to be 'just like Vincent Price'. Vincent Price (aged 71 at the time), who had always been a great voice-over artist, narrates little Vincent's melodramatic adventures:

> Vincent Malloy is seven years old,
> He's always polite and does what he's told.
> For a boy his age he's considerate and nice,
> But he wants to be just like Vincent Price.

The boy does not know much outside his small but very uncanny world consisting of old horror movies and Edgar Allan Poe's nightmares. He imagines himself to be a mad genius who would 'rather share a home with spiders and bats' than with human beings. He dreams of dipping his aunt in wax, for her statue would undoubtedly make a curious display in his wax museum. Little Vincent Malloy then proceeds to experiment on his dog 'in the hopes of creating a horrible zombie'. At the same time, Burton insists that the boy's:

> thoughts aren't only of ghoulish crime,
> He likes to paint and read to pass some of the time.

When he is not painting, reading or 'searching for victims in the London fog', Vincent has to cope with the demands of the outside world, especially with his mother's insistence that he behaves like a normal seven-year-old. For, a normal boy would not dig out their parents' flowerbed having mistaken it for a grave of his beautiful wife – just to make sure that she had not been buried alive.

Whereas his mother sees him as a drama-queen, Vincent is very serious in his intention to remain sad and unhappy. He even ends up imagining his own death. He does not want to be ordinary; 'the norm' is the main enemy of the artist. It kills off imagination; it masks the imbalance between the light and dark forces in the psyche. Darkness is needed as a driving force – to keep up the movement, to retain the creative process. Just as Jung saw psychological complexes as vital for the individual because without them psychic activity would come to a fatal standstill, Burton sees the conflict of dark and light as crucial to the artist's creativity (Jacobi 1942/1973: 38).

Tim Burton has always been interested in the genesis, psychology and fate of the creative person. Actually, in his films he tends to reuse certain archetypal images and situations, especially elements of the child-God myth. He reworks and elaborates the story of a talented but lonely and tormented boy who has a troubled relationship with his father. The father, in his turn, is far from perfect. He is fallible and does not live up to the son's expectations. Often, the son is betrayed or left by the father. The motif of abandonment is important for our argument because Burton's favourite myth, by his own admission, is that of the Frankenstein monster. The 'unfinished monster' myth has often been interpreted by its critics as a mockery of the biblical Genesis. In his films and animation features, Burton rewrites the story of a sensitive, misunderstood, unfinished creature striving for acceptance while only meeting with misunderstanding and rejection. This story obviously has a strong personal – and, in a way, religious – resonance for the director.

In the very method of 'making' a hero Burton follows conservative mythologies. The main creator is the father. His characters rarely have a mother, and when they do, she does not have much significance for the story. The heroes are presented to us as already having a father complex – but nothing is said about a mother. The basis of childhood, the nourishing, comforting female element, is removed from Burton's fairytales. The boys are born into a cruel and cold world to a male parent who, for various reasons, fails to provide adequate care for them. In Jung's own terms, the child is separated or isolated from its background (the mother) and nothing in the world welcomes this new birth. Mother Nature, absent from the picture, is not able to take the child under its wing and nourish and protect him (Jung 1959/2002: 168).

Still, a mother cannot be easily replaced or even completely erased from the picture. Actually, the father figure – whether he is a generous, wise god like the Inventor in *Edward Scissorhands* (1990), the young, irresponsible creator like the little boy Oliver from *Frankenweenie* (1984), Willie Wonka's overstrict father, or Penguin's unsympathetic parent – is always the cause of his son's unhappiness and misery. Sometimes the father is too young (and careless), sometimes too old (and feeble), but he is invariably flawed in some way. The result is that he is unable to care properly for the human being he has created. The child is abandoned. The absence of love and the trauma of betrayal are inevitably transformed into the conflict of the light and dark forces in Burton's characters.

The sons' 'otherness', their eccentricity, is often exteriorized as physical ugliness, as monstrous, inhuman appearance. Ugliness becomes a metaphor for the deficiency of love given to them. In the absence of the mother, there is nobody to love the monster. This myth can be easily translated into the language of human psychology. In his book on the structure and dynamics of the nascent personality, Erich Neumann wrote of the importance of the mother figure for the child (Neumann 1973/2002). Without a mother, the child would have no understanding of positive tolerance towards, and acceptedness of, the outside world, for there will not be anyone to compensate for the child's own bad, unpleasant experiences, such as fear, rage and pain:

> Through the maternal function of compensation and appeasement, the child invests in its ego the positive integral tendency which the mother exemplifies and which she embodies over and over again in her contact with the child. In this way there arises a positive-integral ego capable of integrating positive and negative factors in such a way that the unity of personality is guaranteed and is not split into antagonistic parts.
>
> (Neumann 1973/2002: 58)

Following Neumann's reasoning, a disturbance in the primal relationship will lead to the appearance of a child who perceives the world tragically and has, at the same time, narcissistic tendencies. Deprived of the experiences of security, love and confidence, he mistrusts the outside world and avoids contact with it. The child is also over-subjective in his judgements of people; his views, opinions and behaviour are filtered through his limited, tragic and panicky perception of the environment. He feels that the world has been cruel to him, and that humans have been betraying and abandoning him. Narcissism, in this case, is a manifestation of the survival instinct; it is the 'expression of an ego reduced to its own resources' (ibid.: 78).

It is typical of Burton's male characters to be reduced to their own resources. They find the world a hostile place and communication with it a painful business. They cannot see themselves *in* it; moreover, they often cannot see *beyond* themselves. Like their cinematic prototype, Boris Karloff's heavily made-up monster, Burton's creatures are both menacing and naïve; they want to be loved – but nobody taught them how to love; they want to touch but end up destroying. In the famous 'river' scene in David Whale's *Frankenstein* (1931), the Karloff monster makes friends with a little girl and throws her into the water, naïvely thinking that she will float like the flowers they have been playing with. When, to the utmost surprise of the monster, the girl disappears in the river instead of staying on the surface, he becomes upset and scared. Like a little helpless child, he raises his hands in disappointment, not knowing what to do and is completely baffled as to what has happened. He certainly did not mean it to end up like this.

EDWARD SCISSORHANDS

In *Edward Scissorhands* Tim Burton reworks the Frankenstein legend and stages his own version of the myth of creation. Edward Scissorhands is a punk-looking creature who, having been created in a Gothic castle that happens to be situated just next to a small suburban American town, has no idea of how to live among ordinary people. The director explains the origins of Edward as a character in a book of interviews entitled *Burton on Burton* (1995). There Burton asserts that Edward the misfit was born out of his own inability to comply with the norms of American suburbia, out of his teenage fears and frustrations:

> The idea actually came from a drawing I did a long time ago. It was just an image that I liked. It came subconsciously linked to a character who wants to touch but can't, who was both creative and destructive – those sort of contradictions can create a kind of ambivalence. It was very much linked to a feeling. The manifestation of the image made itself apparent and probably came to the surface when I was a teenager, because it is a very teenage thing. It had to do with relationships. I just felt I couldn't communicate.
>
> (Salisbury 2000: 87)

Not surprisingly, Edward cannot communicate either; actually, he was created and brought up in an isolated environment. In line with the conservative myth of creation, which excludes women from the process, Edward was made out of various bits and pieces by his father, a typical reclusive 'mad scientist'. Interestingly enough, for the role of the father, Burton chose his own childhood hero Vincent Price. In the scene of the Inventor's death, Price's character gives Edward a pair of new hands for Christmas, and for the next few moments the camera concentrates on the boy as he is touching and admiring the gift. Suddenly, the sharp blades that Edward has for hands pierce the soft material of the gift and cut the rubber limbs into pieces. This happens because the man, who was holding them and handing them over to Edward, loses consciousness and collapses. The Inventor, a beautiful old sage, dies of a heart attack before completing his creation, leaving him with skeletal, scissor-like hands. (Uncannily, this also was Vincent Price's last role; he died of lung cancer in 1993.)

For Edward, Paradise is lost. Human hands, the symbol of 'normality' in the movie, are inadvertently destroyed by the boy – and he will never be complete. By actually having a heart attack, the Inventor undermined his status as an omnipotent, magnificent god. Even he, the most perfect of Burton's cinematic fathers, betrays and abandons his creation, if only in the most exceptional of circumstances. Thus, Edward has come to grips with his father's humanity and mortality. By being imperfect and by dying, the

Inventor causes distress to his son who also inherits his father's divine imperfection – along with the gift of creativity. In Tim Burton's movies imperfection and creativity go hand in hand. Edward may be interpreted as some kind of Gothic Jesus, and his father is also different from the sanitized God of Christianity. He is darker, more ambiguous, more controversial, and his son inherits the inseparable trinity of transgression, humanity and creativity.

A metaphor for the creative artist, Edward exists in his shadowy little world and is willing to be a part of society but ends up alienating everyone around him, even the friendly Boggs family. While living with the Boggses, he manages to find himself an occupation, a place in the community's life: he becomes a tree sculptor and a hairdresser. Like his father's, Edward's creativity is controversial; it is inseparable from death and destruction – his tools are sharp blades, yet the sculptures that they cut out are beautiful.

Edward does his best to control the danger that he poses for the people around him. His sharp hands are the metaphor for anger, pain and frustration that a child experiences when he first meets with the dark and unjust side of life. It is as if this horrible darkness is projected onto Edward; he seems to take it upon himself and attempts to redeem it. He tries to release it in his acts of creativity.

In line with the cinematic Frankenstein tradition, the community turns against the freak and wants to destroy him. With his paradise and faith gone, and his god dead, the only thing left to Edward is to lock himself up in his Gothic castle away from the stupidity, lust and greed of the common people. He returns to his dark home that feels and looks friendlier than the radiant, artificial suburban hell in the valley below. Death, which this Gothic home symbolizes, looks like a better choice than superficial existence in the land of mediocrity.

The miserable Edward reminds us of the Biblical Job who falls victim of the imperfect, neglectful side of God. Job, who has nothing to lose, challenges God and tells him that he regrets having been born at all (Job 3: 2).

Edward's suffering also invites parallels with the accounts of crucifixion from the New Testament, especially of Jesus's dramatic appeal to his father: 'My God, my God, why hast thou forsaken me?' (Matthew 27: 46).

BATMAN RETURNS

Burton, who does not write his own screenplays, seems to instinctively choose material that contains this kind of existentialist angst and loneliness. Angst and rebellion are the result of the weakening or loss of faith in the absolute divinity and holiness of the paternal figure. The dark, introverted individualism of many of Burton's main characters is shown through the prism of their relationship with their parents, especially the father. For instance, the Penguin from *Batman Returns* (1992) is born on Christmas Eve, but his parents are so horrified by the child's ugliness that they decide to dump him in the sewer in a cradle. Danny Elfman's music certainly introduces a very 'christmassy' and magical feeling into the floating cradle scene that is constructed so as to emphasize the contrast between the child's purity and innocence, and the cruelty of the world. This scene was obviously intended as a parodic parallel with the birth of Moses. When the cradle reaches the sewer, some stray penguins, who incidentally happen to live there, fish the basket out and take care of the child.

When the Penguin grows up, he takes over Gotham city with his army of freaks and clowns. He is both horrifying and entertaining, and he clearly exhibits tricksterish qualities. In the true Burtonian 'dark child' style, he is also destructively creative as the director of the deadly shows, and he enjoys the public's panicky reaction to them. For Penguin, staging a show in which he is the main actor is a good way to attract attention to his persona and exploit his 'abandoned child' image. In a way, he behaves like the offended Frankenstein monster, punishing mankind for being insensitive to his needs and rejecting him. Another good parallel is E. T. A. Hoffman's Little Zaches, an ugly little despot terrorizing the town of Kerepes with the help of a fairy – the only creature who sympathizes with him, and who also uses the power of magic to make Zaches appear likeable.

Unlike the more 'civilized', clever mayor, who can manipulate people and circumstances with ease, Penguin is crude in his political methods. In fact, because he never grows up, or grows out of his feeling of abandonment, he does not have any political methods. All he has is a blind desire to be noticed. Even when he dies, killed off by the tortured hero Batman, he still remains a lonely, unwanted, freakish child, whose desire for human love and respect had mutated into an angry, ugly will to power. He dies among his favourite (and deadly) oversized toys; the only creatures who mourn him are the penguins.

BIG FISH

Interestingly enough, Burton's more recent movies have a more positive stance to them: they offer a solution to the conflict instead of simply presenting the audience with a pessimistic teenage rebellion against the unjust world. For instance, journalist William Bloom from *Big Fish* (2003) thinks that his salesman father is an embarrassment, an old clown who, as long as William remembers him, has kept telling stupid tales in which he imagined himself as a hero of various quests. Only when the old Edward Bloom is about to die does his son realize that some of his father's magical quests are closer to truth than anyone would have thought. William decides to accept his father as he is – a man who may be weak and only human, but who at the same time possesses a great talent of transforming a travelling salesman's stories into magical, meaningful fairytales. The son realizes that his own profession as a writer and journalist – in other words, the teller of stories – is also a gift of creativity from his father.

CHARLIE AND THE CHOCOLATE FACTORY

The theme of forgiving, understanding and accepting one's father is also prominent in Burton's rendition of Roald Dahl's *Charlie and the Chocolate Factory* (2005). The father–son conflict, absent from the book, is introduced into the movie by Burton in order to explain Willie Wonka's unusual demeanour. Wonka is an eccentric, genius chocolatier who invents new amazing candies, and his rivals dream of stealing the recipes. One day the worst does happen – the recipes get leaked, and it looks like the secret has been sold to the rivals by one of the factory's employees. Wonka, who feels betrayed by his own people, closes down the factory and reopens it three years later without hiring new workers. Then he announces that five lucky children will get a tour of his factory and a lifetime supply of chocolate. While Wonka is very fragile and childlike himself, his hobbies and toys, such as the weird melting wax dolls and dangerous candy-making machines, are curiously dark and Gothic. His first appearance in the film is Burton's tribute to the 1953 horror movie *The House of Wax*, in which a horrible disfigured sculptor (played by the one and only Vincent Price) opens up a House of Wax in New York, using the wax-covered bodies of his victims as his displays. In *Charlie*, Burton makes Wonka emerge amongst the burning dolls, whose faces are melting and eyes popping out, while the baffled and disgusted visitors are staring at him with alarm.

As the film came out in the middle of the Michael Jackson trial, the press immediately drew a parallel between the Burton–Depp interpretation of Willie Wonka and the scandalous celebrity Jackson. Indeed, both Wonka's appearance and his behaviour are reminiscent of Jackson. With his unnaturally light skin and high-pitched voice, Wonka has enough money to buy strange and expensive toys, is obsessed with being young, and generally behaves in an unpardonably infantile manner. He is a big and mysterious celebrity who does not have many friends and is scared of being betrayed and used by people, because he had been betrayed before. He also became such a famous person both thanks to and in spite of his father's strict parenting methods. Wonka's father was a dentist whose methods of bringing up children bordered on torture: his son was made to wear a horrible metal frame on his face (braces) and was prohibited from eating sweets. Having run off, Wonka re-constructed his own appearance and personality and altered it so much that his own father would not be able to recognize him. The only thing left of the old Willie were his ideal teeth – symbolizing the connection between his father's vision of his son and Willie's contradictory, rebellious re-making of the self.

Overall, Burton's vision of the fate of the artist remains rather pessimistic. A typical Burtonian protagonist has a tendency to be ambiguous and dialectical. He can be simultaneously pure and evil, beautiful and ugly. His paradoxical personality is a baffling combination of the demonic and the saintly. The artist's relationship with 'ordinary humanity' is very limited. He wants to touch but ends up damaging and often fails in his attempts to communicate his desires and feelings to the outside world. Favourable metaphorical descriptions aside, the Burtonian protagonist can also be loosely defined as childish, self-centred, egotistical and pathetic because of his chronic lack of interest in anything but his own – often exaggerated – pain and suffering.

Coming back to the mythological interpretation, the crowd uses the tortured artist as a projection figure for its dark qualities and wants to destroy him. He, in his turn, perceives the world tragically and senses that it is his father's fault that he is so different. The father's darkness and light, his humanity and divinity, are inherited by the son. Although the 'dark child' does not entirely understand the complexity of the conflict that he received from his father, he instinctively uses creativity to redeem it.

REFERENCES

Garfield, Simon (2002) 'Beetle Mania', in Paul A. Woods (ed.), *Tim Burton: A Child's Garden of Nightmares*, London: Plexus, 34–9.

Jacobi, Jolande (1942/1973) *The Psychology of C. G. Jung* (8th ed.), trans. Ralph Manheim, New Haven: Yale University Press.

Jung, Carl Gustav (1959/2002) 'The Psychology of the Child Archetype', in C. G. Jung, *The Archetypes and the Collective Unconscious*, London: Routledge, 151–81.

Neumann, Erich (1973/2002) *The Child: Structure and Dynamics of the Nascent Personality*, London: Karnac Books.

Salisbury, Mark (ed.) (1995/2000) *Burton on Burton*, London: Faber & Faber.

Woods, Paul A. (ed.) (2002) *Tim Burton: A Child's Garden of Nightmares*, London: Plexus.

Part II

Challenging the critical space

Chapter 9

Stripping bare the images

Don Fredericksen

INTRODUCTION

The present essay traverses a luxuriant field I have already chewed through on several earlier occasions (Fredericksen 2002, 2005a, 2005b). This field comprises our Jungian relationship to the image, most particularly the image explicitly constructed for consumption by others; it contains fast-growing grasses, and, to my mind, at least a few weeds. So, I am going to chew my cud through the tall grasses and weeds again, from a somewhat different angle, with the help of insights from the Rumanian émigré poet Andrei Condrescu.

Jungians of all kinds – analysts, academics, and daubers – have recently discovered the moving image with an attitude approaching *iconophilia*. Books published and in-progress, doctoral theses, essays and reviews, workshops, a first-ever special issue of *Spring: Journal of Archetype and Culture* on 'cinema and psyche', and even an analyst who tells us that he has helped Hollywood bring what he calls 'archetypal coherence' to some of its films, all testify to this recent love affair (Conforti 2005: 54–70). Within it is a potentially dangerous *naïvete*, and too little awareness of where the psychologically richest registers of the moving image are. I do not believe that these are matters of bad faith, but they do call for cautionary reflection of a critical sort that is nested within some larger understanding and experience of the image *per se*. In other words, the issues raised by this *iconophilia* are not confined to our relationship to the moving image, but extend into Jungian cultural studies in general, and into the analytic rooms where psyche is engaged in personal and sometimes transformative ways.

The bases for my caution are two observations made by Jung. In *Memories, Dreams, Reflections* Jung remarks that he has observed persons become neurotic because they content themselves with inadequate or wrong answers to the questions of life (Jung 1965: 140). This observation applies as well to collectivities, and certainly to the current technologically-driven and image-saturated culture of the globalizing West. This culture now holds not just personal life but the life of the species and the planet in its hands. Secondly, in discussing our attempts to explain archetypal material to ourselves, Jung cautions that a 'bad explanation means a correspondingly bad attitude to those psychic organs we tag as archetypes'. In 'dreaming the myth onwards' (in his famous words), 'whatever explanation or interpretation does to it, we do to our own souls as well' (Jung 1949/50: para. 271). In this light, the issue is about explanation and interpretation, and the way we determine the quality of our experience of the psyche by our explanations and interpretations.

Unfortunately Jung himself has provided a basis for our *iconophilia* and for misunderstanding our present cultural condition. We all know and repeat the Jungian mantra 'psyche is image'. One could devote a rather long essay to unpacking this cryptic statement whose logical form contains ambiguities that can – and do – lead us to unwarranted love affairs with images. I will mention just a few questions we might well put to this statement as it stands *by itself* – which is how it is typically utilized: Is Jung asserting an equivalence or an identity between psyche and image? Or is this a cryptic nugget of the Kantian critique of what we can and cannot know? Does Jung mean to make a universal affirmative claim? If so, which one? Is it 'all psyche is all image'? Is it 'psyche is all and only image'? Is it 'all and only psyche is image'? Or is it, perhaps, 'all psyche is image, but so are other things as well'? And so on, into logical vertigo. Vertigo or not, an answer to these questions is important if we Jungians are going to use 'psyche is image' to justify our relationship to the image, moving still, or non-visual. This latter qualification points to the fact that Jung's use of the word 'image' is itself ambiguous. For example, his claim that 'language itself is only an image' aborts any identity between image and visually manifested picture (Jung 1949/50: para. 271). When Jung adds in another place that 'to understand the psyche, we have to include the whole world', his generalities leave us with the task of making some necessary differentiations (Jung 1954/56: para. 114). Does Jung himself come to our aid here? Thankfully, yes.

THE NECESSITY OF SYMBOLS

Help comes first in his differentiation into two types of those things we take to be carriers of meaning: those which are known things standing in our mind for other known things he defines as signs, and the corresponding attitude toward meaning as semiotic. On the other hand, those which are known things standing in our mind for relatively unknown or ultimately unknowable things he defines as symbols, and the corresponding attitude toward meaning as symbolic. Elsewhere I have discussed in detail the implications of this differentiation for Jungian film studies and cultural studies (Fredericksen 2001, 2002, 2005a, 2005b). The point to be drawn from it at the present is simply this: if we accept that 'psyche is image' in one or more of the logical possibilities named above, then we must nonetheless accept the fact that the images that are taken to be psyche appear as, or as taken as, either signs or symbols. One danger is that we, in our love of *psyche*, will take every *image* as symbolic, confusing signs for symbols. A converse danger is the distinct possibility that the culture presents us with *signs dressed up to appear symbolic, or dead symbols trotted out to look like living symbols*. I will return to these tandem issues shortly.

Jung's differentiation of meaning into semiotic and symbolic registers issues into his more specific differentiation between what he calls the psychological and visionary modes of art, which can as well be tagged the semiotic and symbolic modes of art, respectively (Jung 1950: paras. 136–154). (For those familiar with the history of literary theory, some similarity with Coleridge's differentiation of fancy from imagination will be evident here [Beardsley 1966: 256–8].)

Jung himself, therefore, points in these two foundational differentiations to the need to draw distinctions between sign-images and symbol-images, and between semiotic and symbolic attitudes toward images. This differentiation is an ontological one about the nature and function of the image *per se*, but it obviously implies tandem apperceptive psychological processes as well. *An ontology of the image is a necessary accompaniment to a psychology of the image*, and, in this instance, a corrective to naïve *iconophilia*. What is most worrisome about our collective (here not just Jungian) *iconophilia* is the mistake of taking a symbolic attitude toward the semiotic register. One of the reasons this occurs is that we indeed see archetypal images in the semiotic register; they are there. This seems undeniable. But we have to ask ourselves: *what does archetypal imagery in the semiotic register serve?*

We delude ourselves if we believe the semiotic manifestation and use of archetypal images serves the functions of the symbol as Jung understood them, and we, as self-designating Jungians, should be saying this to the world in which we find ourselves. Quite simply: there is an ethical obligation to do so.

Let us be very clearheaded here: we live in a deeply semiotic culture, among whose governing values stand efficiency and monetary profit. The appearance and experience of the living symbol in this culture is antithetical to its operation. Efficiency requires that persons and processes continue on a path dictated by the *status quo*, and the rationalizations necessary for its maintenance. In a very real sense, the appearance of the living symbol is an experience of arrest, infused with wonder; the Greeks took the latter to be the genesis of philosophy. Perhaps the experience of the living symbol is the time when philosophical wonder, spiritual quest, and psychological reflection are commingled and experienced with an intensity that is difficult to maintain, but which can define the vocation of a person or a culture. Henri Bergson's elegant characterization of what he (not Jung) calls intuition could be said as well of the living symbol: 'itself obscure; it dissipates obscurities' (Bergson 1970: 36). A beautiful line by the American lyric poet Theodore Roethke intimates a similar experience: 'at first the visible obscures; go where light is' (Roethke 1961: 103).

The Rumanian émigré poet Andrei Codrescu has important observations to make about these matters from the perspective of the viability of the creative imagination. The 'Outside' and the 'Inside' are his respective spatial images for the symbolic and semiotic realms. The Outside exists in two dimensions: a physical, geographical one, 'where [humans] speak with animals with or without shamans', and a metaphysical one, 'that place of dreaming, accessible by imagination and poetry . . . the place of the original creative gesture' (Codrescu 1990: 200). In Codrescu's partially metaphoric geography semiotic culture tries to get everything 'Inside' by the brunt of turning everything into signs. Its job, Codrescu states, is the erasure of possibility, the absolute occupation of the unknown by what is known, the obliteration of mystery (Codrescu 1990: 206). When things – including persons – are taken as signs, they can be manipulated; control is the name of the culture's semiotic game. 'Imagination must be destroyed by the manipulation of images,' says Codrescu (ibid.). Listen further to his description of what happens to the unconscious register of the psyche in semioticized culture:

> Where is the unconscious today? . . . The fact is that the unconscious is gone. According to a psychoanalyst of my acquaintance, every attempt to penetrate below the surface these days produces nothing but television jingles . . . Asked how he is feeling, the patient replies: 'The more you look the more you like.' The earliest thing he remembers? 'Reach out and touch someone.' Identity crisis? 'I wish I were an Oscar Meyer weiner.' . . . What does he want from life? 'Double your fun.' Questioning the primal things, he gets: 'G.E. brings good things to life.' It isn't just that the history of television populates the ontological pipeline. *It is as if there are no more individual secrets: they seem to have melted into one huge secret, now in the keeping of the military-industrial-entertainment complex* [my emphasis], instead of the Oedipal one.
>
> (Codrescu 1990: 138–9)

The 'Outside' we call the unconscious has here been filled with the advertising slogans of the 'Inside', with what Codrescu rightly calls 'fake imagination.' This imagination is pre-digested for easy and economically effective consumption – *often using archetypal imagery*.

THE LOSS OF THE REAL

Blaming the military-industrial-entertainment complex cannot let the consumers of the image-products of the entertainment industry off the hook. We seem, in fact, to be hardwired to favor of what cognitive psychologists call 'processing fluency.' Experiments are reported to show that 'when an object is easy to perceive, people evaluate it as more beautiful than when it is difficult to perceive; similarly, when a statement is easy to process, people are more likely to accept it as true than when it is difficult to process' (Schwarz 2006: 136). The ease of processing can be, and is, manipulated by those 'Insiders' who construct images for our aesthetic, intellectual, economic and political consumption. We need to nest our *iconophilia* within an on-going reflective awareness of this fact. Again: our psychology of the image carries ethical obligations.

Let's return to Codrescu for more bad news: what has happened to the outer 'Outside', to nature, while our inner 'Outside' has been disappearing into clichés? It too is disappearing, into what Codrescu calls 'institutional nature':

> This new nature has little to do with ideology, it is rather a function of the technological structures that now link everyone in a new electronic nervous system . . . We are being castrated of expression but kept excited for consumption . . . We are being fed salt-peter, on the one hand, and ginseng on the other.
>
> (Codrescu 1990: 199)

From psychological and spiritual points of view, the loss of natural wilderness is perhaps the most troubling aspect of the disappearance of the outer 'Outside'. I believe Laurens van der Post has his eye on this when he states that 'wilderness is an instrument for enabling us to recover our lost capacity for religious experience' (van der Post 1985: 48). The religious experience of which he speaks, and for which he finds an 'incredible nostalgia rising in us', is an experience of the living symbol. Whether or not this nostalgia will find succor in the generations that follow us is now very much in doubt.

So where does this bad news leave us in Codrescu's view – and not just his? His harsh solution is worthy of our serious attention as Jungian academics, analysts, and artists:

> To guard from its own detritus, and to survive, the role of the imagination in a commodity-driven culture is to strip bare the images. To imagine *nothing*, or rather the nothing behind all the layers of simulacra and false nature, becomes the primary mission. Imagination, in our image-clogged *fin de siecle*, must become an image destroyer, a torcher of imitations: not a maker of images, but a maker of truth, a philosopher . . . Imagination cannot be utopian: utopia is now the business of mass production, Disneyland. Anti-utopian, anti-artistic, anti-imaginary, imagination in the West today must meet monastic exigencies and display, above all, a great *sobriety*. Imagination has become the custodian of the real, and because of this it must defend itself from illusion, a job made immensely difficult by the complete hold of illusion on everything,

especially desire . . . Eventually we may become mere images. In another generation people raised by images will not be able to escape.

(Codrescu 1990: 112–13)

How might Jungians respond when a poet as perspicacious as Codrescu advocates a radical iconoclasm that issues ultimately into *aniconism* – the refusal to make images – and what he calls a 'great sobriety'? We might first notice that other artists of the 'Outside' have made similar advocacies. For example, this one by Werner Herzog, a German filmmaker in whose films the symbolic register sometimes appears, is similarly blunt. Indeed, in some ways Herzog is even more aggressive in his critique than Codrescu:

> There is a lot of damage to our ability to envision things; we are losing visionary abilities just by television, by TV commercials. They pack their message within ten or fifteen seconds, and the effect is devastating. You can see the devastating effects on children who watch television for hours a day . . . They lose imagination; they become lonesome and sad. We all become lonesome and sad . . . Our grandchildren will blame us for not having tossed hand-grenades into tv stations because of the commercials.
>
> (Herzog 1979: 44)

On the other hand, Herzog offers a positive suggestion that points, I believe, in the right direction:

> We have to find adequate images again. What have we done to our images? What have we done to our landscapes? A civilization like ours, without an adequate language or adequate images, will fade away like dinosaurs. It is a very, very dangerous moment.
>
> (Herzog 1979: 44)

This notion of adequate images, of adequacy for 'living by', is crucial; it issues into questions about adequate narratives, about the stories adequate to the sustaining of human life in ways that do not close off the symbolic register. But this is not simply a question of adequate images. It is also a question of adequate attitudes, and habits of perception and apperception, and of adequate institutions for the nurturing of adequate images and adequate attitudes. Does our *iconophilia* serve these commingled needs?

Herzog has an unexpected suggestion for how we find our way into these several adequacies, addressed, however, specifically to those of us engaged in the academic study of the moving image: 'What worries me more and more is our academic approach toward cinema . . . [It] is so, so bad or horrifying because there's a profound absence of pain . . . and that's devastating for human beings' (Herzog 1979: 41).

We live in a culture that is hell-bent to satisfy our desire to erase pain of all kinds; it is a close cousin to our equally human desire to escape the limits of embodiment. But to try to escape these limitations in some ultimate way is to try to bring the mystery of embodiment from the 'Outside' into the 'Inside'. This is a fatal personal and cultural flaw, because without a living sense of our limitations, which is the precise task of individuation, we lack the way to experience the infinite, which is the bedrock upon which the symbolic attitude can be maintained. In these matters Jung is himself quite blunt: 'The decisive question for man is: Is he related to something infinite or not? . . . The feeling for the infinite, however, can be attained only if we are bounded to the utmost . . . In such awareness we experience ourselves concurrently as limited and eternal' (Jung 1965: 325).

In our sustained experience of ourselves as this 'united double nature' lies our firmest basis for an adequate symbolic attitude, within which we can awaken to the fact that our most intimate living symbol has been with us all the time – our embodied selves on this embodied earth. When we can hold in tandem-awareness the presence of Codresu's inner 'Outside' and outer 'Outside', and know that the knowing itself is radically 'Outside', then, perhaps, our *iconophilia* can find its true domain and its true calling.

REFERENCES

Beardsley M. (1966) *Aesthetics from Classical Greece to the Present*, New York: Macmillan.

Bergson, H. (1970) *A Study in Metaphysics: The Creative Mind*, Totowa, N.J.: Littlefield, Adams.

Codrescu, A. (1990) *The Disappearance of the Outside*, Reading, MA: Addison-Wesley.

Conforti, M. (2005) 'Archetypes, Coherence, and the Cinema', *Spring: A Journal of Archetype and Culture*, 73 (2005), 54–70.

Fredericksen, D. (2001) 'Jung/Sign/Symbol/Film', in C. Hauke and I. Alister (eds.), *Jung and Film: Post-Jungian Takes on the Moving Image*, Philadelphia: Taylor and Francis, 17–55.

—— (2002) 'Jungian Film Studies and Jung's History of the Symbol', conference paper, First International Academic Conference of Analytic Psychology, 8–11 July, University of Essex, UK.

—— (2005a) 'Nesting Jungian Commentaries on Film', conference paper, Second International Academic Conference of Analytic Psychology and Jungian Studies, 7–10 July, Texas A&M.

—— (2005b) 'Why Should We Take Jungian Film Studies Seriously?' *Spring: A Journal of Archetype and Culture*, 73 (2005), 31–40.

Herzog, W. (1979) 'I Feel That I'm Close to the Center of Things', *Film Comment* Vol. 15, No. 6 (Nov.–Dec.), 40–48.

Jung, C. G. (1949/50) 'The Psychology of the Child Archetype', in *The Collected Works of C. G. Jung*, vol. 9:I, Princeton: Princeton University Press, paras. 259–305.

—— (1950) 'Psychology and Literature', in *CW* 15, Princeton: Princeton University Press, paras. 133–62.

—— (1954/56) 'Concerning the Archetypes and the Anima Concept', in *CW* 9:I, Princeton: Princeton University Press, paras. 111–47.

—— (1965) *Memories, Dreams, Reflections*, New York: Vintage.

Roethke, T. (1961) *Words for the Wind: The Collected Verse of Theodore Roethke*, Bloomington: Indiana University Press.

Schwarz, N. (2006) 'On Judgments of Truth and Beauty', *Daedalus: Journal of the American Academy of Arts and Sciences*, Spring 2006, 136–8.

van der Post, Laurens (1985) 'Wilderness – A Way of Truth', in C. A. Meier, *A Testament to the Wilderness*, Zurich: Daimon Verlag, 45–57.

Chapter 10

Psyche and imagination in Goethe and Jung

Or, living for love and loving life

Paul Bishop

In this paper I shall use a poem by Goethe to explore the parallels between psychological theory and German aesthetics. A 'Jungian' approach to this text can, I suggest, open us up to an awareness of the dominant cultural tradition to which C. G. Jung belonged (and of which he forms a part). By examining the concepts of anima and imagination in this work by Goethe, I wish to uncover the relation between Jung's psychology and a cultural tradition that understands the arts in terms of their relation to the psyche.

DEDICATION(S)

Written in August 1784 during his first years in Weimar, the poem 'Dedication' [*Zueignung*] was first published as the prologue to Goethe's *Schriften* of 1789 (Goethe 1983: 88–95).[1] Goethe had originally intended the poem to form the introduction to his unfinished epic poem, 'The Secrets' [*Die Geheimnisse*], but the poem came to stand as an introduction to Goethe's works in their entirety. Although 'Dedication' can be read in terms of neo-Platonist allegory (Gombrich 1937) or even in terms of medieval theology (Larrett 1978; Walzel 1932), arguably its most important context is Goethe's complicated relationship with Charlotte von Stein (1742–1827), for whom the poem was originally written. Given its content, the production of the poem for Charlotte – Goethe asked Herder to forward the poem to her in a latter dated 8 August 1784, and himself wrote to Charlotte in a letter of 11–13 August 1784, 'you will take from the poem what is for you' [*Du wirst dir daraus nehmen, was für dich ist*] – is clearly significant (Boyd 1966: 213). But what might that significance be?

In the opening stanza of 'Dedication' the poet wakes up and, in the freshness of the dawn, climbs a mountain path. Here, amid 'a white and filmy mist', he encounters 'a godlike woman' [*ein göttlich Weib*], a feminine presence which he recognizes from his childhood years. ' "Did I not see your tears, your heart's endeavour?" ', she asks, ' "Even as a boy you craved for me." ' ' "Yes, I know you now!" ' is his reply. The divine feminine tells the poet that, although he is no longer a child, he is not a superhuman [*Übermensch*], and so he must do two things, one epistemological, one existential. Following the advice of the Delphic oracle, she urges: ' "Now know yourself [. . .]" '; and, following Goethe's precept that one cannot know oneself without knowing the world,[2] she commands him: ' "[. . .] live with the world in peace!" ' The poet clearly derives a therapeutic benefit from his dialogue with this figure ('She smiled, at once my heart regain its lightness, / The spirit in me leapt to rapture high'), who presents him with a veil – *Der Dichtung Schleier aus der Hand der Wahrheit* (literally, 'the veil of Poetry from the hand of Truth'). Thus the divine feminine, revealed as Truth, reveals in turn the therapeutic function of Art, and the poet is enjoined to deploy the veil of poetry as follows: ' "Throw it into the air when underneath / The blaze of noon you and your friends are glowing, / Fragrance of flowers and spices you will breathe" '. 'That is the way to live, in joy secure', the poet concludes; thus, when we live aesthetically, even after our death 'still must our love [*unsere Liebe*] endure', and bring our children, and our children's children, 'delight' [*Lust*].

Charlotte, the wife of a prominent court official at Weimar, was the woman with whom Goethe entertained an intense relationship for many years, although its exact nature – was their love platonic? was it erotic? – remains a matter for dispute among scholars (Koopmann 2002).[3] Now, an earlier poem of 14 April 1776 bears its dedication – 'To Charlotte von Stein' [*An Charlotte von Stein*] – as its title, and opens with the lines: 'Why confer on us the piercing vision?' [*Warum gabst du uns die tiefen Blicke*] (Goethe 1983: 60–61). Here Goethe had told Charlotte: 'From an old existence we were sharing, / You're the wife, the sister I forgot' [*Ach, du warst in abgelebten Zeiten / Meine Schwester oder meine Frau*], lines which carry an echo of doctrines of reincarnation or metempsychosis that were not uncommon in the eighteenth century (Benz 1957; Kurth-Voigt 1999). Such beliefs find an echo in Goethe's comments in his letter to Christoph Martin Wieland (1733–1813) of April 1776, in which he had confessed: 'I cannot explain the importance, the power of this woman over me except by the transmigration of souls. Yes, we were once man and wife. Now we recognize each other, veiled in the atmosphere of the spirit. I have no name for us – the past – the future – all' (Goethe 1962: 212).[4] Four years later, in his letter to Lavater of 20 September 1780, Goethe was to write: 'Little by little [Charlotte] has inherited the place of my mother, of my sister, and of all the women I have loved' (Goethe 1962: 324). Of Goethe's poem to Charlotte, and of the attitude expressed in it, one critic has commented: 'Few poems have been more personal in origin; few achieve such universality of meaning' (Timms 1982: 64).

In the figures of Helena in *Faust* and of Suleika in the *West-östlicher Divan* the Swiss medical clinician Frank Nager has found evidence of Goethe's own 'healing anima' [*heilkundige Anima*] (Nager 1994: 140). In addition, Nager cites the fifteenth stanza from the 'Elegy' [*Elegie*] in the 'Trilogy of Passion'

[*Trilogie der Leidenschaft*] (1823–1824) – written in the wake of Goethe's rejection in the late summer of 1823 at Marienbad, at the age of 74, by the nineteen-year-old Ulrike von Levetzow (1804–1899) – as a recapitulation of the moment of encounter with the feminine, in terms reminiscent of the earlier 'Dedication'.[5] In Nager's view, Goethe succeeded, not just in the 'apprentice's task' of coming-to-terms with the shadow, but also in that much rarer 'masterpiece' of integrating the anima – the complete development of the unconscious, feminine soul-image [*Seelenbild*] (Nager 1994: 310–11).

Over and above these historico-intellectual and biographical contexts, Goethe's poem 'Dedication' strikingly illustrates an approach to the feminine, to the imagination, and to art, that suggests a fundamental affinity between German classical aesthetics and Jungian psychology. Nor should this affinity surprise us, given that Jung considered himself a spiritual descendant of Goethe, and that his writings are saturated with references to him. What Jung senses is that proximity between the imagination and the feminine that Goethe intuitively grasped in another of poems from his early Weimar years when he identified his 'goddess' with imagination [*die Phantasie*].[6]

ANIMA AS ARCHETYPE AND PSYCHE

In his discussion of archetypal presences in his paper 'The Significance of the Father in the Destiny of the Individual', Jung pondered the correspondence between 'inherited systems' and typical 'human situations', ones that go back to the dawn of time (Jung 1909/1949). Such situations or conditions include youth and age, birth and death, or typical relationships such as sons and daughters, fathers and mothers, or other pairings. Even if, as conscious individuals, we encounter such moments in our life for the first time, for the body and the unconscious these moments do no more than confirm age-old instincts and, in this sense, have been 'preformed' (ibid: para. 728). (In 'The Concept of the Collective Unconscious', he equates an archetype with a 'typical situation', suggesting 'there are as many archetypes as there are typical situations in life' [Jung 1936: para. 99].) Referring to such 'congenital and pre-existent instinctual models or 'patterns of behaviour' as 'archetypes', Jung refers to the earlier poem written by Goethe for Charlotte – in which he suggests that, in an earlier life, she had been his sister or his wife – lines which, we are told, capture the 'mysterious feeling' [*das ahnungsvolle Gefühle*] that accompanies the archetype (Jung 1909/1949: para. 728).

In a sense, it could be argued, Jung's entire theory of the anima is derived from his reading of Goethe. In his lecture called 'Mind and Earth', he applied these lines from Goethe's poem to the specific archetype of the anima. For whenever this archetype is projected, Jung claimed, there arises 'a strangely historical feeling' which Goethe 'clothed in words' in these lines (Jung 1927/ 1931: para. 85). And in 'Concerning the Archetypes, with Special Reference to the Anima Concept', he spoke of the anima as being 'ready to spring out and project itself at the first opportunity, namely, whenever a woman makes an impression that is out of the ordinary' (Jung 1936/1954: para. 141). He even suggested that Goethe's experience with Charlotte von Stein informed his poetic portrayal of Mignon (in *Wilhelm Meister's Journeyman Years*) and Gretchen (in *Faust*) – although how it might have done, he does not explain.[7]

In *Psychological Types* Jung's praise for the power of *Phantasie* in the precise sense of the imagination knows no bounds. In this work one charismatic paragraph follows on another, in which Jung speaks of *Phantasie* as the central aspect of the psyche, defining it as 'just as much feeling as thought', 'intuition just as much as sensation'; as 'the clearest expression of the specific activity of the psyche'; and as 'the mother of all possibilities, where, like all psychological opposites, the inner and outer worlds are joined together in living union [*Innenwelt und Außenwelt lebendig verbunden sind*]' (Jung 1921: para. 78). Equally, for Jung – following Goethe – there exists an intrinsic connection between the imagination and the feminine, between *Phantasie* and 'anima'.

In Jung's writings as a whole, the relationship between the anima as an image of the 'soul' or psyche, and the anima as a separate archetype, remains an area of contestation. The distinction appears to be primarily a chrono-logical one: in Jung's early writings, 'soul' seems to be identical to what he later called 'psyche', whereas the 'anima archetype' becomes more closely identified with the 'soul', in the more traditional (classical) sense. In 1921 and 1928, the phantasy or imagination seems to equate with the anima, which in turn is related to 'personality' [*Persönlichkeit*] (Jung 1921: para. 797). By the same token, the relationship between the concepts 'soul' [*Seele*], 'psyche' [*Psyche*], and 'anima' is equally complex. In fact, this overlap between 'soul' [*Seele*] as, on the individual psychological level, the unconscious psyche, and as, on the archetypal level, the 'anima' (see Jung 1921: paras. 797–807, 808–811) is one of the great, productive confusions of Jung's thought.

In the case of Jung – as well as in the case of Freud, and not just in Oedipal ways, as has increasingly been realized (Sprengnether 1990; Jonte-Pace 2001) – the masculine consciousness orientates itself around its unconscious femi-nine Other. In his chapter on the syzygy of the anima and the animus in *Aion: Investigations into the History of Symbolism*, Jung calls this figure – 'an imago not only of the mother but of the daughter, the sister, the beloved, the heav-enly goddess, and the chthonic Baubo' – the 'anima' (Jung 1951: paras. 24 and 25).[8] In the case of Goethe's poem 'Dedication', the feminine image of the 'godlike woman drift[ing] through the air' borne on a 'glory-cloud' turns out to be the 'Truth' of the masculine psyche. The projections of the anima can prove to be a 'poison of illusion and seduction' (Jung 1951: para. 30), but they can also form part of the individual phantasy that forms the 'mask' of 'personality' (Jung 1928: para. 245), a social 'compromise' (Jung 1928: para. 246), by means of which the 'real' Self can develop and mature.

Jung's theory of the anima is controversial, not least because it apparently lays itself open to the accusation of gender stereotyping. And it is true that his choice of expression is, on occasion, regrettable (Jung 1951: para. 29). Despite its lack of political correctness, however, the *structure* of Jung's thought displays his remarkable insight into the gendered nature of all conscious (social) being. For, under the patriarchal order, what is repressed – and hence what is unconscious – *must*, of logical necessity, include the feminine. Leaving aside Jung *the person*, his *psychological system* reveals itself as profoundly feminist in its insights and implications.[9]

Jung always emphasizes that the archetypal is located, not in some metaphysical never-never land, but in the here-and-now of our relationships, both social relationships and those internal to the individual (Jung 1951: paras. 30–31, 29). As allegory, Goethe's poem 'Dedication' enacts a moment of *active imagination*, as the masculine engages with its Inner Feminine: the poet 'gets in touch', so to speak, 'with his "feminine side" ' inasmuch as he receives, from the hand of the goddess Truth, the 'veil of Poetry' – not illusion-as-delusion (false appearance, *falscher Schein*), but illusion-as-revealing-the-truth (beautiful appearance, *schöner Schein*). This image of the veil and the concomitant image of weaving represents a major point of intersection between Goethe and Jung.

WEARING THE VEIL

The imagery of weaving and interweaving is central in many texts by Goethe, including 'Dedication' – 'Woven of sunlight and the morning dew', the poet is handed, from 'the hand of Truth' herself, 'the veil of Poetry' [*der Dichtung Schleier*]. In *Faust*, Part One, the forces of nature, the secrets of which Faust seeks to understand, are symbolized by the Earth Spirit [*Erdgeist*], whose actions are presented as 'the gigantic shuttle of a divine weaver', 'an eternal wave, / Turning, returning, / A life ever burning: / And thus I work at Time's whirring wheel, / God's living garment I weave and reveal' (Goethe 1987: 19). And later, in the 'Mothers scene' of Part Two, Faust visits the equivalent of the Greek myth of the Moiræ, the Roman myth of the Parcæ, and the Nordic myth of the Norns (perhaps via, according to Eckermann's conversation with Goethe of 10 January 1830, Plutarch's *Lives*). These myths hark back to those goddesses and Great Goddesses of the earliest human civilizations, those 'mistresses of time, of the span of human life', and to the idea that, in their work, 'spinsters and weaver-women perpetually open and close the cycles which affect individuals, nations, and the cosmos itself' (Chevalier and Gheerbrant 1956: 1093). The three-fold activity of Goethe's Mothers – 'formation, transformation, / The eternal mind's eternal delectation' [*Gestaltung, Umgestaltung, / Des ewigen Sinnes ewige Unterhaltung*] – and their position around a tripod, echo this tradition, and twice they are referred to as 'enveloped' [*umschwebt*] by vital primordial images – by 'life's forms' [*Des Lebens Bilder*] and by 'the whole world of creatures [. . .] as images' [*von Bildern aller Kreatur*] (Goethe 1994: 53, 58, 54).

Goethe elsewhere uses the image of (inter)weaving, of insertion and extraction, to describe different psychological attitudes. In one of his maxims, for example, he writes that 'some see themselves in the fabric of the world [*Weltgewebe*] as the weft', or the woof, the threads carried by the shuttle, and 'the others' see themselves 'as the warp', the threads stretched out in the loom, into and across which the other threads are woven, although all people alike are determined by 'the scissors of the Parcae, the Fates' (Goethe 1953: 519). And in his letter to Humboldt of 17 March 1832, Goethe uses the analogy in another psychological context, writing that 'consciousness and the unconscious are related as the weft is to the warp, an analogy that I like to use', and one that clearly indicates Goethe's polaristic as well as dynamic conception of the psyche (Goethe 1967: 480). This interaction of consciousness and the unconscious anticipates Jung's own complementaristic conception of the psyche.

The function of the veil is dual one: it reveals, even as it conceals. Yet some veils conceal more than they reveal, and thus the problem of illusion [*Schein*] arises: some illusions are delusory [*falscher Schein*], others reveal the truth [*wahrer Schein, schöner Schein*]. Some veils, those 'woven of sunlight and the morning dew', and delivered 'by the hand of Truth' from a 'godlike woman', the archetypal Feminine, reveal truth; other veils disguise and distort it. But which is which? And how does one tell them apart?

In *Transformations and Symbols of the Libido* (1911–1912), Jung insisted on the necessity for full creativity of engaging with the unconscious, symbolized by the archetypal maternal feminine, just as, in *Psychological Types*, he emphasized the importance of the role played by the imagination, or fantasy, in the life of the healthy psyche. Thus desire, or as Jung called it, 'libido', is both something sexual and something other (or more) than sexual, something which becomes, in the hands of the talented individual, the basis of art. 'The creative process', Jung states in 'Psychology and Literature', 'has a feminine quality, and the creative work arises from unconscious depths – we might truly say from the realm of the Mothers' (Jung 1930/1950: para. 159). And thus the libido becomes, as he argued in *Transformations and Symbols of the Libido*, the basis of culture, as it gradually, imperceptibly, becomes 'spiritual' [*geistig*] (Jung 1911–1912: para. 342).

Nevertheless, in the same work Jung also drew attention to the dangers of remaining trapped within the unconscious. Years later, in *Aion*, he warns again of the deceptiveness of unconscious illusion, harking back to the Hindu concept of *maya*, introduced from the Upanishads into the intellectual discourse of Europe by Friedrich Creuzer, when he writes of the anima, 'as a personification of the unconscious', and 'the projection-making factor' of the unconscious, in terms of what the East calls 'the spinning woman', or Maya – 'the dancer who produces illusion' [*die illusionserzeugende Tänzerin*] (Jung 1951: para. 20). With reference to the power of the (feminine) unconscious to ruin a man's life just as surely as, so it seems, Jung believes a woman can (and, in his case, the voice of the feminine unconscious as recorded in *Memories, Dreams, Reflections* nearly did), he speaks of 'an unconscious factor, which spins the illusions that veil him and his world' (Jung 1951: para. 18).

A TRAGIC HEDONISM?

Thus the imagery of the Orient, as well as the symbolism of dreams, makes the link between 'the enveloping, embracing, and devouring element' and 'the mother, that is, the son's relation to the real mother, to the imago, and to the woman who is to become a mother for him' (Jung 1951: para. 20). In a footnote to this paragraph, Jung could not make his position vis-à-vis the identity of this mother clearer: 'The word "mother" is not meant in the literal sense but as *a symbol of everything that functions as a mother*' (Jung 1951: para. 20, n.2; my emphasis). Thus Jung 'unveils the sexualized mythology at the heart of creation myths the world over' (Griffin 1988: 168).

Our problems arise, however, when we become *excessively* engaged with our fantasy, with our unconscious, and we forget the world – when, in Jung's words, the *eros* of the man becomes 'passive like a child's'; when 'he hopes to be caught, sucked in, enveloped, and devoured'; and when 'he seeks, as it were, the protecting, nourishing, charmed circle of the mother, the condition of the infant released from every care, in which the outside world bends over him and even forces happiness upon him' (Jung 1951: para. 20). For to behave like this is to fail to come to terms with the world. Jung highlights the dangers of passive erotic delusion, when a 'secret conspiracy' between mother and son helps them both, in his words, to 'betray life' (Jung 1951: para. 21). The ultimate arbiter of illusion-as-delusion and illusion-as-revealing-the-truth is – life itself.

Both in its conception and in its expression, Jung's thought in *Aion* is less delicate (on occasions, more violent, even) than Goethe's, but in their writings both embrace what might be termed a philosophy of 'tragic hedonism'. Goethe's poem 'Dedication' envisages life in terms of joyful transformation – 'That is the way we live, in joy secure' [*So leben wir, so wandeln wir beglückt*] – just as Jung understands that 'the world and happiness may be had as a gift' (Jung 1951: para. 22). Both men aim at 'happiness', yet also know that, in life, we can be burdened with 'the load / Of heavy cares', as Goethe puts it, or be troubled by its 'imperfections', its 'laborious adaptations and manifold disappointments', as Jung calls them (Jung 1951: para. 23). The 'gift' of 'the world and happiness' may come from the mother, yet the boy still has, more often than not, to prove himself appropriately masculine and to engage with the world. For the world 'does not fall into his lap' – rather, it 'has to be conquered' (Jung 1951: para. 22).

Goethe's poem 'Dedication' reminds us that, for Jung, there exists an intrinsic connection between the psyche and the imagination, between the soul and the feminine, between *Phantasie* and *Anima*. So does this mean that for Jung, as for Goethe, the quest for happiness is inextricably bound up with the aesthetic? No Art would mean – no joy? Certainly, the parallels between Goethe and Jung give us good reason to believe in the importance for both of the role played by the aesthetic in the construction of a successful subjectivity. Such a subjectivity would be one truly capable of love – and what is love? In Goethe's *West-östlicher Divan* (a text well-known to Jung), the poet, Hatem, brings together the themes of love and recognition, Self and Other, mask and veil, in the following lines, addressed to his lover, Suleika – lines which, in turn, echo the opening motif of the earlier poem 'Dedication':

> A thousand forms to hide in you discover
> Yet, All-beloved, I at once see you;
> To dress in magic veils is yet another,
> All-present-being, I at once see you.
> [. . .]
> And when on mountains morning strikes and blazes,
> Then, All-things-brightening, I at once greet you;
> Above me sky its vault pure rounding raises,
> All-heart-expanding one, then I breathe you.[10]

NOTES

1 The translation in this volume is by Christopher Middleton.
2 See 'Significant Help Given by an Ingenious Turn of Phrase' [*Bedeutendes Fördernis durch ein einziges geistreiches Wort*] (1825) (Goethe 1988: 39–41).
3 According to the latest theory Goethe was not in love with Charlotte at all, but with the Duchess Anna Amalia (1739–1807), mother of the prince of Sachsen-Weimar-Eisenach and Goethe's friend, Carl August (Ghibellino 2004).
4 For further discussion, see Angelloz 1958: 101–2.
5 See Goethe 1983: 251, where the poem is translated by John Frederick Nims.
6 The opening lines of 'My Goddess' [*Meine Göttin*] (1780) (Goethe 1983: 74–79, where it is translated by Michael Hamburger).
7 At the end of chapter 2 of *Aion*, Jung intimates that the recognition of the anima is preceded by the integration of the shadow (just as Faust must encounter Mephistopheles, before meeting Gretchen – and, later, Helena?), and that further stages in 'the analytic process' follow (Jung 1951: para. 42).
8 I am grateful to Alberto Lima and the Executive Committee of the IAJS for inviting me to post a comment on the IAJS website's discussion seminar, which prompted me to look at this section of *Aion* in more detail.

9 Hence Jung's thought has shown itself amenable to 'feminist revision' at the hands of Susan Rowland (Rowland 2002).
10 *In tausend Formen magst du dich verstecken* (Goethe 1998: 345).

REFERENCES

Angelloz, J.-F. (1958) *Goethe*, trans. R. H. Blackley, New York: The Orion Press.

Benz, E. (1957) 'Die Reinkarnationslehre in Dichtung und Philosophie der deutschen Klassik und Romantik', *Zeitschrift für Religions- und Geistesgeschichte*, Vol. 9, 150–75.

Boyd, J. (1966) *Notes to Goethe's Poems*, vol. 1 *(1749–1786)*, Oxford: Basil Blackwell.

Chevalier, J., and A. Gheerbrant (1956) *A Dictionary of Symbols*, trans. J. Buchanan-Brown, Harmondsworth: Penguin.

Ghibellino, E. (2004) *J. W. Goethe und Anna Amalia: Eine verbotene Liebe*, 2nd edn, Weimar: Denkena Verlag.

Goethe, J. W. von (1953) *Werke* [Hamburger Ausgabe], ed. E. Trunz, vol. 12, Hamburg: Christian Wegner.

—— (1962) *Briefe* [Hamburger Ausgabe], ed. K. R. Mandelkow, vol. 1, Hamburg: Christian Wegner.

—— (1967) *Briefe* [Hamburger Ausgabe], ed. K. R. Mandelkow, vol. 4, Hamburg: Christian Wegner.

—— (1983) *Selected Poems*, ed. C. Middleton, Boston: Suhrkamp/Insel Publishers.

—— (1987) *Faust: Part One*, trans. D. Luke, Oxford and New York: Oxford University Press.

—— (1988) *Scientific Studies*, ed. and trans. D. Miller, New York: Suhrkamp Publishers.

—— (1994) *Faust: Part Two*, trans. D. Luke, Oxford and New York: Oxford University Press.

—— (1998) *Poems of the West and East: West-Eastern Divan – West-Östlicher Divan*, trans. J. Whaley, Berne: Peter Lang.

Gombrich, E. (1937) 'Goethe's "Zueignung" and Benivieni's "Amore" ', *Journal of the Warburg and Courtauld Institute*, Vol. 38, 331–39.

Griffin, R. (1988) 'Jung's Science in *Answer to Job* and the Hindu Matrix of Form', *Studies in Iconography*, Vol. 12, 161–70.

Jonte-Pace, D. (2001) *Speaking the Unspeakable: Religion, Misogyny, and the Uncanny Mother in Freud's Cultural Texts*, Berkeley: University of California Press.

Jung, C. G. (1909/1949) 'The Significance of the Father in the Destiny of the Individual', in *The Collected Works of C. G. Jung (CW)*, ed. H. Read, M. Fordham, and G. Adler, 20 vols, London: Routledge & Kegan Paul, 1961, *CW* 4, 301–23.

—— (1911–1912) [*Transformations and Symbols of the Libido*] *Psychology of the Unconscious*, trans. B. M. Hinkle, London: Routledge, 1991.

—— (1921) *Psychological Types*, in *CW* 6, London: Routledge & Kegan Paul, 1971, 1–495.

—— (1927/1931) 'Mind and Earth', in *CW* 10, London: Routledge & Kegan Paul, 1964; 1970, 29–49.

—— (1928) 'The Relations between the Ego and the Unconscious', in *CW* 7, London: Routledge & Kegan Paul, 1953; 1966, 121–239.

—— (1930/1950) 'Psychology and Literature', in *CW* 15, London: Routledge & Kegan Paul, 1966, 84–105.

—— (1936) 'The Concept of the Collective Unconscious', in *CW* 9/I, London: Routledge & Kegan Paul, 1959; 1968, 42–53.

—— (1936/1954) 'Concerning the Archetypes, with Special Reference to the Anima Concept', in *CW* 9/I, London: Routledge & Kegan Paul, 1959; 1968, 54–72.

—— (1951) *Aion*, in *CW* 9/II, London: Routledge & Kegan Paul, 1959; 1968.

Koopmann, H. (2002) *Goethe und Frau von Stein: Geschichte einer Liebe*, Munich: C. H. Beck.

Kurth-Voigt, L. E. (1999) *Continued Existence, Reincarnation, and the Power of Sympathy in Classical Weimar*, Rochester, NY: Camden House.

Larrett, W. (1978) '*Der Dichtung Schleier*: From Theology with Love to Aesthetics', in C. P. Magill, B. A. Rowley, and C. J. Smith (eds), *Tradition and Creation: Essays in Honour of Elizabeth Mary Wilkinson*, Leeds: W. S. Maney & Son, 89–100.

Nager, F. (1994) *Goethe: Der heilkundige Dichter*, Frankfurt am Main and Leipzig: Insel Verlag.

Rowland, S. (2002) *Jung: A Feminist Revision*, Cambridge: Polity Press.

Sprengnether, M. (1990) *The Spectral Mother: Freud, Feminism, and Psychoanalysis*, Ithaca: Cornell University Press.

Timms, E. (1982) 'The Matrix of Love: "Warum gabst du uns die tiefen Blicke" ', *German Life and Letters*, Vol. 36, No. 1, 49–65.

Walzel, O. (1932) ' "Der Dichtung Schleier aus der Hand der Wahrheit" ', *Euphorion*, Vol. 33, 83–105.

Chapter 11

Jung's function-attitudes in music composition and discourse

Byron Almén

JUNG AND MUSIC

Among the arts and humanities, music occupied a most tenuous position for Carl Jung. Jungian *literary* critics can draw inspiration from many sources: his lecture 'On the Relation of Analytical Psychology to Poetry' (Jung 1931), his article 'Psychology and Literature' (1950), his monograph on James Joyce's *Ulysses* (1934b), and his expansive seminar notes on Nietzsche's *Also Sprach Zarathustra* (1934–40/1988). Jungian *art* critics can look to his musings on Picasso (1934a) or to Aniela Jaffé's 'Symbolism in the Visual Arts' (Jaffé 1964). But what do Jungian music theorists have? – a handful of off-hand remarks in the *Collected Works*, an occasional reference to music in dream amplifications, and one or two letters and biographical anecdotes. Jung, who was scarcely shy about venturing into new fields of study, apparently felt disinclined to weigh in about music.

Indeed, the little evidence we have suggests that Jung experienced a lifelong ambivalence towards music – both as a therapeutic modality and as an artistic medium. He appeared to consider music both precious and dangerous, reacting to it as though it were a manifestation of his own inferior function or anima, as a treasure to be feared and protected. He once remarked to a journalist: 'Bach talks to God. I am gripped by Bach. But I could slay a man who plays Bach in banal surroundings' (Sands 1955: 249). Late in life, he told an American pianist and music therapist: 'I know the whole literature – I have heard everything and all the great performers, but I never listen to music any more. It exhausts and irritates me . . . [b]ecause music is dealing with such deep archetypal material, and those who play don't realize this' (Tilly 1956: 274). His daughter Marianne observed: 'I have always loved music, but he has never understood it, and this was a barrier between us' (ibid.: 275).

Given Jung's professional interests, and the place music may have occupied in his own psyche, Jung's approaches to music tended to emphasize the roles it played within the personal, cultural, and collective *unconscious* – as a compensation of the feeling function, as reflecting or reacting against a social Zeitgeist, or as a mirror of unconscious processes. In his 1929 dream seminar, for example, he analyzed the dream of a respectable and overly rational businessman in which the dreamer attends a concert with his brother-in-law. From his patient's associations, Jung concludes that the brother-in-law represented, 'another side of the dreamer; he is not as efficient as the patient but has a plus on the artistic side' (Jung 1938/1984: 11). 'Music', he said, 'is symbolic of a more rounded outlook for the dreamer; it is the art of feeling par excellence' (ibid.: 11).

In Jung's example, music works beneath the surface of the psyche, largely inaccessible to consciousness and standing for those parts of the personality that require development and attention. It is undeniable that music, like all the arts, derives some of its potency from invoking unconscious contents. But, like any cultural artifact, music is also a product of conscious control. We might, for example, cite a counterexample to the brother-in-law dream in Jung's writings. In 'On the Psychology of the Unconscious' from the *Two Essays*, Jung describes an aesthetically sensitive analysand who is dealing with issues of sexuality in his sessions (Jung 1943). When he dreams of beautiful organ music during a particularly painful separation dream, Jung argues that the patient's conscious involvement with music provides a point of stability, allowing him to stave off a psychic regression resulting from the breaking of relational ties (ibid.: 108). In this example, music is representative of the conscious mind coping with the assimilation of unconscious elements.

If a Jungian theory of music were to approach its object as a manifestation of both the conscious and unconscious parts of the psyche, then I think it is capable of offering many productive insights. In particular, Jung's model of the differentiated conscious mind – his theory of psychological types – reminds us that we can interact with the world in very different ways. This insight is critical to understanding how music communicates to (and through) us.

JUNG'S TYPOLOGICAL MODEL

In the course of his therapeutic practice, Jung observed that individuals tended to encounter, manipulate, and understand the world in certain preferred ways. In mapping these preferences, he argued that all of us employ the same finite number of cognitive strategies, but that the preferred weightings and comfort levels of these strategies were different from individual to individual. Some strategies were strongly accessible to consciousness and could be used with facility and assurance; others were only partly accessible to consciousness and could be used only with a degree of strain or unfamiliarity; while others were almost entirely inaccessible to consciousness and were therefore unpredictable and potentially dangerous when employed.

Jung identified eight cognitive strategies which he called *function-attitudes*, since they resulted from the combination of four *functions*: thinking, feeling, sensation, and intuition, and two *attitudes*: extraversion and introversion.

The four functions were further subdivided into 'rational' (thinking and feeling) and 'irrational' (sensation and intuition) pairings. Each pair of functions or attitudes contained mutually opposed psychological approaches that could not be used in tandem but only in succession. For example, the (rational) thinking function is employed to organize reality according to objective criteria, while the (rational) feeling function is employed to organize reality according to evaluative criteria. Likewise, the (irrational) sensation function perceives reality in terms of experience and the senses, while the (irrational) intuition function perceives reality in terms of implications and possibilities. Finally, the extraverted attitude is oriented toward objects and events in the outer world while the introverted attitude is oriented toward the individual psyche.

Jung considered these eight function-attitudes (extraverted sensing, introverted feeling, and so on), to be weighted in each individual according to certain principles. The details of this functional profile are beyond the scope of this study and are complicated by issues of development, social and environmental pressures, and life experience. It is sufficient for our purposes to note that two function-attitudes – a *dominant* and an *auxiliary* – are typically most accessible to consciousness in any individual. In most cases, one of these function-attitudes comprises a rational function and the other an irrational function; likewise, one comprises an extraverted attitude and the other an introverted attitude. (The reason for this is probably pragmatic, in that each individual thus develops one kind of competence for dealing with all aspects of life – the inner vs. the outer and the organization vs. the perception of reality.) As an example, if one's dominant function were introverted intuition (an irrational function), one's auxiliary function would likely be either extraverted thinking or extraverted feeling (both are rational functions).[1]

MUSIC AND TYPE: MISCONCEPTIONS

What does this model say about our experience of music and the way that type interacts with it? Let's start with two contradictory generalizations about music that one frequently hears: first, that musical pieces – like people – have different types, and second, that all music is representative of a single type or type configuration, as with Jung's comment that music is 'the art of feeling par excellence' (Jung 1938/1984: 11).

At a type conference in Australia a few years ago, the keynote speaker used short musical excerpts to illustrate each of Jung's eight functions – so, there was an 'introverted feeling' piece, an 'extraverted intuiting' piece, and so on. Now, this presentation was rather light-hearted, and the speaker was attempting to capture the 'energies' of each function rather than to establish firm correlations. Nevertheless, the audience's expressions of recognition suggested that there may be something to this analogy. Websites devoted to individual MBTI types have observed a surprising conformity of music preferences among their contributors. Music companies are increasingly tailoring their offerings to specific target audiences by invoking psychological categories: the website allmusic.com, for example, allows you (as of 2006) to search for titles based on a specific configuration of moods (there are currently 179 of them, including 'cerebral', 'passionate', 'paranoid', or 'suffocating', just to name a few). It seems to make sense that, if people with common personality characteristics are drawn to certain musical works more than others and if there are ways to predict these preferences in advance, then musical style must have some relation to type.

There are problems with too closely linking musical piece and type, however. Most importantly, these observed correlations tend to break down across temporal or cultural boundaries due to the fact that music communicates via culturally specific conventions and semantic codes that the audience must understand to appreciate. To see what I mean, consider the Beethoven 'Pastorale' Symphony. At its original performance, the largely upper-class audience would have picked up on certain conventional references. For example, the simple harmonies, the repetitive gestures, and the drone-like low pitches would have been recognized as an evocation of an idealized lower class that was thought to be in closer harmony with nature. The stylized bird calls that pepper the movement and the musical evocations of storms, in combination with the autobiographical, confessional style of art criticism of the period, might have built up for that audience a narrative of a young man traversing a natural landscape and seeing his emotions echoed in its displays.

For audiences hearing the same work today, the conventions are significantly different. Apart from the fact that many modern listeners might miss the specific conventional references (especially if unaware of the programmatic title), this work now occupies a very different place in a larger musical universe. As a 'Classical' work, it might, for example, be heard as 'highbrow' or 'old-fashioned.' It has thus acquired a new set of subsequent associations not present at the original performance; the newly circumscribed role of Classical music in the cultural landscape means that that music will be appreciated by a different subset of music consumers – and for different reasons. Furthermore, a listener who had never before encountered European art music would have a very different reaction – in this instance the musical syntax would be unfamiliar and certain features of the discourse would be submerged. This is not to say that music is meaningless or entirely subject to cultural pressures, but that there are no one-to-one correlations between music and the way it will be perceived.

Likewise, the association of music with a single function like feeling has more to do with the social function of music, and the preconceptions of the interpreter, than it does with the feeling function per se. We tend to conceive of music as emotional or instinctive, yet in the first half of the eighteenth century, mechanical and architectural metaphors were frequently employed as descriptors of musical structure and form. Music was thus ideally an exemplar of Enlightenment rationality, with each element and part playing its assigned role and contributing to the whole. Music, thus understood, sounds more like the product of extraverted thinking – the sorting of constituent parts according to logical criteria – than of extraverted or introverted feeling – the sorting of constituent parts according to cultural value.

It thus appears that music can acquire different associations and characteristics depending on the predispositions of the individual or community perceiving it. Any artistic medium involves a play of symbols and conventions, and the typological preferences of the community – whether composer, performer, or listener – combine with social context to influence the way any piece of music is understood. The piece may set certain limits to interpretation, but I would argue that music is semiotically complex enough to accommodate a multiplicity of interpretations.

TYPOLOGY AND SCHOLARLY DISCOURSE: EARLY TWENTIETH-CENTURY HARMONIC THEORY

My contention is that the different functional configurations in individuals and cultures lead to distinctly different ways of encountering and understanding music, and that these differences have less to do with universal musical types or meanings than with a flexible interplay between the musical work and our preferred functions. In other words, musical meaning is far more malleable and dependent on interpretation than we tend to assume. One way to illustrate this dependence of meaning on function is to consider the many ways that the emphasis on different functions can shape the terms of scholarly discourse about music. We will see that, even when theorists are exploring the same kinds of music and musical issues, they come to very different conclusions about music, conclusions that I would argue are based in part on functional preference.[2]

My illustrations are drawn from the decades before and after 1900, a time of grand theoretical syntheses for music scholarship. The rise of musicology as a discipline had resulted in a new awareness of the way that musical styles changed over time, and the increasing harmonic and formal complexities in the music of Franz Liszt, Hugo Wolf, Richard Strauss, and Gustav Mahler were answered by a handful of sophisticated analytical approaches. One such approach was the product of the great pedagogue and theorist Hugo Riemann, whose writings appear to me to display the characteristics of a dominant introverted thinking function in its articulation of a simple principle explaining complex musical phenomena without sacrificing that complexity.

Hugo Riemann and introverted thinking

This principle, for Riemann, was a notion that apparent oppositions mask an underlying unity, and he applies this concept at every turn. At the most basic level of his harmonic theory, for example, is the notion that major and minor triads, the primary harmonic entities in tonal music, although distinct on the surface, are derived in the same manner as mirror images of each other: in the simple major triad the intervals of M3 and P5 are measured upward from the lowest pitch, while in the simple minor triad those same intervals are measured *downward from the highest pitch*. This derivation places Riemann at odds with the traditional doctrine that both the major and minor triads are measured from their harmonic root. Further, it appears to have no immediate practical usefulness, and has the unfortunate side-effect of requiring a different perceptual strategy for minor than for major. Riemann's innovation is incomprehensible unless one understands the consequences that follow from it. First, it is not intended primarily to be a practical innovation, but a theoretical and conceptual one. Regardless of how one hears the relationship between major and minor in practice (and Riemann clearly understood major and minor to be inflected variants of one another), the essential feature of major and minor for Riemann is that they are equivalent in their theoretical treatment and in their practical behavior. When the most common motions between chords in a key are mapped out schematically, the relationship between constituent harmonic functions in major and minor tonalities are shown to involve absolutely identical transformations (see Klumpenhouwer 2002: 467).

Arnold Schoenberg and extraverted sensing

There is a quality to Riemann's writings that corresponds well with the introverted thinking function. By contrast, consider the theoretical writings of the composer-theorist Arnold Schoenberg. Although he is best known today for his compositions, where he introduced atonal and serialist principles, he is also one of the twentieth century's most significant pedagogues of tonal music.

Unlike Riemann's pedagogical method, which at all times remains focused on the issue of unity-in-complexity, Schoenberg's approach is concerned with securing for the musician the largest degree of creative flexibility and freedom. Here I observe the prevalence of an extraverted sensing functional preference. For Schoenberg, music is a vehicle for making an artistic statement, and a theory must not interfere with the choices of the artist by laying down arbitrary rules or restrictions. Rather, its function is organizational and pedagogical: it clarifies the available options with respect to a musical domain without closing off possible avenues of exploration. This functional perspective is centrally concerned with issues of *utility* and *application*: a theory must be useful to be worthwhile.

Whereas most music textbooks of the time (and today) inculcate a hierarchy of more- and less-preferred compositional choices (what chords to use and when, when to reuse melodic material, etc.), Schoenberg's *Harmonielehre*, published in 1911, instead reads like an experimental recipe book, exhaustively listing alternative choices without imposing a value spectrum upon them. He shows how chords can be altered by substituting different tones, and then shows how these chords might be employed in practice. What is important for Schoenberg is not the theoretical justification for the chord alteration. Instead, it is his absolute indifference to traditional distinctions between the displayed harmonies, combining the most unobtrusive with the most bizarre, that is significant. He does not erase the distinctions between possible options but, in true extraverted sensing fashion, conveys a profound sensitivity to aesthetic differences of detail.

> To hell with all these theories, if they always serve only to block the evolution of art and if their positive achievement consists in nothing more than helping those who will compose badly anyway to learn it quickly.
>
> (Schoenberg 1911/1983: 9)

Heinrich Schenker and introverted sensing

As a third example, consider Heinrich Schenker, a piano teacher and theorist who probably represents the single greatest influence on modern music theory. Schenker was an exact contemporary with Schoenberg, but his work exhibits a completely different spectrum of functional preferences. In contrast to the 'do-what-works' approach of the latter, Schenker saw himself as a staunch defender of a musical tradition that he believed to be under threat from the rise of atonality and extreme chromaticism. His writings illustrate the striking combination of dominant introverted sensing with auxiliary extraverted thinking.

The significance of the introverted sensing function for Schenker is clearest in his analytical method, which is characterized by a pervasive attention to comparative choices and to a multi-leveled hierarchy. This method involves the determination of the precise role that each pitch of a piece plays within the framework of the whole – every pitch is at some level shown to be an embellishment or prolongation of another, more important pitch, resulting in layers upon layers of interpretive levels that include greater or lesser amounts of detail. Listen to the functional preferences emerge in the following quote:

> Having finally regulated the number of tones, their rising development, and their falling inversion, the artist could now face the task of defining quite precisely the sacrifices which each tone had to make if a community of tones was to be established usefully and continued stably. In particular:

> if [two pitches were in conflict, one would have to yield to the other],
> whose superiority was warranted by its root-tone character.
>
> (Schenker, 1906/1980: 40)

There is a strong prescriptive component to both the constitution and the critical employment of Schenker's method. His analytical preferences are modeled on the compositional techniques of the great tonal masters. The stylistic language of these composers determines what analytical choices are made, and the degree to which the method yields 'correct' results, when applied to a piece, becomes a critical tool for judging the relative worth of that work. The auxiliary extraverted thinking function is revealed in the classificatory tendency and hands-on practicality of 'Schenkerian analysis'. His theories, more than the others discussed above, condense into a coherent method that must be put into practice to be effective.

Ernst Kurth and introverted intuition

Finally, consider the very different configuration of functions revealed in the writings of another contemporary, Ernst Kurth. Here we see the combination of dominant introverted intuition with auxiliary extraverted feeling. Kurth was opposed to what he perceived as the atomistic, mechanical way in which theorists isolated musical phenomena in order to generalize about these phenomena. The result of such an approach, he argued, would be the exclusion of the most essential aspects of music, namely, the significations that they acquire in a particular context. Kurth's analyses of the music of Richard Wagner, Anton Bruckner, and J. S. Bach seek to uncover the psychologically potent meaning that lies between all the various musical motions. His analytical terminology is much more diffuse than that of Riemann, Schoenberg, or Schenker; for Kurth, analysis must attempt to articulate the ineffable, and his terms frequently work like extended metaphors that seek to flesh out that which cannot be directly stated. Listen to his use of an analogy between musical process and energy flow (an analogy that is strikingly similar to that used by Jung in his description of the unconscious):

> The real hallmark of this technique of harmonic shading, however, is the *pliability* with which originally tonal chords in late Romanticism accommodate individual tones to the manifestation of a single direction. It is the reaction of harmonies to the slightest energetic tensions ... The harmonies of the high Romantic style become so sensitive that, like a light, thin and extraordinarily sensitive film, they instantly stretch as the current ebbs and flows. Even a slight wisp darkens and discolors them. A slight darkening often depresses the whole mood with a single chromatically deviating tone, and can at times evoke

wonderful shadings of faint melancholy . . . The most subtle brightening effects, however, are also induced by the reverse process of raising a tone.

(Rothfarb 1991: 103–4)

Note Kurth's personalization of music through reference to the psyche, his empathic engagement with anthropomorphized musical activity, his suggestion that meaning is both ubiquitous and hidden, his penchant for metaphor and allusion, and his impressionistic use of language.

CONCLUSION: OTHER DIRECTIONS

In comparing these four theorists and their theories, one has to be struck by the extreme variety of approaches to what is essentially the same literature. Each of these men has had a strong impact on the field of music theory, and yet their conclusions are scarcely reconcilable with one another, to the degree that they seem to be talking about completely different music. The fact that the *same* music is under discussion is an indication that music does not speak to us only in one way. Art acquires meaning only through *our interactions* with it, and functional preferences are like filters that encourage certain interpretations and effects while excluding others.

Beyond an awareness of functional differences, there are other paths that a Jungian-based perspective on music might take. We might, for example, examine theoretical disputes between scholars or disciplines to see whether they arise from different functional configurations. Schenker's and Schoenberg's public misreadings of one another offer a fine subject for such a typological analysis. Alternatively, we might approach a piece of music by trying on each function or function pairing to increase the range of our insight, to look for our methodological blind spots, or to achieve a balance of perspectives. We might compare the compositional, perceptual, or performative strategies of composers, listeners, or performers with different functional preferences to look for common or distinguishing features. Or we might interrogate the musical conventions and communicative paradigms themselves. Do they, for example, communicate with equal clarity or direction to all types or only to some? Did these conventions and paradigms themselves emerge from a cultural nexus with a functional bias?

Most important is the perspective of flexibility and openness to alternatives that characterizes the Jungian worldview. If we break apart the notion that musical works have fixed meanings, we can counter potentially repressive structures of power in our academic communities. If we also offer a way to map out and value distinctly different interpretive valences, we can provide an appealing alternative to an entropic rhetorical relativism. The Jungian perspective and the type theory contained within it offer this possibility. And just as Jung finally embraced the value of music therapy near the end of his life when he saw what it could accomplish, so too do I hope that the disciplines of music and Jungian studies will develop a fruitful rapprochement in the years to come.

NOTES

1 The most elaborate published treatment of Jung's typological theory is found in Jung 1921/1971.
2 The following comparison of Riemann, Schoenberg, Schenker, and Kurth derives from a more extended treatment – related to the four psychological temperaments – in Almén 2005. See also Almén 2006 for other examples of discourse analysis informed by Jungian typology.

REFERENCES

Almén, Byron (2005) 'Musical "Temperament": Theorists and the Functions of Musical Analysis', *Theoria*, Vol. 12, 31–68.
—— (2006) 'Modes of Analysis', *Theory & Practice*, Vol. 31, 1–28.
Jaffé, Aniela (1964) 'Symbolism in the Visual Arts', in C. G. Jung (ed.), *Man and His Symbols*, New York: Dell Publishing, 255–322.
Jung, Carl Gustav (1931/1966) 'On The Relation of Analytical Psychology to Poetry', in *The Spirit in Man, Art, and Literature* (*CW* 15), ed. R. F. C. Hull, Princeton, N.J.: Princeton University Press, 65–83.
—— (1934a/1966) 'Picasso', in *CW* 15, 135–41.
—— (1934b/1966) ' "Ulysses": A Monologue', in *CW* 15, 109–34.
—— (1943) 'On the Psychology of the Unconscious', in *CW* 9, 3–119.
—— (1950) 'Psychology and Literature', in *CW* 15, 84–105.
—— (1921/1971) *Psychological Types*, *CW* 6.
—— (1938/1984) *Dream Analysis: Notes of the Seminar given in 1928–1930 by C. G. Jung*, ed. William McGuire, Princeton, N.J.: Princeton University Press.
—— (1934–40/1988) *Nietzsche's Zarathustra: Notes of the Seminar given in 1934–1939 by C. G. Jung*, 2 vols., ed. James L. Jarrett, Princeton, N.J.: Princeton University Press.
Klumpenhouwer, H. (2002) 'Dualist Tonal Space and Transformation in Nineteenth-Century Musical Thought', in Thomas Christensen (ed.), *Cambridge History of Western Music Theory*, Cambridge: Cambridge University Press, 456–76.
Rothfarb, Lee A. (ed.) (1991) *Ernst Kurth: Selected Writings*, Cambridge: Cambridge University Press.
Sands, Frederick (1955) 'Men, Women, and God', in William McGuire and R. F. C. Hull (eds), *C. G. Jung Speaking* (1977), Princeton, N.J.: Princeton University Press, 244–51.
Schenker, Heinrich (1906/1980) *Harmony*, trans. Elisabeth Mann Borgese, Chicago: University of Chicago Press.

Schoenberg, Arnold (1911/1983) *Theory of Harmony*, trans. Roy E. Carter, Berkeley: University of California Press.

Tilly, Margaret (1956) 'The Therapy of Music', in William McGuire and R. F. C. Hull (eds), *C. G. Jung Speaking* (1977), Princeton, N.J.: Princeton University Press, 273–75.

Chapter 12

Jung in the twilight zone

The psychological functions of the horror film

Angela Connolly

INTRODUCTION

Until recently the horror film tended to be seen as a unified genre, and 'the privileged and critical tool for discussing the genre' was, as Noel Carroll notes, psychoanalysis (Carroll 1982: 16–24). The result was a universalizing tendency to read horror only in terms of repressed infantile desires and, as Waller states, a 'tendency to disregard the complex relationship between a genre and the social, political and cultural values and institutions that make up our world' (Waller 1986: 12). This led critics such as Carroll and Freeland to reject *tout court* the relevance of psychoanalysis to film studies, suggesting instead that horror is concerned with the social construction of differences and of evil (Freeland 2000: 2).

Just as horror cannot be reduced only to the psychological, equally however it cannot be explained *only* in social or historical terms, important as they are. Horror is a way of exploring what film academic Peter Hutching, in a discussion on horror, calls 'beyondness', the idea that there are realms of experience that take us outside ourselves and 'engage our imagination in creative, speculative and unexpected ways' (Hutchings 2004: 105). It is this aspect of horror that is perhaps most open to the application of Jungian theory and concepts, and it is somewhat paradoxical that Jungians have paid little attention to what Robin Wood sees as 'currently the most important of all American (film) genres and perhaps the most progressive' (Wood 1979: 127–30). In particular, recent developments in Jungian thinking provide exciting opportunities for revisioning the psychological *and* cultural implications of horror films. The introduction of Henderson's concept of the cultural unconscious (the idea that there is a culturally mediated area of the unconscious lying between the personal and the archetypal unconscious; Henderson 1990) provides Jungians with a sound theoretical basis for the study of the concrete manifestations of universals in different social and historical contexts. I propose to utilize the cultural unconscious and Jung's concept of the Shadow to analyse the structure and the functions of the horror film.

THE JUNGIAN SHADOW

In Jung, the experience of the uncanny is linked to the encounter with the Shadow – the dark, unknown part of the personality that lies in the unconscious, 'the sinister and frightful brother, our own flesh-and-blood counterpart' (Jung 1953: para. 51). The term shadow encloses within itself all Jung's theorizations on the subject of evil. Jung is opposed to the Augustinian doctrine of the 'privatio boni' for he sees evil as 'a genuine force to be reckoned with in the world', as Murray Stein puts it. He is equally opposed however to the dualistic idea that evil is an independent and integral part of nature, and for this reason, as Stein says, 'Evil is not quite, or not always, archetypal for Jung' (Stein 1995: 7). Jung does insist however that the Shadow is an archetype and that what is archetypal in the shadow experience is the universal tendency to project our own evil into external reality. For Jung, both from an individual and a collective point of view, this universal tendency plays a vital role in the way in which we experience otherness, and it explains why he insists that judgements of good and evil differ from individual to individual and from culture to culture.

Jung however also uses the term shadow in another, more poetic way, as a pregnant metaphor that translates an experience that we have every day of our lives, the knowledge that we have a 'twilight zone', an obscure part of ourselves in which many presences reveal themselves. Within the multiplicity of meaning enclosed within this metaphor, Mario Trevi discerns various strands of linguistic ambiguity: shadow as that part of the body that gives us corporeality and depth; shadow as the outlines that we see in the dark that give definition; shadow as the realm of death. To reduce the shadow to any-one of these contents, signifies, 'an impoverishment of this emotive experience, of this imaginal and affective mass' (Trevi 1986: 127–30). The Shadow for Jung is as much a collective phenomenon as an individual one, and just as the shadow of a person defines him or her as individual, so too the capacity of a culture or society to encounter and assume its shadow, plays a role in a passage from limits to definition.

THE CULTURAL COMPLEX

Working from the concept of the cultural unconscious, Singer and Kimbles have suggested that complexes also exist within the psyche of the group. Like the individual complex, the group or 'cultural complex' is envisioned as 'an emotionally charged aggregate of ideas and images that cluster around an archetypal core', which works to structure our emotional experiences, our beliefs and our actions. This term is 'a way of describing how deeply held beliefs and emotions operate in group life and within the individual psyche by mediating an individual's relationship to a specific group, nation or culture'

(Singer and Kimbles 2004: 188). They impose constraints on the way in which we structure our identities and on the way in which we perceive, imagine and react to difference and 'otherness'.

Jung stressed that the psyche is marked by the tendency to dissociate into complexes, and he suggested that this is a normal part of life, linked to the difficulty of affirming the 'whole of one's nature' (Jung 1934: 92–104). Singer and Kimbles suggest that cultural complexes are arranged in bipolar systems and that when the group consciousness aligns itself with the affect proper to one pole of the complex, the other pole is assigned to a suitable object which will then evoke emotions such as attraction or fear. If the function of horror is to express and give form to the cultural shadow complex of a given society, the work of these authors suggests that the cultural shadow complex is organized around two opposing poles: the victim pole and the monster pole.

THE AESTHETICS OF HORROR

In *The Philosophy of Horror*, Carroll argues that the horror provoked by the monster is evoked by its un-natural character, 'they [monsters] . . . are cognitively threatening . . . monsters are in a certain sense challenges to the foundations of a culture's way of thinking' (Carroll 1990: 34). This cognitive threat depends essentially on the fact that monsters are categorically interstitial, that is to say they blur the boundaries between categories.

The horror film is associated however with another emotion, terror, and any definition of the function of the horror film necessitates making a clear distinction between horror and terror, as there are important semantic differences between these two psychological modes. It suggests that at the individual and collective level, they may play different roles. As Susan Rowland states in *Jung: A Feminist Revision*, 'Whereas "terror" signifies the expansion of the conscious self under sublime pressures, for example, in the erosion of borders between natural and supernatural in a ghost story, "horror" means a reverse direction of recoil and even self-fragmentation' (Rowland 2002: 156).

This erosion of boundaries creates an aesthetics of indeterminacy and uncertainty, principal characteristics of the Sublime. Central to much psychoanalytical film criticism is Freud's hypothesis, developed in 'The Uncanny' (1919) that the production of uncanny feelings depends on the return of the repressed. If we look more carefully at Freud's text however, it is clear that, despite all his struggles to contain the uncanny within the framework of the repressed, he has failed to confute Jentsch's contention that the uncanny is linked to intellectual uncertainty about the status of an object, real or imaginary.[1] This suggests that in the horror film the categorical interstitial nature of the monster should tend to elicit uncanny feelings of terror rather than horror, and that horror is linked more to monsters that lie outside the border of the human; that is to say they are abject or monsters that are too close to ourselves in that they are all too human.

The uncanny is one of the founding and characteristic experiences of modernity, although each age will formulate the anxieties expressed in the uncanny in its own way and the images that terrorize one age may seem slightly ridiculous to another. What does not change is our need for these terrifying experiences, as the terrors and the uncertainties of the sublime moment attest the infinite possibilities of the human subject and its struggle against the limits of human knowledge.

The aesthetic response to the horror film cannot however be limited only to horror or terror. As Alex Neill has pointed out in *Empathy and (Film) Fiction*, the concept of empathy is important in any discussion of the aesthetic response to film fictions (Neill 1996). According to this author it is necessary to distinguish between three kinds of reactions: emotional reactions where our focus of concern is oneself, sympathy where I feel for the other, and empathy where I feel with the other. Empathy is an imaginative activity in which the spectator is able to represent to him or herself the thoughts, beliefs and desires of the other as though they were one's own (Neill 1996: 187).

When we think about our empathetic response to the horror film it is natural to think first about our empathy with the victim, for as Clover states 'our primary and acknowledged identification is with the victim' (Clover 1996: 71); but I would suggest that it is our aesthetic response to the monster that is the most important factor and that it is this that allows us to differentiate between the three, separate categories of horror film, each with its own characteristic aesthetic response and each with its own particular way of coming to terms with the cultural shadow complex: abject horror, repressed horror and sublime horror.[2]

THE CULTURAL FUNCTIONS OF HORROR

In 'abject' horror monsters such as that of *Alien* are represented as totally evil and alien others which provoke only disgust and revulsion. Here the monster is no longer interstitial as it falls outside of the boundaries of humanity and it is utterly abject. There is no attempt at subjectivization, the motives for the creature's behaviour are meaningless and unintelligible, it is devoid of any interiority and all empathic identification is impossible. The split between the victim and monster poles is total, with collective consciousness completely aligned with the victim pole while the monster pole is projected onto a suitable scapegoat. There is no elaboration of collective guilt and no change in the dominant ideology, which is rather reinforced. The monster can only be expelled into the void from where it will return in an endless spectacle of meaningless destruction.

In 'repressed' horror, monsters such as Mr Hyde or the werewolf evoke mixed emotions of horror and pleasure and they are more human than inhuman. They are partially subjectivized as they have desires and fears with which we can unconsciously identify as they represent our own repressed fears and desires. So although we accept the necessity of their destruction, nevertheless we feel some sympathy with their pain and suffering.

In 'sublime' horror, the aesthetic response to monsters such as Norman Bates in *Psycho* is one not of recoil and rejection, but rather that of terror in the face of the impossibility of determining once and for all the category to which the monster belongs. In the same way, the boundaries between the monster and the protagonist, between monster and spectator become blurred through a process of empathy with its subjective position. This opens the way to the possibility of a process of dis-identification with the victim and of recognition of collective guilt and an enlargement of collective consciousness. As Jung says, 'Without guilt, unfortunately, there can be no psychic maturation and no widening of the spiritual horizon . . . if collective guilt could only be understood and accepted, a great step forward would have been taken' (Jung 1945: paras. 440–43).

The moment in which we recognize the other in ourselves and ourselves in the other is a sublime moment of 'unlimiting of the imagination' from which we can emerge with an increase in consciousness and in self-knowledge. To illustrate these three categories I will look at three different representations of one of the most enduring monsters, the vampire. The figure of the vampire which emerged as an historically unified concept in early modern Central and Balkan Europe, synthesizes various traits from different sets of magical beliefs such as the werewolf and the revenant. The vampire can be interpreted as a new way to represent evil which was now linked to death itself, to a contagion that sprang directly from the dead body and all that it represented (Klaniczay 1990: 168–88). This figure has continued to haunt Western society until the present day, especially in times of social crisis.

NOSFERATU: ABJECT HORROR

F. Murnau's 1922 *Nosferatu: A Symphony of Horror* is a classic of the German expressionist cinema but it is also a film that reflects the shadow complex of the Weimar Republic. Based on Bram Stoker's novel *Dracula*, it has important differences from the original text, that reflect the way in which the film articulates the anxieties of its particular socio-cultural context (Stoker 1890). If Stoker's Count Dracula is anything but an attractive character, Murnau's Count Orlok, with his talons, his pointed ears and his rat-like features, is a truly repulsive figure.

Jancovich suggests that Stoker's Dracula represents the articulation of bourgeois fears about the erosion between the private and public spheres essential to the social organization of bourgeois society (Jancovich 1992: 49), but Nosferatu articulates much more primitive and archaic fears. Through his contagious presence, he is a threat to society in its entirety: he not only invades and pollutes the sacred boundaries of the bourgeois home; he infects the whole city of Bremen with the plague. Murnau accentuates his non-humanness so that he seems more a corpse than a living being, more an animal than a man, thus increasing his abject character. The most fascinating and drastic change is however, as Wood notes, the transformation of the heroine, Nina. Whereas in Stoker's version, the feminine is split between Lucy, sexually active and thus evil and impure, and Mina, the incarnation of the pure and passive feminine allied with patriarchal values, Murnau all but eliminates Lucy and accentuates the equation between Nina and the evil represented by the vampire. As Wood points out, 'Nina herself, emaciated and bloodless, ambiguously resembles both vampire and Christian martyr; at once Nosferatu's destroyer and potential mate' (1996: 374–75). If her sacrifice saves patriarchal male subjectivity, the price of her victory is her own destruction so that, as Wood says, 'patriarchy is left empty, without the ratification of the adoring woman to venerate the brave, strong, pure men' (Wood 1996).

In a discussion of the predominance of images of sexual murder [*Lustmord*] and mutilated female corpses in so many of the avant-garde productions of the Weimar Republic, Maria Tatar has suggested that these images can be seen as an aesthetic strategy for dealing with the profound crisis in male subjectivity brought about by the First World War and the political and economic instability that followed the defeat of Germany (Tatar 1995). The incapacity to reflect on the cultural shadow, and on the collective guilt for the horrors of the war, produced a radical split between the victim and the monster poles of the shadow complex, leading to a profound sense of victimization on the one hand, and on the other, a search for an evil monster responsible for the unleashing of evil.[3] From *Nosferatu* onwards, collective consciousness was haunted by the image of the vampire, an image that could be projected indifferently onto sexually active women such as prostitutes, serial killers such as Peter Kurten, or Jews, as in Artur Dinter's 1919 novel, *Sin against Blood*. *Nosferatu* shows us how the profound split and dissociation in the shadow complex that would eventually lead to the Holocaust was already active in the collective psyche as early as 1921.

BROWNING'S *DRACULA* AND UNCANNY HORROR

The rise of Hollywood horror coincided with the darkest hours of the Depression, and once again the role the vampire plays in the cultural unconscious can be seen in terms of a crisis of male subjectivity and of the dominant ideology. The 1930s Universal horror films are often seen as 'responses to and even expressions of, fears and anxieties associated with the Great Depression' (Hutchings 2004: 25). They represented at one and the same time, a way of

escaping from the real horrors of the economic situation, a search for a
suitable scapegoat onto which to project collective guilt about the excesses of
the Jazz Age and a way of expressing the profound feelings of impotent anger
and passivity linked to the loss of social identity. If the Jazz Age was marked
by the transgression of traditional gender roles by figures such as the New
Woman, the Vamp and the Homosexual, the Depression began a puritanical
backlash and a return to repression of transgressive sexuality.

Although Tod Browning's 1931 *Dracula* is often compared unfavourably to
Nosferatu, in fact the Universal pictures have much to recommend them for
as Jancovich argues, they unite 'the visual style of the German horror films
with a strong grasp of popular narrative forms' (Jancovich 1992: 55). Between
them, Browning and Bela Lugosi add as Freeland points out, 'an erotic
charge ... a hint of Byronic or Romantic-satanic male figures' (Freeland
2000: 133) to the character of Dracula that was absent from both Stoker's or
Murnau's versions. It is difficult to imagine a more striking contrast than that
between Max Schrenck's repulsive Nosferatu and Bela Lugosi's portrayal of
an erotically appealing, foreign aristocrat. He represents the threat posed to
American society by an alien 'other' who opposes a decadent aristocratic past
to a progressive bourgeois future, savage individualism to patriarchal order
and collective male solidarity. Yet he is above all a threat to proper gender
division. Lugosi's Dracula is both a potent masculine sexual predator and a
parody of the 'vamp' with his pale skin, eyeliner and accentuated dark lips. If
he is interstitial, he represents not so much the blurring of the boundaries
between life and death as between masculine and feminine. In his ambiguity
he represents the dangers of male and female bisexual desires that patriarchal
gender divisions repress for as Showalter remarks, the 1931 version is 'much
more explicit about bisexuality than later versions' (Showalter 1990: 182).
Jancovich too stresses the transgressive character of the film, which overturns
the sexual politics of the bourgeois home.

> Ironically, once the women become Dracula's victims and slaves they
> acquire an active and even aggressive sexuality which is traditionally
> defined as the prerogative of the male. The men on the other hand, are
> placed in a position of sexual passivity and victimization previously
> associated with femininity.
>
> (Jancovich 1992: 50)

Dracula offers the possibilities for the audience to participate in guilty pleas-
ures that society repressed while at the same time it punishes the screen characters for giving way to this participation. Renfield, an effeminate figure who
falls under Dracula's spell in a highly eroticized scene, is punished for his
homosexual desires by madness and death in the same way that Lucy is
punished for her active sexuality.

Dracula is however a more complex film than *Nosferatu* in its articulation of the cultural shadow complex. If *Dracula* suggests that it is transgression and blurring of gender divisions that is responsible for the social disorders of the Depression, it equally undermines the equation between gender confusion and evil through the feelings of sympathy that it evokes with the monster, that are absent from both Stoker's and Murnau's versions. Through the introduction of humour such as in the lines when Lugosi remarks that 'I don't drink ... wine', through his erotic appeal and through the suggestion that he is capable of suffering, a relationship is created between the monster and the audience. Such a relationship, Jancovich notes, 'lessens his impact as a monster' and thus weakens repression and the dissociation between monster and victim poles of the cultural shadow complex (Jancovich 1992: 55).

DREYER'S *VAMPYR* AND SUBLIME HORROR

Vampyr, first shown in 1932, has been rightly called 'one of the most powerful projections of the uncanny in the history of the cinema' (Prawer 1980: 139). In *Vampyr* evil is no longer depicted as something alien coming from the outside, but rather it is already there, in the heart of the peaceful French village of Courtempierre. As Prawer puts it 'the forces of evil are as natural a part of the landscape as the human beings who inhabit it and as the force of good' (Prawer 1980: 158). *Vampyr* is very loosely based on Sheridan Le Fanu's novella *Carmilla* about a lesbian female vampire (Le Fanu 1872), but what Dreyer has absorbed from Le Fanu is not the theme of deviant sexuality, which is eliminated, but his sense of a militant supernatural. This is the idea that the intrusion of the spirit world upon the proper domain of matter is something that can happen at any time and any place.

David Bordwell argues that the systematic dismantling of secure relations between the elements within the whole film, acts to undermine the stability of the spatio-temporal continuum (Bordwell 1981: 103), and Dreyer seems to delight in disrupting the intelligibility of the relationship between body and reflection, between substance and shadow. The result is a misty dream world of spectral figures whose identities seem to shift and change, where shadows detach themselves from bodies and take on the semblances of reality and bodies loose their materiality and their confines. In the end, neither Gray nor the spectator can ever be certain of the reality of what they hear and see.

If *Dracula* creates the beginnings of a process of sympathy with the monster through the knowledge of his inner state, in *Vampyr* the process of empathetic identification is carried to the extreme limit in three fundamental scenes of the film. In the first, Léone who is being drained of her blood by the chief vampire, is beginning to turn into a vampire herself. Through a close-up shot of her face, Dreyer conveys to the spectator both the evil of the vampire's blood lust, and the self-disgust and guilt of Léone when she sees the terror in her sister's face.

In the second scene David Gray has been convinced by the evil doctor to donate his blood to Léone and as he rests after the transfusion he suddenly hallucinates the image of his blood dripping onto the floor. Blood is a recurring image in Dreyer, yet here blood is not a symbol of sexuality or contagion but a way of entering into contact with the vampire. It is through this exchange of blood that Gray is able to vicariously participate in the subjective experience of the vampire, as we can see from the famous coffin scene.

Gray dreams that his shadow detaches itself from his body and sees himself lying in a coffin. In a series of reverse shots the camera moves back and forwards from Gray looking down at himself to Gray looking out of a glass window set into the coffin lid to see the vampire gazing down at him. This scene is remarkable because it represents a complete reversal of the classic vampire scene in which the hero discovers the vampire lying in his coffin. Through his dream it is as though Gray is participating in the central subjective experience of the vampire, the horror of being neither dead nor alive. As M. Grant says, 'In *Vampyr*, the dead are conscious of being dead and so are unable to die. They induce us to approach them but in doing so, we find ourselves as other, where what we hear is the echo of our own step, a step towards silence, towards the void' (Grant 2003: 154). Nevertheless it is exactly this conscious participation of Gray in the terror of the indeterminacy of the boundary between life and death that constitutes the sublime moment in which victim and monster come together and recognize themselves in the other. In this way, the acceptance of the cultural shadow complex creates the possibility of the passage from limits to definition, from a morality based on abjection and repression to a truly ethical attitude.

CONCLUSION

In the foreword to *The Couch and the Silver Screen*, Laura Mulvey suggests that 'cinema exists on a razor's edge between reality and illusion, so that it ultimately throws doubt on both . . . uncertainty offers a better position from which to understand reality, for certainty must, of necessity, be illusory' (Mulvey 2003: xvii). Horror has various different cultural functions as I have tried to show in this brief discussion of three classic vampire films. At its best it provides a 'royal road' to the understanding of the 'shadow side' of our culture and to the possibility of an increase in consciousness.

NOTES

1 See Nicholas Royle (2003) *The Uncanny* for a fuller discussion of this point.
2 I have already discussed these categories in a previous paper. See Connolly (2003).

3 The Mitscherlichs' discussion of collective guilt and victimization after the Second World War is equally applicable to the situation after the First World War (1975).

REFERENCES

Bordwell, D. (1981) *The Films of Carl-Theodor Dreyer*, Berkley and Los Angeles: University of California Press.

Carroll, N. (1982) 'Nightmare and the Horror film: the Symbolic Biology of Fantastic Beings', *Film Quarterly*, Vol. 36, No. 3, 16–24.

—— (1990) *The Philosophy of Horror or Paradoxes of the Heart*, New York: Routledge.

Clover, C. J. (1996) 'Her Body, Himself: Gender in the Slasher Film', in B. K. Grant (ed.), *The Dread of Difference*, Austin: University of Texas Press.

—— (2000) *The Naked and the Undead*, Boulder and Oxford: Westview Press.

Connolly, A. (2003) 'Psychoanalytical Theory in Times of Terror', *Journal of Analytical Psychology*, Vol. 48, No. 4, 407–552.

Freeland, C. (1996) 'Feminist Frameworks for Horror Films', in *Post-Theory*, (eds) David Bordwell and Noel Carroll, Madison: University of Wisconsin Press.

Freeland, C. (2000) *The Naked and the Undead*, Boulder and Oxford: Westview Press.

Freud, S. (1919) 'The Uncanny', trans. James Strachey, *Pelican Freud Library*, vol.14. Harmondsworth: Penguin, 1985: 229–268.

Grant, M. (2003) 'Cinema, Horror and the Abominations of Hell', in Andrea Sabbadini (ed.) *The Couch and the Silver Screen*, Hove and New York: Brunner-Routledge.

Henderson, J. (1990) 'The Cultural Unconscious', in *Shadow and Self*, Wilmette, Il: Chiron Publications.

Hutchings, P. (2004) *The Horror Film*, Harlow UK: Pearson Longman.

Jancovich, M. (1992) *Horror*, London: B.T. Batsford.

Jung, C. G. (1934) 'A Review of the Complex Theory', in *Collected Works*, vol.8, London: Routledge & Kegan Paul, 1960: 92–107.

—— (1943) 'On the Psychology of the Unconscious', in *Collected Works*, vol.7, London: Routledge & Kegan Paul, 1953: 3–123.

—— (1945) 'After the Catastrophe', in *Collected Works*, vol.10, London: Routledge & Kegan Paul, 1964: 194–218.

Klaniczay, G. (1990) *The Uses of Supernatural Power*, Oxford: Polity Press.

Le Fanu, J. S. (1872/1999) *In a Glass Darkly*, ed. Robert Tracy, Oxford: Oxford World Classics.

Mitscherlich, A. and M. (1975) *The Inability to Mourn*, New York: Grove Press.

Mulvey, L. (2003) 'Foreword', in Andrea Sabbadini (ed.) *The Couch and the Silver Screen*, Hove and New York: Bruner-Routledge.

Neill, A. (1996) 'Empathy and (Film) Fiction', in David Bordwell and Noel Carroll (eds) *Post-Theory*, Madison: University of Wisconsin Press.

Prawer, S. S. (1980) *Caligari's Children*, New York: Da Capo Press.

Rowland, S. (2002) *Jung: A Feminist Revision*, Cambridge, UK: Polity.

Royle, N. (2003) *The Uncanny*, Manchester University Press.

Showalter, E. (1990) *Sexual Anarchy*, London: Virago Press.

Singer, T. and S. Kimbles (2004) 'The Emerging Theory of Cultural Complexes', in J. Cambray and L. Carter, *Analytical Psychology: Contemporary Perspectives in Analytical Psychology*, Hove and New York: Bruner-Routledge.

Stein, M. (1995) *Jung on Evil: C. G. Jung*, London: Routledge.

Stoker, Bram (1890/1993) *Dracula*, Hertfordshire: Wordsworth Classics.

Tatar, M. (1995) *Lustmord: Sexual Murder in Weimar Germany*, Princeton: Princeton University Press.

Trevi, M. (1986) *Metafore Del Simbolo: Ricerche sulla funzione simbolica nella Psicologia Complessa*, Milan: Raffaello Cortina Editore.

Waller, G. A. (1986) *The Living and the Undead*, Chicago: University of Illinois Press.

Wood, R. (1979) 'An Introduction to the American Horror Film', in R. Woods and R. Lippe (eds) *The American Nightmare: Essays on the Horror Film*, Toronto: Festival of Festivals, 7–28.

—— (1996) 'Burying the Undead', in B. K. Grant (ed.), *The Dread of Difference*, Austin: University of Texas Press.

Chapter 13

Writing about nothing

Leslie Gardner

INTRODUCTION

Both C. G. Jung and Jacques Lacan wrote very differently about 'nothing' in ways I will explore here. This is part of a wider study of Jung's stylistics, and the differences between these psychologists. I will conclude here by finding Jung's methods more authentic.

In establishing this discussion, I will be defining what this 'nothing' stands for in relation to Jung and Lacan's critiques of the chosen 'faux' texts, their choices and mine. The texts I have chosen come from Lacan's volume, *Ecrits* and from Jung's late work, *Mysterium Coniunctiones* (Lacan 1977; Jung 1963). My purpose is to contrast their treatment of their chosen texts.

I will investigate how Jung engages directly with his hoax text through etymology in his commentary on the Bologna enigma. (Elsewhere in my broader discussion, I explore Jung's use of paraphrase and amplification in his discussion of this text.) In his very different way, I will also examine how Lacan engages logical structural analysis, and approaches his missing non-text indirectly in his seminar on Edgar Allan Poe's short story, 'The Purloined Letter' (1845). A hoax text (Bologna) and an invisible text (the Queen's letter in the Poe story that is never revealed) both amount in my investigation to being 'un-real' i.e. 'nothing'.

My larger project is the study of the relationship of Giambattista Vico's rhetorical principles to Jung's writings. This broader research leads me to begin with the texts that are 'nothing' by using the epistemological strategy that both Vico and Jung frequently engaged in: etymology.

ETYMOLOGY

In the early part of the eighteenth century, Giambattista Vico, a Neapolitan philosopher and jurist, was working in the department of law and rhetoric at Naples' university, producing lectures and books in relative obscurity. Eventually in 1725, he published his ground-breaking discovery of the laws of a poetical science, published in *The New Science* (actually three drafts/ editions, each shorter than the other to accommodate diminishing financial support). Increasingly recognised, as his work was disseminated by French romantic historian Michelet, the German poet Herder and later by political theorist Georges Sorel, his work also later influenced Karl Marx, S. T. Coleridge, Benito Mussolini, James Joyce and Marshall McLuhan. Vico was a seminal thinker whose notions of the cognitive and symbol-making capacities of the imagination influenced ideas of history, sociology, anthropology, communication and psychology.

Vico used etymology as his primary investigative tool. The deep history and associations of words to their origins were crucial to him. It is also a favourite ploy used by Jung and by many Jungians since it implies a respect for the authority of primordial language (which Jung and many Jungians think also to be 'pre-logical'). Tracing a word back through the layers of time and overlaid meaning gets to what it really signifies, Jung believed. But etymology is brimming over with ideological choice, and while that is not my main point here, it is another aspect of how Jung and Vico used etymological derivations. I will myself employ etymology to lead us into the discussion of what it is about these texts that leads me to call them 'nothings'.

Vico has often been called the 'philologiser of history' (Auerbach 1973). Vico set out to demonstrate that each era has its own stylistic characteristics. Correspondingly, the writers in each period conform to that style, or else they may deliberately set it aside, as Vico claimed he did in his own era. I will use a specific example here for our purposes.

Early on in Vico's book, *On the most ancient wisdom of the Italians, unearthed from the origins of the Latin language*, the translator, L. M. Palmer, adds a footnote, explicating Vico's choice of the word 'effigy' in association with certain archetypal ideas Vico explores in the text (Vico/Palmer 1988: 60). Vico is complaining there that such 'imaginative ideas' as he finds in use are misconstrued by philosophers, historians and artists. He has been attacking these groups for their mindless 'distortions' of historical truth, which imputes an absolute reality to events. They, historians and poets, narrate events and justify how they are ordered by:

> [H]unting out the ultimately distinctive circumstances of the situations [to] . . . uncover the causes peculiar to them . . . they thrive on imitation [painting, ceramics, poetry] and embellish an archetype taken from common nature with traits that are *not* common . . . or they set off an archetype first expressed by another artist, with better features of their own . . . Some of these archetypes can be better *feigned in effigy* than others, because the models always surpass their copies.
>
> (Vico/Palmer 1988: 61)

Of course this is the familiar complaint of the Platonist who decries false imitation. Vico goes on, however, to establish that imitations do lead 'upwards [eventually] to the supreme, best, and greatest God' (ibid.). But, for my discussion here, Vico's point is that the laws of history are based not on cause but on common-sense ideas discerned by the *prudent* observer. They are discovered, not invented, and they abide in events and words about them from their inception. Human cognition functions in these imitative ways. To impute any other explanation to our human way is ignorant.

I want to focus on his use of the words 'feigned' and 'effigy'. Palmer explains Vico's choice etymologically. An etymologist isolates words, taking them out of their lexical context, and investigating their semantics, unlike the structuralist approach to linguistics of an I. A. Richards or J. L. Austin, who gather the meaning from contexts within a sentence or in a phrase. Palmer, following Vico's lead, focuses on the associations of the words on their own to make her point. The choice of the word 'effigy' aligns the word with the related word from the Latin, 'feign': it is from the Latin *confingi*, past participle of the verb *confingere:*

> [T]he mathematician [says Vico] *feigns* intellectual elements of God's spiritual activity; the artist only feigns the phenomenal things of ordinary natural consciousness. If imitating God's creative activity is feigning, then it seems appropriate to call copying God's created works 'feigning in effigy'.
>
> (ibid.)

'Feigning', 'effigy', and 'fiction' all share one source in the old Latin. When we look at the definition and derivation of the word 'fiction' in the OED – we see it comes from the Latin, originally, via Old English, and Old French Provencal:

> **Fiction**   from M. L. fictitus, a misspelling of L. ficticius 'artificial, counterfeit', from fictus, pp. of fingere . . . something invented, 'from L. fictionem (nom. fictio)' a fashioning or feigning, from fingere 'to shape, form, devise, feign', originally 'to knead, form out of clay', from PIE *dheigh- (cf. O.E. dag 'dough').
>
> (The Online Etymological Dictionary)

'Fiction' associates with narrative remnants. These 'fashionings' are the human way, and as they become more distant from source, i.e. copies of copies, they devolve into effigies. But, always *fingere* remains embedded in that word 'effigy'. Lifeless statuary is related to the original, creative 'shaping' that fiction is. 'Feigning', 'effigy' and 'fiction' with their abiding connectedness stand revealed in a meaningful relationship.

As we note, Vico had an argumentative purpose in contrasting the backdrop of these words, and it reveals his stance when he does so. Fiction and 'faux' or hoax texts, 'nothings' stand revealed as associated concepts.

'NOTHING' AND FICTION: LACAN v. JUNG

The next step, then, is to connect 'fiction' and the hollow, hoax memorial text, or 'effigy' Jung explores, with 'nothing' and to explore the same connection in Lacan's examination of a story about a missing letter. Their approach to 'nothing' is *revealed* in Jung's case, and is *logically set out* in Lacan's analysis and thereby makes evident their different psychologies.

In Lacan's opening seminar in *Écrits*, he explores Poe's story 'The Purloined Letter' (Lacan 1977). He explores a fiction. Fiction is a 'nothing' inasmuch as it is a creation, or a shaping of what was not previously there, an imitation – a secondary or tertiary level in Vico's neo-Platonic hierarchy. Lacan uses Poe's story which has the further fictive complication of including a deliberately missing text at its core. We never learn the dangerous content of the Queen's letter which is the pivotal object of the story. The story, then, is an imitation of an imitation of nothing. It contrasts two kinds of pursuit of this 'nothing', a comparison which forms the heart of the story, as I shall show.

Jung's problematical text appears in *Mysterium Coniunctiones* (Jung 1963). He critiques centuries of commentary on an anomalous passage which putatively appeared on a memorial stone in Bologna. This text is anomalous for several reasons. First of all, the text is a riddle; and, secondly, it has been exposed as a hoax, written as a joke. It is a 'nothing'. Moreover there is also reason to doubt it ever existed.

Now we need to turn more closely to each text.

THE BOLOGNA ENIGMA: JUNG'S HOAX TEXT

To review briefly the premise of the Bologna enigma: Jung tells us that the:

> [E]pitaph is sheer nonsense, a joke, but one that for centuries brilliantly fulfilled its function as a flypaper for every conceivable projection that buzzed in the human mind.
>
> (ibid.: para. 52)

Paradoxically, and yet fully aware of this paradox, Jung joins the ranks of commentators. He cites the memorial poem in Latin alongside its German translation. Here is part of the English translation as rendered by R. F. C. Hull:

> He knows and knows not (what) he raised up to whom.
> (This is a tomb that has no body in it.
> This is a body that has no tomb round it.
> But body and tomb are the same)
>
> (ibid.: para. 51)

Jung points out the riddles: old women are referred to as young brides; coffins and cradles are contrasted. Further, information is set out in the negative, i.e. x is not y, nor is it z. It is a poetical list of negations and contradictions. The riddle opens up broad considerations of gender, alongside its overloaded nonsense, with recurring themes of fatality and loyalty, and includes consideration of suppressed alchemical motifs of containment (which Jung is especially excited to excavate). Jung recounts the works of important commentators who tease out the meanings in parlance that reflect their own motifs. The most successful fit for Jung, he tells us, are the accounts of the alchemical pundits. Well, he would say that, wouldn't he? He writes, well aware that we readers know his inclinations:

> The Enigma of Bologna and its commentaries are, in fact, a perfect paradigm of the method of alchemy in general. It had exactly the same effect as the unintelligibility of chemical processes: the philosopher stared at the paradoxes of the Aelia inscription, just as he stared at the retort, until the archetypal structures of the collective unconscious began to illuminate the darkness.
>
> (ibid.: para. 88)

Additionally, we are told by Jung, commentators rely only on the testimony of a Milanese scholar who read about the text in a secondary source, centuries ago. But this did not stop earlier commentators, nor does it stop Jung exploring the possible meanings of this vanished work.

> [W]ithin the limits of psychic experience, the collective unconscious takes the place of the Platonic realm of eternal Ideas. Instead of these models giving form to created things, the collective unconscious, through its archetypes, provides the *a priori* condition for the assignment of meaning.
>
> (ibid.: para. 101)

Jung concludes that image and meaning are identical – a phrase in a nutshell that reveals Jung's Vichean approach to imagination (ibid.: para. 93). Meanings are excavated from the memory whose primary tool is the imagination. Without those memories, and without the imagination, there is nothing. But, paradoxically, that is all there is. In any case, the meaning and the existence of the hoax text are the result of imputed 'truths' – instantiations of projections. There is nothing there, so the meanings are all that is there. And, I propose, Jung extends this to say that the imputation of meaning makes up all there ever is, especially meanings that scholars discover. Jung reports on the conclusions of one of the commentators he admired most, Richard White. In this regard, to show that overwhelming meaning abides, as ever, in the psyche he says that White discovers the meaning of the inscription as the soul printed on matter (ibid.: para. 93). Therefore the enigma text directs us to the mysteries of the psyche again.

The powerful trigger set off by this particular 'nothing' (admittedly a paradoxical statement about the text of Bologna) inspired reams of evocative and authentic scholarly work, Jung's included. Jung makes the case that these investigations are not only the exempla of human exploration, i.e. paradigms of human endeavour, but also are emblematic of substantive 'reality'. 'Reality' is made of this dynamic 'nothing'.

As he investigates the conclusions of analysts over the centuries, and also examines the phenomenon of centuries of theoretical scrutiny of this hoax text, Jung concludes that the paradox of human expression is emblematic itself of the recurring eruptions of the collective unconscious. Evidence of the collective unconscious is discovered in these projections and in their persistent reappearance over long periods. His discovery that the tools of Jungian psychic analysis help him investigate the text is thereby shown to be viable and authentic.

LACAN'S TEXT: 'THE PURLOINED LETTER'

To begin my exposition of Lacan's style, I will first note that there is renowned and extensive critical literature about this seminar. Notable examples are: Anthony Wilden's commentary and various other writers from Jacques Derrida to Barbara Johnson, whose critiques I will refer to here while making my own observations (Johnson 1977, Wilden in Lacan 1981, Derrida 1987).

The story goes like this: the police fail to retrieve a letter containing evidence of something that the Queen wishes to conceal. It was stolen openly from in front of the Queen herself. The thief, a Minister who relishes having the Queen in his thrall, hides it where the most exhaustive searches fail to uncover it. In despair, the police come to Poe's famous imaginary detective, Dupin and his friend, who narrates the story, asking for help. They have searched the perpetrator's apartment with no success. By appealing unknowingly (as Lacan explains it) to Freud's 'repetition compulsion', the enigmatic Dupin locates the crumpled letter hidden in open sight in the Minister's front room.

Lacan approached Poe's story in his own way. He does not trawl through commentary or existing scholarly literature in the way Jung did in his approach to the Bologna enigma. Any persuasive appeal the authority of the past may have does not move Lacan. Previous commentators do not engage him.

In fact, near the conclusion of the story, Dupin uses a neat etymological display to reveal the Minister's personality, which Lacan ignores. This is curious, in light of Lacan's own logical approach to psychoanalysis, for its rational leaning might have been applicable to his purpose. Rather Lacan's goal, it appears, is to reveal, by any means, the psychoanalytic triad operating in Poe's story: an investigation to locate the Oedipal coordinates. However, ironically, Poe's Dupin's etymological excursion seems to disparage the kind of analysis Lacan engages in. (Is that why he missed it out?) Here is Dupin's exposition:

> With an art worthy a better cause, for example, they [mathematicians] have insinuated the term 'analysis' into application to algebra. The French are the originators of this particular deception; but if a term is of any importance – if words derive any value from applicability – then 'analysis' conveys 'algebra' about as much as, in Latin, '*ambitus*' implies 'ambition,' '*religio*' 'religion,' or '*homines honesti*' a set of honorable men.
>
> (Poe 1845/1999: 468)

In other words, Dupin tells his friend, these derivative meanings are suspect, or, we might say, 'rhetorical'. Similarities in spellings do not necessarily make for significant associations. Hidden meanings are not out in the open with such obvious clues. (This plays into Dupin's investigatory method that the letter is out in the open and not hidden.)

But there are further problems with Lacan's misconstrued analysis.

Barbara Johnson complains that Lacan focuses on the 'wrong' issue in thinking about Poe's recounting of police misinterpretation (Johnson 1977). It is true that the police looked everywhere possible for the hidden letter. But it is their nomenclature that has distracted them – they call their hunt a search for something 'hidden'. In fact, the letter is in plain sight. It is, therefore, in the very nature of how they search for meaning, for something 'hidden', that leads to their failure to find it. Johnson points out that it is the 'trauma of interpretation' rather than the 'compulsion to repeat' that Lacan should have commented on – a failure to focus on the meta-issues – contexts, intentions and specific content (ibid.). Lacan is not looking into the primary situation of the text as un-reality, as 'missing' object, but with its transparent and evident significance. (Dupin does. And Jung does when he looks at the Bologna text.)

Derrida complains that in Lacan's *formal* analysis of the story Lacan mistakes the product (Derrida 1987). Lacan eschews mention of the narrator, which is a crucial literary and thematic device in Poe's story. He leaves this element out because the triadic coordinates don't work when that extra fictional device, the narrator, is included.

Lacan throws away too much of the story – he avoids close examination of the fictional text itself. He abstracts a structured scenario that fits his theoretical idea of the 'imaginary'. Here, meaning and image are not identical – the analysed image points to a 'deeper' Oedipal construction. He leaves out discussion of the crucial narrator; he leaves out mention that this is one of three stories in which Poe featured Dupin (i.e. the context of this story) – in fact,

Derrida protests, Lacan reduces the story, and then he treats it as if it were 'real' occurrence i.e., as if it were not fiction, not 'nothing'.

JUNG'S DEDUCTIONS ABOUT FICTION, ABOUT NOTHING

Jung has already characterised such theorists as Lacan in his essay on the Bologna enigma as liable to the 'wildest fantasies and speculations' (Jung 1963: para. 50). His argument is that these scholars are not aware of the underlying nature of what they are exploring, i.e. that it is a 'nothing' they are examining, and missing the point, they are led astray. And they do not let the text speak for itself. (Are their patients treated in this way?)

The missing element in Lacan's examination seems to be his ignorance of the anomalies of psychic reaction. Lacan believes that the underpinnings of human product are rational, and so the elements must fit a causal and logical ordering. In an earlier essay, 'On the nature of the psyche', Jung argues that 'the soul was never able to get a word in as the object investigated' by psychologists:
He continues,

> The position of psychology is comparable with that of a psychic function which is inhibited by the conscious mind: only such components of it are admitted to exist as accord with the prevailing trend of consciousness.
>
> (Jung 1947/1954: para. 347)

Lacan is one such unaware psychologist, at least on the evidence of his seminar on 'The Purloined Letter'. Jung's playful awareness of the ambiguities and paradoxes of all written or verbal 'text' makes his propositional approach authentic. By delving into what is familiar to humans, the artifice of 'nothing' or 'fiction', as the foundation of the human psyche; such a method results in genuine engagement with the human matter.

Jung's exploration is concerned with human modes of discovering meaning. He examines the text in its paradoxical totality, as something significant and 'real' (in its fictive way), by using productively its reception by commentators. Of these commentators, especially the medieval mind, it is hard to differentiate between 'tomfoolery' and 'creativity', yet the text remains charged with affective unconscious contents (Jung 1963: para. 52).

Indeed that reality, of a mixture of farce and creation, is all the reality we can expect of any text, or, indeed, of any human product. The contexts, the formal structures, the significance are the three elements comprising the paradox of human imaginative creation. These elements are all taken on board as a totality in assessing human invention and in understanding human communication.

REFERENCES

Auerbach, Erich (1973) *Scenes from Drama of European Literature*, Massachusetts: Peter Smith Press.

Derrida, Jacques (1987) *The Postcard*, trans. Alan Bass, Chicago: University of Chicago Press.

Johnson, Barbara (1977) 'The Frame of Reference: Poe, Lacan, Derrida', *Yale French Studies*, vol. 55/56, 457–505.

Jung, C. G. (1947/1954) 'On the Nature of the Psyche' in *CW* 8, trans. R. F. C. Hull, London: Routledge, 159–167.

—— (1963) *Mysterium Coniunctiones*, trans R. F. C. Hull 'The Enigma of Bologna' in *CW* 14, London: Routledge, 56–88.

Lacan, Jacques (1977) *Ecrits*, trans. Alan Sheridan, London: Tavistock Publications, originally in French 1966.

—— (1981) *The Language of the Self: The Function of Language in Psychoanalysis*, trans./commentary Anthony Wilden, Baltimore: Johns Hopkins Press.

Poe, Edgar Allen (1845/1999) *Tales of Mystery and Imagination*, Virginia: University of Virginia Press.

Vico, Giambattista (1710 /1988) O*n the Most Ancient Wisdom of the Italians*, trans. L. M. Palmer. New York: Cornell University Press.

Part III

Making/interpreting art in the world

Chapter 14

The poetical word

Towards an imaginal language

Elenice Giosa

INTRODUCTION

The emphasis upon rationalization in education promotes a poor thin language lacking in poetry. Against it, in this essay, language is considered to be a symbolic mediator – that means treating language as a process, not as a final product of grammatical structures. The poetic word I refer to is the 'animic' word, fruit of the image–dialogical process established in the classroom. I describe an experience with Brazilian students who wanted to read texts in English. The experience is an attempt to create together an 'Education of Sensibility', a pedagogical expression that re-unites the person with the nature of their surroundings – towards our individuation process.

My aim is to join two theoretical backgrounds: the Analytical Psychology of Carl Gustav Jung and the Anthropology of the Imaginary of Gilbert Durand, which concerns the importance of the imagination to the psychological development. Durand (2001) bases on Jung's theories his statement that imagination is important in obtaining and maintaining anthropological equilibrium for individuals and groups. What must be reached through the homeostasis between rationality and imagination, is what we call 'Education of Sensibility' (Ferreira Santos 2004) or Education with Soul' (Carvalho 1995).

My larger research involves an analysis of British culture through the myths of King Arthur and the Knights of the Round Table as I consider mythical language a pathway towards an imaginal language. Nevertheless, here I will only describe my first steps towards a poetical word in a practical classroom experience – which afterwards became my data for exploring the Arthurian myths more deeply. So, I consider, firstly, text as image (Benjamin 1994); secondly, the notion of 'the poetical word' (Bachelard 2001, Durand 2001, Jung 1992, among others); and thirdly, Education of Sensibility or Education with Soul (Carvalho 1995, Ferreira Santos 2004). Finally I am using ideas of data analysis developed by Bachelard (1989) and Gilbert Durand (2001). All these emphasize language as a symbolic presentation of images that are brought up in the classroom interaction. I bring to this my own experience with a group of students. Here, I try to make a brief link with the Arthurian legend, more specifically with the hero's attitude and the role of the Grail as container of the group.

THE POETICAL WORD IN THE CLASSROOM

I will concentrate on the analysis of some classes that I consider special and meaningful to me, because they show my first steps towards the search for an imaginal language to permeate the teaching–learning background. I emphasize that these classes were not previously prepared. The data and the idea of collecting data were brought up throughout the classes. As I belonged to a Jungian study group, I went to these classes keeping in mind how, in my classroom teaching of English as a foreign language, the students and I could establish a dialogue with the images of our souls, the texts's images and with the images constructed by the group in that interaction, which could lead us to a meaningful teaching–learning experience. In fact, I began to question what the word 'image' meant in this classroom where the teaching and learning process was involved.

The group I worked with consisted of six women aged around forty, who are all psychologists studying Jung's theories, and wanted to read texts in English as part of the tasks required for their studies. So, these psychologists had the idea of forming a group to improve their knowledge of the language through reading texts.

You are going to notice that the descriptions of the images are also done in the mother tongue so that the students do not interrupt the stream of the description. Keeping the word and image closer to each other – we consider the 'narrative' as 'image' (Benjamin, 1994), 'image' as 'meaning' because according to Bachelard (2001) image has its own emotional value. When the emotional value of the image is experienced together with the person's sensibility field (smell, hearing, touching, viewing, tasting), it helps the person to create her own poiesis, to imagine, giving back the depth that the word deserves. Bachelard also says that the person gives herself to the image, listening to it, feeling it and having her soul cultivated by the images. Being so, my intention is that, facing the word in the imaginative field, the interaction proposed in the classroom can be sensualized, bringing the teaching–learning experience closer to sensorial reality. When I say 'sensualize', I mean to minimize the rationalization process that is, for most of the time, imposed in the classroom, as discussed by Edgar Morin (2001).

This processual way makes me try to recover the magical power of the word. And that is the topic of this small case study. Imagining the language, connecting its inner images and relating them to ours, we can really feel it, more than repeating automatically its structures. Recovering some parts of my classes, I chose a moment when the students brought to the class their own individuation images. For example, student Claudia brought a poem, in Portuguese, called 'Hóspede' [Hostess], by Guilherme de Almeida, through which the word–image of a key symbolized her individuation process. The others listened to her silently. After reading, she said how that poem reminded her of her old memories (the wooden box where she used to keep some important objects and the keys of her grandparents' house with whom she spent her childhood). At this moment there emerged a discussion about the word 'wood'. The students didn't know the meaning of that word. So, I always made them think about the meaning of the words for them, in this intense moment of image. So, I asked, in Portuguese, questions such as, 'Which meaning do you prefer? Why?' – without giving them the translation.

Throughout the discussion, they immediately got the meaning, saying that it could only be so, as that box referred to Claudia's memories. I was particularly impressed with the key because it reminded me of the rusted keys from my grandparents' house in my childhood times. To my surprise, in the next class Claudia brought me a similar key as a gift, and the poem. Then she began to read some sentences in English that were built after the interaction with the group. (I write exactly what the students said. So, some language mistakes may be found).

> The key is a individuation image
> It keeps secrets
> It opens and closes the doors. It releases entrances and exits
> It means the access to the unconscious in this depth revealing and
> > freeing.
> It links places and people
> Individuation is connection and join, but also release and separation.

In the next class, we began with student Isa's presentation. But before she began, Claudia brought out another poem, now from Alberto Caeiro (one of Fernando Pessoa's poetic identities) that compared the depth of the poetry to the beauty of a sunflower. With the poem, she brought the photo of a beautiful sunflower – this was the individuation image previously presented by another student. Silence again, while the student read the poem. After the reading–listening session, the group discussed, in Portuguese, how this poem expressed the individuation process. They pointed to the words: movement, process of life and death.

Then, Isa showed her image: a stone. Together with it, she brought another poem, this time by Carlos Drummond de Andrade entitled 'Há uma pedra no caminho' [On the way there's a stone] – which was previously discussed in our other group of Jungian studies by our professor. Throughout the discussion, the group said that the stone reminded them of persistence, sustaining qualities; it is heavy; in deep places we find precious stones; the stone protects, constructs. Curiously, the same student said that when she arrived at home, she watched a soap opera in which one of the main characters said the following sentence: 'she is where only the stones can hear'. For an instant, there was silence in the classroom. Also, she brought another poem about a stone.

I began to realize that the students were completely involved at an imaginative level in the discussions, as they usually brought either poems, extracts of soap operas or films, drawings or objects. I began to understand in my teaching what syncronicity meant, as described by Jung. Isa's sentences in English in interaction with the group were:

> Each stone has its own beauty.
> She is where only the stones hear.
> The stone is unique and exceptional.
> The stone has many formats.
> I like Drummond's poem 'Pedras no caminho'
> The stone is very heavy
> The stone builds beautiful and strong houses
> I want to have a stone house to take my friends to eat a barbecue
> We find precious stones in the deepness
> The stone protects us from bad spirits
> It is difficult to find a stone on the way.

Another syncronicity moment was when I was invited by my friend Rose (who didn't belong to this group of psychologists) to share with her a class for a group of ladies around sixty. For discussion, I took the theme 'rose' (considering my friend's name) and I proposed a Brazilian song, 'As rosas não falam' [roses don't speak], a samba composed by a Brazilian author, Cartola. Then I talked about the myth of Tristan and Isolde, emphasizing the symbol of the rose. At the end, I gave a rose to my friend, symbolizing my feelings about her invitation.

Well, in the classes with the group of psychologists, the following happened: Student Glauce's image was a red rose. Then, she began saying what that symbol meant to her: the pruning that is an aspect of individuation, because when the branches are carefully cut, not only the rose becomes stronger, but the branches can be planted, to become rose trees – which represents the process of birth, life and death: the cyclic movement of nature. Student Drica immediately mentioned a song – which was 'As rosas não falam', the same song I had taken to the group of ladies – showing the close relationship between a man and a rose. So, she left the room and came back moments later with seven beautiful big roses, carefully wrapped to give to each of us. It was a great and welcome surprise, because I could realize how each image reflected the soul of each student. Each of us smelt the rose deeply, touched by the act of Drica. The sentences produced by Glauce were:

For me, the rose is the symbol of the cyclic aspect of life
The rose needs a fertile sole to grow
The rose has thorns
My husband gives me red roses all the time
The rose is one of the manifestations of beauty
The rose personifies the perfum of the loved woman
The process happens from outside to inside
With the courteous love, the rose became a symbol of the lovers.

Curiously, as Drica was also a singer, some weeks after she presented a show in which she sang the song 'As rosas não falam', dedicating it to the English group. For me, these are also examples of syncronicity through the image of a rose which permeated and constructed our own symbolic relation.

Besides their individuation images, the group also built the images each one had about the group. Very briefly, Isa saw the group as a mountain and the sea, as she said that in the mountain, there are stones, the sunflower, roses, the key. All the symbols mentioned by Isa were the ones previously drawn by each one in their individuation images. Drica didn't draw anything, but she wrote the following words and sentences in Portuguese: 'o grupo traz o novo' [the group brings newness], 'pluralidade' [plurality], 'um elemento estranho' [a strange element]; 'leva-nos ao desconhecido e à infância' [it takes us to the unknowning and to childhood]; 'ajuda-nos a ter um outro tipo de experiência com a língua inglesa' [it makes us experience another kind of relationship with the English language]. She also wrote some words in English, referring to the group: 'new, the other, memories of the children, childhood, deconstruction, know, don't know'. Glauce mentioned the affectivity of the group and drew some inter-related hearts. One central heart in blue – where the group appeared, a red one meaning each of us and a green one – which meant going beyond the knot among the three hearts.

Finally, we finished the semester working with sandplay – as it was suggested by Isa. As a sandplay therapist, she suggested that we go to her office and have a collective sandplay experience. We built a beautiful scene with a jazz band and its seven musicians, my Arthur bear, a cave, a bridge, some trees and other objects. I also recorded the class and I mention some sentences created by the students in the analysis below.

ANALYSIS OF THE CLASSES: IMAGES AND LANGUAGE

How silence was faced

According to Bachelard, silence can be an encounter with the soul (2001). He says that 'facing the sleepy water, the dreamer adheres to the reveries of the world' (Bachelard 2001: 189). Taking his words, I would say that facing each material object, we got closer to the reveries that lived inside us. The presence of each object made us dive into our own reveries, showing what we felt because we allowed the object to feel. Silence was clearly lived out when the students recited the poems. This gesture is as if the students were diving into their own souls. Afterwards, while discussing these classes, the students said that I heard their silence, encouraging them to imagine the silence.

Gestures

The poetic word becomes an inherent part of the body. The group's attitudes were reflected in their individual gestures. One example was the delivery of the key to me by student Claudia, as if it were a call for me to know her, which also activated my own sensibility field, putting myself in communication with my ancestrality (the rusted keys of my grandparents' house). Then the delivery act reappeared with Drica (giving roses to everybody), in the poem by Isa that was dedicated to the whole group and in the song sung by Drica in her musical show.

According to Durand (2001) image provokes a dive into the ancestral experience that nourishes the soul, promoting growth and wisdom. The author says that some of these gestures – like the gesture of delivery (in the case of this study, the 'key' and the 'rose'), the act of 'smelling' – in our case, smelling the rose as soon as we received it – reflect images of the sub-myth of containment, suggesting symbolic representations of intimacy, shelter, protection and some sensations, like shyness, compassion, friendship. These word–images appear in the language used by Glauce who referred to the cyclic aspect of life. She said, 'For me, the rose is the symbol of the cyclic aspect of life./ The process happens from outside to inside'. So, the rose seems to appear as a regeneration symbol, whose thorns are part of its trajectory as well as ours – as if it were our own Grail. More than that, it seems to show the transformation that the students began to live through language. Through this rose/Grail they are in contact with the soul of this language created by the group, a contact that touched their own souls. So, I can say that 'roses don't speak, they bloom'. The image of a continent is also expressed by Drica who built a jazz band in the sandplay activity, with seven musicians (without counting them) – that curiously is equivalent to the number of people in our English group – and in her attitude of dedicating the song 'As rosas não falam' to the group, in her musical show.

These images point to a lunar hero – that means, a hero who not only raises his sword to attack, but also dives with it into the deep waters in order to minimize his fighting. This movement among students and teacher is what I call, in education, 'Education with Soul' or 'Education of Sensibility', an attempt to sensualize reason, to alternate opposite energies. I consider this experience as a 'call', so that I could open myself to the encounter with my soul through the images that were presented to me in the symbolic class-room interaction: gestures of the students that activated my own lunar sensibility.

Also, what was very meaningful to me was that the students said that I nurtured them to do what Jung said: to stay with the image. As pointed out by Bachelard (1989), each symbol emerging evokes a poetical image that comes from its inside. Also, Bachelard shows that it is the imaginal activity of the images that form the ' "imagined image", putting the image as an "adventure of perception" ' (2001: 3). I consider that it is this imaginative exercise that brought the syncronicities developing throughout these classes. Such 'meaningful coincidences' permit us to consider syncronicity as part of our imaginative and creative process, which also dynamizes a deeper involvement among teacher and students. This symbolic and poetical movement of kaleidoscopic images characterizes a path towards the 'Education of Sensibility' or 'Education with Soul' – towards the mythopoiesis – that is the next step to be analysed in my research. So, language is a symbolic mediator that leads us to weave our own poiesis, the narrative of our own personal myth: our life story.

Language is image and so is strictly related to our psychological development. According to Jung, image is symbolic because it unlocks the unconscious and it is gifted with deep emotion. Viewing language as the symbolic mediator in the context of Western culture, I try to bring Jung's thoughts to a perspective of alterity.

As we who are privileged with this knowledge wish to share it, our students' feelings could be better explored by using this pedagogical context. This is because it not only strengthens the ties between the people involved in the process, but also augments the meaning of learning. For instance, the study of a different language can be considered as a way to attract new perceptions and experiences. A language may be considered as more than a communication instrument. Rather it is the door to our own soul living inside us. Student Glauce said: 'English for me now has meaning. It is an amplification not only of the language but of meaning'.

So, definitely, the words feel.

It is the consciousness that life has a wider meaning that puts man above the simple mechanism of getting and wasting.

(Jung 1992: 89)

REFERENCES

Bachelard, Gaston (1989) *A água e os sonhos: ensaios sobre a imaginação da matéria*, São Paulo: Martins Fontes.
—— (2001) *A poética do devaneio*, São Paulo: Martins Fontes.

Benjamin, W. (1994) O narrador: considerações sobre a obra de Nikolai Leskov, in *Magia e técnica, arte e política: ensaios sobre literatura e história da cultura*, trans. Sérgio Paulo Rouanet, São Paulo: Brasiliense (Obras escolhidas), 197–221.

Carvalho, J. C. de P. (1995) *A educação fática: construção, vieses e projetividade*, Ver. De Educação Pública, Cuiabá, Vol. 4, No. 6, June/Dec. 1995.

Durand, Gilbert (2001) *As estruturas antropológicas do imaginário*, São Paulo: Martins Fontes.

Ferreira Santos, M. (2004) *Crepusculário: conferências sobre mitohermenêutica e educação em Euskadi,* São Paulo: Zouk.

Jung, C. G. (1992) *O homem e seus símbolos*, Rio de Janeiro: Nova Fronteira.

Morin, Edgar (2001) *Ciência com consciência*, 5th ed. Brasil, Rio de Janeiro: Bertrand Brasil.

Chapter 15

Healing with the alchemical imagination in the undergraduate classroom

Lee Robbins

INTRODUCTION

In this essay I will describe how Jung's understanding of the alchemical imagination helped to facilitate an experience of psychological transformation and healing for a team of five students enrolled in a course called 'Alchemy and the Transformation of Self'. The course was offered for the second time at the Gallatin School of Individualized Study at New York University. Gallatin is unique because it is a non-traditional liberal arts college within a traditional university. The curriculum is interdisciplinary with a focus on experiential learning supported by the rigor of classical texts. This explains why a course as subversive as alchemy is integrated into the curriculum. Moreover, Gallatin is the only school in New York University where Jung has been welcomed into the academy without suspicion. Primary and secondary sources by and on Jung are incorporated into the handful of courses I teach, including a course primarily devoted to Jung called 'Jung and Postmodern Religious Experience'.

There are three reasons for designing a course focused on the theme of healing through the alchemical imagination. The first reason is presented in the first part of the essay, where I explain the nature of transformation, how it is used in the context of the course, and the way it is related to imagination. In addition, I present an exposition of the interdisciplinary theoretical foundations of the course. These selected readings – ranging from Jung and alchemy, to object relations, quantum physics, Buddhist thought and poetics – highlight the theme running through all the texts, that healing emanates from the non-ego or unconscious realm of the psyche.

Describing the fundamental characteristics of the alchemical imagination from within the tradition and the role it plays in the process of transformation and healing comprises the second reason for offering the course and is presented in the second part of the essay.

In the third and final section I describe the creative process through which five students channeled their knowledge and understanding of the relationship between transformation and the alchemical imagination into an assignment called the alchemy project. The alchemy project unfolded in three stages during the course of the semester, based on the work of Austin Clarkson, who has devised a non-traditional method of experiential learning based on Jung's model of the unconscious.[1] Edward Edinger's *Anatomy of the Psyche* was the primary text that guided the project, proffering students the academic background to play with alchemical symbols intelligently (Edinger 1985). The purpose of the assignment was to bridge the divide so common in university curriculum, between intellect and emotion, experiential and academic learning, individual and culture. Therefore, for the project to accomplish the intention of healing and transformation a safe learning environment would need to be fostered for students to harness the experiences of wounding and suffering that many would put into the course.

TRANSFORMATION, INFORMATION AND THE NON-EGO

I introduced the class to the idea and activity of 'transformation' by exploring the etymology of the word. Transformation is composed of the pre-fix 'trans', which comes from the Latin *intrare* or *extrare* that means to pass over to the other side. 'Form', is the shape or outline, the arrangement of orderly or not so orderly parts that gives a person or thing its unique character. Form is distinguished from, yet related to, content in much the same way Jung describes his late definition of the archetype as a predisposition to a form that is empty of content (Jung 1959: para. 155). Implicit in the idea of the archetype and by extension transformation, is that experience is not fixed or static and is in a constant process of change. Indeed, it is possible to move to the 'other side' of a painful event and open to the flow of evolving meaning.

To further clarify the relationship between form and content to transformation I introduced the principle of 'information'. In his book *The Alchemy of Healing* Christopher Whitmont employs the term in the tradition of physicist David Bohm (Whitmont 1993). Bohm understands 'information' as an unbroken movement of energy that manifests in the form and content of both the material and mental worlds or what he refers to as the explicate order. Also known as the implicate order, information is similar in meaning to Jung's understanding of the psychoid unconscious which he perceived as a unified field or *unus mundus* upon which the opposites of matter and spirit rely: '[t]he psyche lies embedded in something that appears to be of a non-psychic nature' (Jung 1946: para. 437). Thus, according to the theory of information forms may dissolve – the most radical example being the body at death, 'but information – that which informs may continue to flow' (Whitmont 1993: 50).

I would suggest to students that from its origins in the archaic cultures of China, India and Africa, through the Middle Ages and into Jung's psychology of the unconscious, the art of alchemy had one goal: to distill from within the mental and physical suffering of both person and world, the unbroken movement of energy that was believed to be the source of life.[2] *Alchemy discovered its unique relationship to this healing source through imagination that I infer belongs to the infinite realm of information.*

Alchemy devised a symbolic system of transformative procedures disguised in the pseudo-scientific language of chemical operations to locate the primordial movement of healing energy. In *Memories, Dreams, Reflections* Jung explains that the language of chemical metaphors is absurd to the rational ego because it describes a kind of active transformation process taking place in the objective psyche that is foreign to the ego (Jung 1963). Moreover, in his commentary on the *Rosarium Philosophorum*, a sixteenth-century alchemical text that Jung used to explain the nature of the archetypal transference, he writes: '[i]f there is such a thing as an unconscious that is not personal – i.e., does not consist of historically acquired contents, whether forgotten, subliminally perceived, or repressed – then there must also be processes going on in this non-ego, spontaneous archetypal events which the conscious mind can only perceive when they are projected' (Jung 1944: para. 501). The symbol system of alchemy therefore is an imaginative projection of transformative events transpiring in the non-ego, the realm of Bohm's information and Jung's psychoid archetype, and students would be given the opportunity to encounter the non-ego realm in the alchemy project.

To support the non-ego perspective that is the distinguishing feature of Jung's psychology and the alchemical opus, readings from East and West were introduced with this theme in mind. In an essay titled 'Self-Transformation', the Buddhist scholar and translator of the Pali Canon Bhikkhu Bodi clearly breaks with the western idea of transformation as simply a means of refining and healing our situation in the world to get more of what we want (Bhikkhu Bodi 1998). According to this author, self-transcendence must be distinguished from self-transformation. For transcendence implies the relinquishment of all attempts by the hungry ego to establish and cling to a solid personal identity rooted in the capitalist idea of aggrandizement.

In his essay 'The Transformational Object', Christopher Bollas describes the search in adult life for objects, either human or non-human, secular or religious that are identified with a metamorphosis of the self (Bollas 1987). What is radical and refreshing about Bollas' thesis is that the transformational object is not located through desire per se, or craving or longing. It arises from the person's imagined certainty that the object will deliver transformation, together with a feeling of deep communion between person and world, opening the heart to the aesthetic moment, which may not always be beautiful.

Portions from Stan Marlan's extraordinary book, *The Black Sun* are an endorsement of the psychological territory that Jung alludes to as non-ego (Marlan 2005). According to Marlan, the conditions for healing and/or transformation are ripe when ego is not protected from, but pushed toward an acceptance of the 'feared unthinkable' and into the core of the void (ibid.: 275).[3] For Marlan, confronting the feared unthinkable is a kind of ego-death comparable to the alchemical *mortificatio*. Yet, according to tradition, it is precisely the *mortificatio* experience that is the gateway to the central mystery of the opus, known as the *lumen naturae*, or the discovery of the dark light of nature hidden in the unconscious. Marlan's insight reverberates with Freud's observation at the turn of the last century, that we would prefer to repress, develop symptoms and become ill, rather than face the reality of our deepest suffering.

For Gaston Bachelard the poetic idea of reverie is a synonym for the imaginative faculty. Reverie describes an interior state of tranquility and deep contemplation, in which *ego is not an independent factor*. Rather, the alchemical rituals of *rotatio* and *circulatio* churning in the unconscious replace ego's reliance on development and secondary process and life is de-formed and re-formed, moment-by-moment, as much by the synchronistic present as by the causal past. Reverie may be compared therefore to the alchemical operation of *solutio* in which the ego, conditioned by psychoanalytic myth of historical determinism, dissolves in the embrace of eternity. It is a psychological attitude that would need to be cultivated in students to bring the alchemy project to completion.

CHARACTERISTICS OF THE ALCHEMICAL IMAGINATION

The challenge before me was to evoke in students a trust and confidence in their own capacity to organize and structure the disorganized *prima materia* or *massa confusa* of the 'feared unthinkable' life event into the medium of the alchemy project. I imagined that the project would function like the *vas hermeticum*, the container or sealed alchemical vessel where 'the matters of psyche could be heated up, cooked, coagulated, distilled and transformed' (Marlan 2006: 289). Identifying some of the fundamental features of the alchemical imagination would begin the process of binding personal experience to the collective symbol system of alchemy.

Jung acknowledges the potency of the alchemical *imaginatio* when he writes, 'the concept of *imaginatio* is perhaps the most important key to understanding the secret of the opus' (Jung 1944: para. 279). Thus, supported by the texts that exclaim 'imagination is the star in man, the celestial or super celestial body' (ibid: para. 277), he equates the healing quality of imagination with the image of a star. *Astrum* or star is a Paracelsan term and means something like 'quintessence'. Jung clarifies the nature of this celestial body. It is not an 'immaterial phantom' but something corporeal, a hybrid phenomenon that is made up of a *different kind of substance* that is half spiritual and half physical. Therefore, when Jung refers to imagination as a celestial body he is moving toward identifying *imagination as the nucleus at the core of the opus that engenders transformation.*

What the texts call the subtle body of imagination may be experienced in a middle terrain between subject and object, or the alchemist and the material she is working to transform. Similarly, Jung describes this area of experience as 'an intermediate realm between mind and matter, i.e., a psychic realm of subtle bodies [or images] whose characteristic is to manifest themselves in a mental as well as a material form' (ibid: para. 278).

Imaginatio, as it was pronounced in Latin is therefore born out of a dialogue between the known and the unknown or we might say between the ego and a non-ego realms. *Meditatio*, also from the Latin is a term used interchangeably with *imaginatio* to emphasize that the emergent third process begins first as 'a living relationship to the answering voice of the other in ourselves' before it extends into a dialogue with the outside world (ibid.: para. 274). Therefore, the dark light of imagination, which has been referred to as the *lumen naturae* is activated through relationship with the radical otherness of the non-ego realm or with the invisible forces of the psyche by means of which things pass from an unconscious potential into a manifest one.

Like the star, which is the quintessence of energy in the heavens, *imaginatio* is nothing less than '*a concentrated extract of the life force, both physical and psychic*' (ibid.: para. 278), in the human being and the source of every conceivable transformation, for good or ill. This is the transformative energy that the student would connect to through the alchemy project. Learning to engage with the flow of experience in the intermediate space fraught as it is with anxiety and fear, together with the expectation of resolution, is according to Jung 'the real secret of the magisterium' (ibid.: para. 392). It is precisely the skill of listening and waiting in the empty realm, in a spirit of reverie, that engages deep structures of the psyche that in turn engender a homeostatic life-fulfilling tendency.

In summary, the alchemical imagination functions firstly as a subtle body conjoining the complete human experience of body and soul, ego and unconscious. Secondly, it is a physical activity and the materialization in the form of the subtle body of the formless energy that engenders life. Additionally, this energy, which is an extract of the life force, may be felt and known as students learn to live in an intermediate space between opposites, through the agency of a ceaseless dialogue or relationship with the unknown. Finally, imagination is the heart or nucleus of the alchemical opus without which there cannot be healing or transformation.

THE ALCHEMY PROJECT

The quilt shown overleaf (Figure 15.1) was created by five young women who applied some of the basic characteristics of the alchemical imagination to heal parts of their lives and come to an acceptance of the 'feared unthinkable'. Composed of five unique forms, the quilt is an image of the alchemical operation *coagulatio* and an example of the transformative effect of the completed project.

Coagulatio is the process that turns something into earth. Earth is one of the synonyms of *coagulatio*. For a psychic content to become earth means that is has become concretized, grounded and confined within the limits of one's personal reality.

In his chapter of the same name from *Anatomy of the Psyche*, Edinger

Figure 15.1

explains, 'that coagulatio is generally followed by other processes most often by *mortificatio* and *putrefactio*' (Edinger 1985: 98). Only what has become fully concretized is subject to transformation for it has become 'tribulation calling out for transcendence' (ibid.: 98).

Tara (tree) was born with a genetic disease known as progressive muscular dystrophy. She lives in pain as the result of multiple surgeries on her back. She makes a royal palm tree and explains that she chooses the tree because it is unique and can't break in storms. It is an image of her deformed spine, made strong and healthy in imagination. The buttons signify a kind of fruit falling from the tree, the fruit of acceptance of her chronic condition in the form of tears.

For Tara the body, a primary image of *coagulatio* is experienced as a prison or tomb. What she discovers through the alchemy project is that she desires disconnection from her body; she cries out for *sublimatio* because her spirit is much stronger than her mortal flesh that restricts every day of her life. She describes the class as being a catalyst for descent into her crippled body and dealing with the hope of no change. 'I am in the third space', she exclaims, 'trying to confront myself and bridge the gap between the insoluble and life, between what I cannot control and what I can'.

Rebekah (mandala). Like the spectrum of Jung's archetype that encompasses the range of experience between spirit and flesh, the imaginal operations of alchemy encompass the worlds of both pleasure and pain. Rebekah, like Tara, experienced only the painful side of *coagulatio* in her body. She suffers from clinical depression. Her feelings of self-loathing are bound to a corpulent figure with sensual desires, needs and appetites that she cannot control. She compares her depression to the archetypal great Fall in Eden when humans became conscious that the flesh is a source of suffering, bringing awareness of 'overwhelming grief and desire, heaviness and impurity'. The cure she exclaims 'is precisely what I fear; disintegration, dissolving or *solutio* into the feared unthinkable, to end the cycle of depression'. Like Tara, Rebekah balances herself 'a top a narrow tower of sublimatio' in the disguise of medication to distance herself from feelings that belong to the dark *coagulatio* and to avoid the descent into the reality of her body. Her quilt square is a symmetrical image of the astrological earth mandala with an image of the womb in the form of a labyrinth at the center. Constructed out of shades of soft green fabric, the mandala is a luxurious and protective image from a feminine source, offering interior permission to feel at home in her body.

Christine (gold square). Edinger writes that for those who are already driven by desirousness *coagulatio* is not the needed operation to promote life experience, but for Christine this is not the case. She suffers from a weakness of desire bordering on anhedonia. She describes her fear of asserting herself, of making decisions, of defending her needs as the 'broken matter' she brings to the vessel of the project. Her yellow/gold square represents honey, which is an alchemical image of the lure of desire and sweetness and therefore an agent of *coagulatio*. The mortal flowers rising from their tulle and honey beds into the sky she describes as an image of the birth of libido. The pearls express the alchemical idea that when a problem or symptom is worked on slowly it forms into a coagulated jewel – the 'Pearl of Great Price' (Hillman 1990: 230). Her square is a projection of the confident yet gentle woman she would like to become.

Samantha's white square is a memorial to the baby sitter who was shot point blank holding the hand of a six-year-old child. Amira was the first person to whom the child expressed her love, and then she was gone. The square is layered with textures of fabric and paper in white and pastel that fade into the distance. The deep red horizontal lines splashed on white remind Sam of the blood shed at the moment of Amira's death. Sam told me she could not really connect to the piece, and I suggested that perhaps being a witness to such a violent act was simply too painful to remember. Bachelard explains, '[i]magination is not the repository of childhood trauma, but the cradle of a renewed world' (quoted in Kearny 1995: 91). Sam would begin to feel renewal as she released the history of traumatic memory into a song she wrote and sang to the class in honor of Amira. 'Music', she exclaims, is thus my form of *coagulatio*, though partially a step towards *sublimatio*, it is music which ultimately beings me back to the ground, to breathing, to chilling, to living'.

Sarah (knitting). The French Lacanian Julia Kristeva in her book *In the Beginning was Love: Psychoanalysis and Faith*, suggests that imagination originates in the affect of utter loss (Kristeva 1987). The loss is experienced by the subject as a feeling of lack or the absence of something or someone deemed essential for life. And yet, this utter feeling of abjection sets an 'imaginary discourse' into motion that she describes as nothing less than a 'discourse of loving play' (ibid.: 58). For Kristeva, the ludic imagination therefore transmutes loss into play by returning it to the 'unable face of the other' or the unconscious (ibid.), pushing the ego beyond its historical conditioning into the non-ego place outside of space and time.

Kristeva's understanding of the origin of imagination is a beautiful frame for understanding how Sarah was learning to cope with the death of her seventeen-year-old brother who died in an accident just a year ago to the day her group was scheduled to give their presentation.

The rectangle composed of dark mottled knitted colors reflects the spectrum of emotional volatility that moves from grief to fear, to disorientation and brokenness, describing herself 'like an amputee patient incomplete without my brother'. The bells in the fabric represent the different noises of grief. Sometime they are silent; other times they give off noise. The knitting needle, still embedded in the wool and connected to a larger ball of yarn speaks to the fact that the depth of her loss has no apparent end. Sarah's knitting therefore is an imaginary discourse of loving play binding together two worlds: her world of living grief with the world of the dead in which her brother now lives.

CONCLUSION

The quilt is more than an isolated image of the alchemical *coagulatio*. It functions as the fulcrum of a dynamic network of emergent individual meanings deriving from a shared emotional experience of human loss, illness, and struggle. Composed of five separate images, the unitary symbol of the quilt is an example of what Edinger calls cluster or network thinking which is a synthesis of ego directed and fantasy thinking elaborated by Jung in *Symbols of Transformation* (Jung 1956: 18). The object of this method is to develop a web of expanded meanings deriving from a central image – in this instance, *coagulatio* (Edinger 1995: 20).

The fruit of the alchemical imagination, the subtle body of the quilt, derives its power to heal from each student's personal experience of *mortificatio*. The symbolic death of the fixed and conditioned ego position leads to what Henri Corbin describes as an experience of *ekstasis* (Corbin 1972: 17). In other words, ego is lifted out of the confinement of subjectivity as the personal story is absorbed into and dignified by the collective human condition. The liberating experience of *ekstasis* derives from the disciplined application of the qualities of the alchemical imagination to the real life situation. For as students learned to dwell in the ambiguous empty realm between the revealed and the obscure, also known as the *mundus imaginalis*, the artwork of the quilt turned pathology and wounding into a free space of possibility or a culture of imagination. Winnicott suggests that it is this kind of cultural experience, fabricated from psychological affliction, that provides the continuity in the human race that transcends personal experience (Winnicott 1977: 100).

The creators of the quilt bear witness to the fact of transformation in the turning of something into other than it is. Such transformation is to be felt and known here and now, in this body, in this emotion and in this class. Their experience is verified by the mythology and philosophy of the original alchemists who mined ores and metals that fell from the heavens into the bowels of the earth. The matter was deemed numinous because it contained the timeless energy out of which the cosmos was generated. To retrieve the mystery in matter (and the human psyche), which had the power to recreate the world and cure the ills of a languishing humanity, eternal time had to be extracted from the metals and condensed into the present. By subjecting the matter to transformative rituals of fire, water and air, this was accomplished. For as one text reads: 'what nature cannot perfect in a vast space of time we can achieve in a short space of time by our art' in this life for the glorification of person and world (Eliade 1978: 51).

This brings me to a concluding remark about the symbol of the quilt. It is not geometrically perfect in the sense of being symmetrical. The shapes are not of equal proportion and the edges are not smooth, yet it is beautiful. Rather the project is a reflection of the real existential life situation of the students who made it and calls to mind Ed Casey's admonition about the image. What is important is not *what one sees but the way one sees*, which is the true *opus contra naturum*, and this transition from a literal to imaginal vision of psyche's suffering is brought about by the emotion of love – love turned toward the imaginal world (Hillman 1972: 185).

I am aware as I complete this essay that the goal I had for the class and for myself was to impel us all more deeply into the alchemical *opus* – the work of refining, purifying, metabolizing and symbolizing psychological experience until it glows with the *lumen naturae* or the light of its own darkness. For as Jung writes: '[t]he goal is important only as an idea; the essential thing is the *opus* which leads to the goal; that is the goal of a lifetime' (Jung 1945: para. 400). With Hillman, I read Jung to be saying the purpose of the goal idea is to impel the psyche into the *opus*. 'We shall have extraordinary and marvelous goals, like gold and pearls (Figure 15.1) because then we shall be motivated to stay the course, that *via longissima* called a lifetime' (Hillman 1990: 236).

NOTES

1 In the preparatory stage the class divided into teams of four or five students. In the incubation stage each team as a whole unit chose an alchemical image, while individuals within the group expanded the meaning deriving from the central image. The illuminative stage culminated in a performance or display or work from each team giving form to the alchemical image in a range of expressive media inviting a dialogue between the conscious attitude and emergent meanings from the unconscious. For a more extended discussion of this process see Clarkson (2002).
2 See Mircea Eliade's *The Forge and the Crucible* for a trans-cultural presentation of the history of alchemy.
3 In the final part of this essay examples are offered to illustrate the way students confronted the feared unthinkable in the alchemy project.

REFERENCES

Bhikkhu Bodi (1998) 'Self – Transformation'. http://www.accesstoinsight.org (accessed 14 February 2006).
Bollas, C. (1987) 'The Transformational Object', in *The Shadow of the Object*. New York: Columbia University Press.
Clarkson, A. (2002) 'Foundations of Creative Imagination: Reporting And Researching the Outcome of a Course Design'. *Jung: the E-Journal*, 1(2): 1–17.
Corbin, H. (1972) 'Mundus Imaginalis'. *Spring: A Journal of Archetype and Culture*, 1–19.

Edinger, E. (1985) *Anatomy of the Psyche*, Chicago: Open Court.
—— (1995) *The Mysterium Lectures*, Toronto: Inner City.
Eliade, M. (1978) *The Forge and the Crucible*, Chicago: University of Chicago Press.
Hillman, J. (1972) *The Myth of Analysis*, Chicago: Northwestern University Press.
—— (1990) 'Concerning the Stone: Alchemical Images of the Goal', Eranos Year-
book: Ascona Switzerland.
Jung, C. G. (1944) *Psychology and Alchemy*, in *The Collected Works of C. G. Jung*
(*CW*), ed. H. Read, M. Fordham, and G. Adler, 20 vols, London: Routledge &
Kegan Paul, *CW* 12.
—— (1945) 'The Psychology of the Transference' in *CW* 16, paras. 353–539.
—— (1952) 'Two Kings of Thinking', in *CW* 5, paras. 4–46.
—— (1956) *Symbols of Transformation, CW* 2.
—— (1959) 'Psychological Aspects of the Mother Archetype', in *CW* 9i, paras.
148–198.
—— (1963) *Memories, Dreams, Reflections*, trans. Richard and Clara Winston,
London: Fontana.
Kearney, R. (1995) *Poetics of Modernity*, New Jersey: Humanities Press.
Kristeva, J. (1987) *In the Beginning was Love: Psychoanalysis and Faith*, New York:
Columbia.
Marlan, S. (2005) *The Black Sun*, College Station: Texas A and M.
—— (2006) 'Alchemy', in *The Handbook of Jungian Psychology*, London: Routledge.
Whitmont, C. (1993) *The Alchemy of Healing*, Berkeley: North Atlantic.
Winnicott, D. (1977) *Playing and Reality*, New York: Basic Books.

Chapter 16

The serenity of the senex

Using Brazilian folk tales as an alternative approach to 'entrepreneurship' in university education

Claudio Paixao Anastacio de Paula

INTRODUCTION

The recollection of our grandparents telling us stories marks the memory of many people. The imaginative use of oral literature in different contexts can evoke situations similar to those in which sacred stories told by our ancestors reconnects the listener to the place of the soul. Fernando Diniz – one of the artists from 'Engenho de Dentro', a psychiatric hospital where he was nurtured by Nise da Silveira[1] – referred to this realm with these words:

> . . . the world of images
> I've moved to the world of images
> The soul has moved to something else
> Images take a person's soul
>   (Diniz quoted in Silveira 1981: 13)

If used skillfully, oral stories may become passages through which people travel to perplexity and fascination. They are journeys to what Henri Corbin called *mundus imaginalis*: a world which lies on the ontological level above the world of senses and below the purely intelligible world, an intermediate world (Corbin 1964). The images awakened by these stories and the need to express them is the urge of the psyche to configure its visions into shapes. Such shapes transform individual drama into character: they are a live mind creating and being created by live stories. The same idea could be proposed in another way: stories are live beings which exist because of men and are shaped by them but, in turn, also shape the human being.

The images evoked by these stories don't invite us to interpret them. They invite us to the possibilities of multiple narratives; to engage in a *bricolage* of ideas and perceptions. They invite us to leave aside a pure and simple analysis of the stories told, any form of categorization, iconoclastic analysis or use of a conceptual language. Rather, they invite us to take risks; to search on our own for the understanding of the analogies and patterns of similarities that the stories told awaken in each of the listeners. So they invite us to educate the way we see, to exchange the operational term which conducts our observation of images (not only these, but also the images from everyday life, from our fantasies, from our dreams). As Hillman (1977) and Adams (1989) put it, the operative term here becomes 'to look like' – 'this looks like that' – instead of what Freud and Jung proposed: 'this *means* that'.

FOLK TALES AND UNIVERSITY EDUCATION

We would like to present an experiment performed with students from the health and education areas in a Brazilian university, which consisted in using folk tales as an alternative approach to 'entrepreneurship'.

In the present context of Brazilian education a new 'era of knowledge' is being advertised, and entrepreneurship is one of its clichés. The 'entre-preneurship fashion trend' has led to a state of cultural amnesia, where many educators seem to ignore one of the foundations of education: education is one generation telling stories to younger generations – the transmission of knowledge. The prophets of 'entrepreneurship education' seem to forget that the transformations called 'History' are reactions to what the previous gener-ation has done. It is a process where previous references should be trans-formed and not discarded with a radical emphasis on the new. The young are encouraged to create their own history while abandoning the history of those who preceded them, in a movement which hypertrophiates the values of *puer*, denying and rejecting *senex*. This is an emphasis on the immediate, on the idea of success, efficacy and puerile combats, instead of deepening, insight, ana-logy, maturity and drama. One is led to ignore that the opposites contain and depend on each other. Nothing can be eliminated. At the most, it can be sent to the unconscious. Even then, one must submit oneself to the consequences of this rejection.

In his studies regarding the *puer aeternus* archetype, Hillman (1979, 1998) emphasizes some aspects which seem fundamental for the present debate. The *puer* represents the need to seek for the generative, the capacity to generate as a father, which is defined within the *puer–senex* polarity. Using an alchemic metaphor, the generation of the new is not linear, but circular, prefigured in the old. The emphasis is on the unity that is *puer-et-senex*, since the division of *puer* and *senex* hinders the capacity of making a spiritual discrimination of the multiple internal voices. Rather division replaces inner voices with a promiscuity of 'philosophies', techniques and globalizing 'formulas' that lead to passive inertia and imprisonment. When separated from *senex*, *puer* lacks order, reflection and limits that are necessary for one to love destiny and be guided by it towards the creation of oneself.

Distance from *senex* means distance from the spiritual father, who offers meaning and order, and is replaced by the mother: magic replaces *logos*. *Puer*, as Hillman states, needs to be acknowledged by his father so as to enable paternity in himself. This can be clearly seen in the Brazilian reality. The absence of a father, the overestimation of *puer* and the imprisonment in the realm of mothers – as well as the passivity, conformism and voracity associated with it – are constellated throughout Brazilian history. This may be one of the reasons for the fascination with *puerile* entrepreneurship.

Before continuing with an analysis of the current 'entrepreneurship fashion trend' in contemporary Brazil it is necessary to talk briefly about the origins of the construction of Brazilian identity and culture, as this is the basis for the *puer*/*senex* conflict mentioned above.

PUER, SENEX AND BRAZIL

Brazilian identity begins in the nation-forming at the end of the seventeenth and beginning of the eighteenth century, which is much later than the official 'discovery' of the territory by the Portuguese in 1500. According to Barreto (2000), even though the question: 'who is the Brazilian?' is a later one, the formation of Brazilian identity begins much earlier – initially with the fusion of Indians (the first, the 'non-Brazilians', the first ingredient of the blend) and Portuguese and later with the Africans and other peoples.[2]

Within this scope, the Brazilian dilemma of either preserving tradition or modernizing has much deeper roots. The initial mixture was accompanied by the destruction of the bases of Indian social life, denial of all their values, despoilment, captivity, slavery and depression which led many Indians to simply lie in their hammocks and die. Moreover, these Indians still suffered the scourge of the missionary preaching, where the 'good God from heaven fell upon them, like a wild dog, threatening to cast them in hell forever. Good and evil, virtue and sin, value and cowardice, everything became confused, "trans-exchanging" beauty for ugliness, evil with good' (Ribeiro 1995: 43).

One of the first consequences of this shock of cultures was the introduction of a social institution which enabled the formation of the Brazilian people: a practice called '*cunhadismo*' [brother-in-lawism]. This practice was an ancient Indian custom to incorporate strangers into the community and consisted in giving them an Indian woman for a wife. As soon as the newcomer took this woman for a wife, he would automatically establish a number of bonds which would make him a relative of all the group members. This was possible due to the Indian classificatory kinship system which relates all the members of the tribe to each other. Thus, his wife would become his *temerico* and the relatives from her parents' generation became his parents or parents-in-law. The same occurred in his own generation, where all became his brothers or brothers-in-law. In the younger generation, all were his children or children-in-law.

The Portuguese knew how to take advantage of this mechanism as an excellent source of free labour for the exploration of the natural resources of the new territory. As it was usual for a Portuguese man to have as many as 30 wives, a great number of bastards were born, lost between two worlds, neither fully Indian, nor Portuguese. Whole generations were marked by shame and failure, not initiated in either of the two worlds, immature, lacking either a Portuguese or an Indian soul. As they were not welcomed by either of these two groups, these lost people did not find shelter in the known human worlds and had to invent their own. The feeling of being abandoned resulted in the Brazilian feeling of orphanhood. The problematic identity (belonging neither to the forest, nor to the village) resulted in a feeling of 'no-onehood'. Up to today the Brazilian mixture is seen as negative by the so-called or self-proclaimed 'superior populations'. This awakens in the half-breed a reaction which is, on the one hand, compensatory (as expressed in a popular Brazilian saying: 'God is Brazilian') and, on the other, an egoic defense characterized by the depreciation of virtues such as patience, self-sacrifice and devotion. At that moment in history this generated the first traces of a culture marked by exploitation, theft and violence against their own peers.

In this new man's mentality, elements of amorality (due to the confusion of the moral references of the two founding groups), astuteness/cleverness trap (as survival strategies) and cruelty/coldness (as a strategy of facing a world which rejects him) are reinforced – the elements of a trickster.

On the other hand, the absence of a paternal principle leads to a proximity with the realm of mothers. The fatherless child travels to the opposite, to the mother, and takes refuge in nature, in search of magical solutions and satisfaction of desires instead of restraint, of collective renunciation in the name of the law and of moderate pleasure. The theme of abandonment – a radical one, where there still has not been a reconciliation with the origins – is complemented by the identification with the 'superior' people with the objective of reproducing a foreign identity as a substitute for the non-formed one.

Difficulties in establishing a fraternal relationship and in striving for a collective project follow the theme of abandonment. These problems include the need for identification, the absence of a father and the non-appreciation of the maternal origins. Such elements form a nucleus which, together with many others, shapes an infantile model for the Brazilian 'heroism'. This is marked by a latent destructivity and a culture of voracity. Here identification with fashion trends easily occurs, sustained by fantasies of power, independence, quick solutions and control, as with the ideas of 'entrepreneurship'.

Another aspect to be considered in the 'entrepreneurship fashion trend' is its perspective concerning the influence of the unconscious on the entrepreneur's attitude. It is a pragmatic perspective, made popular by the business gurus, who preach the manipulation of unconscious capacities as a strategy to improve performance and reach professional success.

The idea of performance in this context includes fantasies of control, efficiency, prestige and growth, which are an amalgam of conventional and

sedimentary ideas resistant to change. Although this interest in the unconscious is quite simplistic, it brings about an enormous potential for a 'work
with the soul' outside the traditional psychotherapeutic setting. The idea of
an effective performance in an enterprise can be used as a source of energy
which could mobilize individuals to engage in a process of amplification
and contact with deeper layers of the soul in a way which is not present in
traditional approaches to the theme.

Entrepreneurship, in this narrow-minded view, is understood as an attitude of conquest, persistence, combat and a struggle to fulfill dreams, corresponding to a *solar heroic* model, or a *diurnal* regime of relationship with the
world. This regime, according to Gilbert Durand (1980, 1988) is characterized by the use of exclusion, contradiction and identity as principles of
explanation. It is extremely efficient in situations that demand an active attitude: the entrepreneur as a stubborn and tireless individual, who never gives
up or retreats. But the refusal to acknowledge the principles of analogy and
resemblance result in an inflexible attitude with difficulty in adapting to
change.

It becomes evident that there is a need to incorporate traits of a *nocturnal*
relation with the world, which emphasizes different explanation principles:
commitment, indulgence and fusion. However, it is not a question of simply
moving from one extreme to the other, as one would be adopting a *mystical*
attitude, marked by withdrawal, perseverance, viscosity (refusal to separate),
sensory realism and miniaturization.

Our objective is to create conditions which enable the participants to bring
together the heroic, solar and 'masculine' principle and the nocturnal and
'feminine' principle, in a *synthetic* regime: an attitude of dissemination and
drama which enables causality and end, a mature confluence of present,
past and future. This goes beyond the narrow view that an entrepreneurship
attitude is linked only to the activity of opening businesses or generating
self-employment.

Story telling, bringing together imagination, experienced history and attitude, to re-elaborate them in the present, with the objective of building a
future, has been a way of representing, experiencing and reflecting about
experience. Establishing a dialogue with these powerful stories, through the
exercise and representation of multiple roles enables one to project images of
the unconscious into the daylit world (as figures, thoughts and actions). This
digestive and fermentative process enables *puer* to meet *senex*. According to
Hillman, we can't get rid of our complexes; it is them who give us up, their
time of decay is longer than an individual existence. It is necessary to give
them voice, to provide them with connotative meaning, establish a dialogue
with them. If they are abandoned, they will operate like a Karma and will be
fulfilled elsewhere.

STORYTELLING AND THE CLASSROOM

Brazil is rich in folk tales originating from the fusion of cultures of the people that formed the country. These folk tales reflect, with amazing clarity, the potentials and difficulties of these people. Four tales from the nineteenth century, gathered by Sílvio Romero (2000), a folklore researcher and literature historian, were selected: 'John plus Mary', 'The Hunter King', 'The Lazy Man' and 'The Black Bird'.

The stories were chosen because they represent the spontaneous effort of the Brazilian half-breed to build an autonomous identity within the colonist framework. Although independent, the tales connect themselves to represent metamorphoses, lack of equilibrium and compensations of a collective path in search of identity and causality.

The tales present a panorama of the Brazilian mythical identity fused in the three matrixes that Penna (1999) identifies as generators of the imaginary regarding Brazil: the notion of paradise, of hell and of the 'El Dorado'. As every culture pictures its present state as one of 'fall' and the previous state as one of lost happiness, the Portuguese colonizer – when faced with the new territory where the new people present themselves in a state of nudity, of apparent innocence and immersion in nature and sensuality – initially experiences a newfound paradise. In this movement, he is forced to promote a synthesis between his medieval and renaissance references of paradise: on the one hand the innocence described in Genesis; on the other, dealing with the erotism, idleness and gluttony which were in tune with the a renaissance re-paganization. 'There is no sin below the Equator!', was an interjection attributed to Gaspar van Baerle (1584–1648), alias Gaspar Barlaeus (1647/1940), which seems to have been a common saying in seventeenth century Europe. This vision of a discovered paradise, ready to be explored, contrasts itself with, for example, the vision of the Puritans who established themselves in North America, who were there, they said, to re-found paradise by their own efforts. This initial view of Brazil as paradise is followed by a vision of hell – a dive into the principle of reality – of a humid, wild place, full of pestilence, unbearably hot, full of beasts and unfriendly savages. It is a place where work was hindered by the heat and even reason becomes lazy and covered in sweat. Finally there comes a synthesis, a dialectical solution for the counter position of the two previous moments. 'The El Dorado', in its Brazilian version, is now the search for precious metals in the wild outback or the 'Legend of the Green Stones', where paradise appears in its new version – the wealth of the emeralds emerging from the green hell of the forests full of snakes and malaria.

The tales also present the condition of a people in the process of 'being made', as proposed by anthropologist Darcy Ribeiro (1995), having their Indian traditions abused, fused by force with the white and the black, originating a new African-Portuguese-Indian Romanity. In the beginning, 'society' really was a:

[C]onglomerate of multi-ethnical people, coming from Europe, Africa or natives . . . activated by the intense mixture, by the most brutal genocide in the extermination of tribal people and by the radical ethnocide in the de-characterization of the Indian and African contingents . . . para-doxically, ideal conditions for ethnical transfiguration . . . forced de-Indianization of the Indians and de-Africanization of the black man. Stripped of their identity, they are condemned to invent a new ethnicity which includes all of them . . . half-bred . . . with a few European white men . . . Surprisingly, what happens is that instead of becoming an over-seas Lusitania these newborn become a people in themselves, which, since then, struggles to become conscious of themselves and fulfill their possibilities . . . In truth, . . . a late and tropical Rome.

(Ribeiro 1995: 448)

Finally, the tales reflect the condition of a people rejected by the Portuguese 'father' and distant from the animic heritage of the Indian 'mother', as proposed by Jungian analyst Roberto Gambini (Dias and Gambini 1999). According to Gambini, in the Brazilian foundation myth, the vital bond between mother and son is cruelly ruptured so development is prevented.

[The relationship] between mother and son, fundamental for develop-ment, is eliminated right at the beginning. Thus the question of uncon-sciousness is already present – he can't know where he came from. He can't be loved, nourished and protected by this mother; he can't mirror her, nor can he relate to a father who is absent from the story. The hero will undertake his journey without the necessary conditions to fulfill his destiny. He doesn't come to the end of his historical path. However, this is, in our opinion, a perfect expression of the hero archetype, as it expresses what happens in Brazil. Here, the hero cannot be complete. What would the non-impeded heroism be? Constitute ourselves fully as an individuality integrating the three races.

(Dias and Gambini 1999: 129)

The first tale, 'John plus Mary' – a reforging of Hansel and Gretel – describes our collective orphanhood (or illegitimacy). The children in this story are not abandoned due to hunger or family tragedy as in the European versions. They are abandoned simply because the parents wanted to be relieved of their obligation towards them. Besides this, John and Mary do not function harmoniously as counterparts, but as elements in conflict. This can be seen when, after the death of the witch, Mary tries to put an end to her brother's life with the help of a lover. The tale presents the limiting aspects of the Brazilian maternal complex and the conflict between the chthonic and spiritual aspects of the feminine, with a constant return to the first. It also shows the dramatic aspects of the imprisonment of the collective identity in this pattern, and the perverse consequences of an absence of paternal moderation, of the privation and immaturity as a consequence of this condition in a culture which is predatory of its peers. The solution of the drama does not, like its European counterparts, lead to the expected return home and reconciliation with the original situation.

The second tale – 'The Hunter King' – presents the dissociation of the Brazilian collective conscious from its foundations, the passivity and precocious aging of a culture which has lost contact with its most profound values. It is a story of a passive quest for renewal and a childish effort of reconciliation with the feminine.

The third tale, 'The Lazy Man', also presents the theme of a radical dependence on a negative maternal complex, leading to a passivity which induces laziness and theft. However, an elderly man is introduced who induces the characters to error, stimulating their negative traits just enough to overcome their lack of initiative. Besides him, there is a hardworking servant (the shadow of the lazy man and his wife). As in the previous tales, the sacrificial theme is present. Here it is considered a fundamental element to awaken a fraternal relationship according to legal principles.

The initiation situation presented in the fourth tale – 'The Blackbird' – enables a reflection about the dialectic of the shadow from another perspective: the variations of racial prejudice, disrespect and oppression which underlie our Brazilian culture. Mediated by a spiritual godfather (the blackbird) we are led to re-encounter the 'Negro Gaforinho', a projection of the 'poor, black and renegated' elements. Starting from the traditional situation of 'the door which should not be opened', stages which cover the realm of the Great Mother, the different forms of relating to *eros*, the virile element and the conjunction of the lunar feminine with the solar masculine are overcome. There is a revitalization of inauthentic and perverted cultural forms presenting a revealing side effect: the adolescent managed to marry the princess, but takes the throne amalgamated to his new identity of Negro Gaforinho. So the new, the half-bred, is born through the impulse to miscegenation which united the princess to 'Pai Gaforinho' (an old, black beggar).

METHODOLOGY

A 'Trojan Horse approach' was used to work with university students. Eager to 'develop entrepreneurship skills' they ended up being exposed to an opportunity of expanding the heroic and solar vision of their own behaviour, with a more synthetic, deep, critical and contemplative perspective. As the students interact with the projection of the Brazilian soul onto the imported European mythologems, they operate with patterns of behaviour still present in their relationship with others, with work and with environment.

The workshop aims to show the participants that the struggle of the *entrepreneur hero* is much more against internal than external opponents. And also that there is another entrepreneurship posture, a *synthetic* one, which unites the combative aspect of the *hero* (explorer, colonizer) and the critical and contemplative aspect of the exploited. This posture connects the active entrepreneurship aspect with a reflective one. It is now possible to use the insight gained in the analysis of external and especially internal difficulties to overcome them.

Operating with a diurnal approach to entrepreneurship, the difficulties are projected onto a figure of 'The Brazilian'. The individual, however, excludes himself from this category, avoiding the unconscious dilemmas and the cultural conflicts which sustain this situation. This is an example of a 'cultural complex' (Kimbles 2000, Kimbles 2003, Singer and Kimbles 2004). These are defined as complexes which operate simultaneously in the collective psyche and in the psyche of each one of the group members, supporting collective beliefs and emotions which operate in the group dynamics. We are faced with the challenge of enabling people to become aware of these complexes, of bringing them to the surface.

The work included exercises where the participants' fantasies and projections were constellated in a concrete way. The following steps were taken:

1   The tales were narrated in the traditional manner.
2   The participants debated the tales, dealing with them as 'business cases'. The associations brought up were discussed by the participants. The facilitators stimulated the debate, but did not, at this moment, interpret any of the contents.
3   The theoretical aspects (associations with theory, interpretations, amplifications) were presented by the facilitators and debated with the group.
4   The contents of the tales were then re-explored with expressive techniques (drawing, hand puppets, painting, etc.).
5   The tales were retold/relived as psychodrama, with the possibility of re-evaluating roles, performing and learning new attitudes.
6   As a final step a new processing session was held where the participants related the tales to their personal history, and shared, among themselves, the associations these tales had awakened in them.

RESULTS

The results were surprising, as these participants often consider themselves highly practical and intellectualized, and thus have difficulty in approaching their own conflicts in the psyche, and consequently, their imaginative force. Telling, reflecting and representing stories mobilized energy, unlocking rich psychic contents. The series of stories retold were a continuous and practical confrontation with contents of the unconscious. In this context, the group acted as a vehicle for the individual encounter with the soul. The process of an encounter with the unconscious, added to the effects produced by the group activity (where the members mutually supported each other), and resulted in a curious experience of initiation: a method or path which makes the internal world accessible. In the exercise of telling and representing, both the psyche and body are activated, making the perceptions in relation to oneself, others and the world clearer and allowing people to understand more precisely, as Jung put it, fantasies of which they only had a vague presentiment.

As an example, one of the participants fell asleep for a few minutes during the debates. Suddenly she woke happy and excited. She then told the group about her past: the many businesses she had set up and which were not successful. While sleeping she had been invaded by a story which seemed to continue the discussions about the tales: she had set up a new business, a textile industry, and was very excited: she would finally be successful because she had found 'the colour which did not exist'.

The overall objective of the work is to guide people to a new dimension of work with themselves, offering them the possibility of going beyond the surface and objectivity of everyday life, to a place where it is possible to find renewal and nourishment in 'colours that did not exist'. The proposal should lead participants to resist speeding up and conformism. Instead, they should seek a re-encounter with the complexity and serenity of *senex*, in the digestion and fermentation which can lead to reflection and transform complexes into a source of generative energy.

In all of the tales there will always be an attempt at stimulating a form of enactment: encouraging creative interaction and dialogue aiming at activating a sense of personal causality and re-encountering personal and collective history. The greatest challenge for any work that aims at approaching intrapsychic issues is finding a way to extend the newfound perspective to everyday activities and routine. In order to amplify and deepen the insights obtained by means of intrapsychic work, the 'Trojan horse approach' was used once again. At the time, the work was continued through an approach which brings together both coaching, common in the organizational environment, and brief therapy to root the new perceptions into daily life. In this case, the coach plays a role similar to that of the Chinese Shi fu: facilitator of the individual encounter with the soul.

The feedback of the participants at the end of the workshop was highly positive. However, we expect the reflections and insights gained in the workshop to be further developed. As many of the results and impacts would only be seen after some time, a precise evaluation is difficult. Some participants were followed in the Psychological Support Department of the school, and a change in posture in many of them could be seen: they have become more reflective, critical and aware of their emotions, conflicts and fantasies. A more responsible and committed attitude has led the participants to a more creative approach towards their difficulties and their own careers.

Experiences such as those narrated by the participants indicate the force, power and the reality of the mythopoetic function of the psyche: we live to produce stories, to claim ownership over them, to transform and be transformed by them. These stories compel the individuals to a succession of sensations, thoughts and emotions which, if welcomed, nursed and digested will lead to a much greater understanding of oneself.

Why do these stories move us? Because of the story told or because we can identify our personal history in them? Because we have the tendency to make our personal history epic? Where does the strength that animates them come from? Perhaps from those primordial stories. From those stories which remind us of the darkness in the caves; of the clearings and the fires lit in the middle of the jungle; of the elders telling stories in the deserts; of the wood-burning stoves which were always lit. Stories that come from somewhere which is neither here nor there, but from somewhere in between. Stories which cross over into our world, coming from the fields of dreams, from the *mundus imaginalis*.

James Hillman refers to these stories as resonance boxes which echo present life or strings which resonate the small melodies of everyday life. The story is sometimes an auxiliary, sometimes a wise mentor. When talking about these stories it is possible to talk about the gods without actually taking them as material entities. It is possible, however, to simultaneously perceive their reality, as everything is in the mind. To what kind of needs did the gods expose the ancients? To what kind of needs do the gods, even if still unnamed, expose our souls? What kind of sacrifices do they – the eternally enigmatic – expect from us?

Perhaps to answer these questions, we should reflect on the words of Hillman:

> Remember: what the Greeks said their Gods asked for above all else, and perhaps only, was not blood; it was not to be forgotten, that is, to be kept in mind, recollected as *psychological facts*. For me, that's the value of history. It keeps events in mind, lest we forget. So, the task is re-finding again and again ways of remembering the divine and human, and not repeating what once worked assuming it goes on working. Above all, the task of re-finding means abandoning complaint, abandoning nostalgia, not bemoaning the lost connection in a *durftige Zeit* (dry time). For the complaint only limns the desolation of today against a vividly meaningful 'history', driving the sacred ever farther from the secular and leaving contemporary life without divine presences, a condition which Giegerich describes in the last desperate sentence of his paper as 'the emptiness, meaninglessness, unrealness'.

> (Hillman 1994: 5)

This is the value of these stories, this is the value of the impressions they awakened and the memories they evoked. Such value is an invitation to look carefully at them and, who knows, indulge oneself in the experience of interacting with them.

NOTES

1 Nise da Silveira (1905–1999) was a psychiatrist from Alagoas state, responsible for the introduction of Carl Gustav Jung's ideas in Brazil. Her life is full of noteworthy facts. She was the first woman to graduate in Medicine from the University of Bahia (the only woman in a class of 150 men). As a pioneer in the use of plastic expression to treat psychotic disorders she fought against the generalization of the use of aggressive treatment techniques which were popular at the time (electroconvulsive therapy, insulin shock therapy and lobotomy). She was arrested for political reasons and sent to prison during the 'New State' (the dictatorial period in Brazil which lasted from 1937 to 1945) where she inspired Graciliano Ramos, a famous Brazilian author, to write 'A terra dos meninos pelados' [the land of the naked boys]. She was a pioneer in the use of contact with animals as an auxiliary psychotherapeutic resource in the treatment of mentally ill patients. She created the Museu de Imagens do Inconsciente [Museum of Images from the Unconscious] at the Engenho de Dentro psychiatric hospital, which has a unique collection of artwork from psychiatric patients, and Casa das Palmeiras [Palm Tree House], an institution to treat people who have left psychiatric hospitals, using expressive activities in an outpatient unit. This anticipated by many years a concept which is now common.
2 This and other reflections on the formation of identity in the Brazilian culture presented in this article are impregnated with ideas from a series of debates with Professor Marco Heleno Barreto (from the Centro de Estudos Superiores da Companhia de Jesus) during the celebration of the 500 years of discovery of Brazil (in 2000). These ideas echo a much broader analysis, developed by Professor Barreto, regarding the 'identity' within the difficult situations of relationship and reconciliation of Brazilian 'heroes' among themselves and with the land, presented in popular folklore tales of the nineteenth century.

REFERENCES

Adams, M. V. (1989) 'Deconstructive Philosophy and Imaginal Psychology: Comparative Perspectives on Jacques Derrida and James Hillman', in Rajnath (ed.), *Deconstruction: A Critique*, London: Macmillan, 138–157.

Barlaeus, G. von (1647/1940) *Rerum per octennium in Brasília et álibi gestarum sub praefectura illustrissimi Comitis J. Mauritii Nassoviae*, Amsterdam: 1647/Clave, 1659/S. Paulo, 1940.

Barreto, M. H. (2000) 'A mãe que entrega a filha ao bicho: uma fantasia brasileira', *Junguiana*, Vol. 18: 41–52.

Corbin, H. (1964) 'Mundus imaginalis ou l'imaginaire et "imaginal" ', *Cahiers International du Symbolisme*, Paris: Berg International.

Dias, L. and R. Gambini (1999) 'Outros 500', São Paulo: Editora SENAC.

Durand, G. (1980) 'As estruturas antropológicas do imaginário', Lisboa: Editorial Presença.

—— (1988) 'A imaginação Simbólica', São Paulo: *Cultrix* / Ed. Da Universidade de São Paulo.

Hillman, J. (1977) 'An inquiry into image', *Spring: A Journal of Archetype and Culture*, Vol. 37: 62–88.

—— (1979) 'A Grande Mãe, seu Filho, seu Herói, e O Puer', in Vitale, Augusto et al. (eds) *Pais e Mães: Seis estudos sobre o fundamento arquetípico da psicologia da família*, São Paulo: Edições Símbolo.

—— (1994), 'Once More into the Fray – A Response to Wolfgang Giegerich's "Killings" ', *Spring: A Journal of Archetype and Culture*, Vol. 56: 1–18.

—— (1998) *O livro do Puer, ensaios sobre o Arquétipo do Puer Aeternus*, São Paulo: Paulus.

Kimbles, S. (2000) 'The Cultural Complex and the Myth of Invisibility', in Thomas Singer (ed.) *The Vision Thing: Myth, Politics and Psyche in the World*, London: Routledge.

—— (2003) 'Five key points on cultural complexes', Seattle: C.G. Jung Society. Online, available at: http://www.jungseattle.org/w03/IP_Winter2003_final.pdf? (accessed 21 December 2007).

Penna, J. O. M. (1999) 'Em berço esplêndido: ensaios de psicologia coletiva brasileira', Rio de Janeiro: Instituto Liberal/Top Books.

Ribeiro, D. (1995) 'O povo brasileiro: a formação e o sentido do Brasil', São Paulo: Companhia das Letras.

Romero, S. (2000) 'Contos populares do Brasil', São Paulo: Landy Editora.

Singer, T. and S. L. Kimbles (2004) *The Cultural Complex*, London: Brunner-Routledge.

Silveira, N. (1981) *Imagens do inconsciente*, Rio de Janeiro: Alhambra.

Glossary

Words marked with [*] are Jungian terms included in this Glossary.

Active imagination* This is the term Jung gave to his therapeutic method of asking a patient to spontaneously fantasize upon an image, usually a dream image. By this method, unconscious* material may be brought into consciousness, and individuation* is promoted. Active imagination is the opposite of conscious invention: it is a method of surrendering the direction of fantasies to the other or the unconscious. Most often, active imagination indicates the use of a person's own unconscious image from a dream, but Jung argued that cultural, mythical or artistic images could also be used.

Alchemy Alchemy was more than the doomed and greedy attempt to turn lead into gold as some Renaissance literature alleges. It also included philosophical and religious beliefs that held that mind, matter and divine spirit existed in a continuum. Alchemists tried to refine the soul from its incarceration in base matter. Gold and lead were the material aspects of substances that were equally psychological and divine. Therefore mental and spiritual work existed alongside the chemical operations that became the precursor to modern chemistry.

Alchemy, Jungian* Alchemy, Jungian is defined by Jung as a projection of psychic contents, specifically the individuation* process, onto the chemical activities of the alchemist. He interpreted alchemy texts as demonstrating the projection of unconscious processes and alchemists as unwitting self-analysts. Alchemists developed symbols. Jung believed that alchemical symbols enabled psychological transformations similar to the role of dreams in his psychology. In his view, alchemists used chemistry and symbolic language to stimulate their own individuation so that they could reach the 'gold' of union with the divine or self archetype*.

Amplification* Amplification is a Jungian therapeutic technique in which a psychic image (such as from a dream) is *amplified* by linking it to a mythological motif. This serves to make the image appear less personal and so suggests something of the 'otherness' of the unconscious.

Consequently, amplification tends to downplay questions of the personal or cultural history of a person.

Anima* The anima is the archetype of the feminine in the unconscious of a man. In that this locates a feminine mode in the subjectivity of the masculine gender, denoting a bisexual unconscious, this is a helpful concept. However, at times, Jung uses his own unconscious anima as a model for designating female subjectivity as 'more unconscious' than males'. Remembering that all archetypes are plural and androgynous mitigates the stress of gender opposition, modelled upon heterosexuality. A male's unconscious is not purely or necessarily feminine or vice versa. (See also animus*, Eros*, Logos*, gender.)

Animus* The animus is the archetype of masculinity in the unconscious of a woman. Like the anima, this does not lock Jungian theory into perpetual gender opposition since the unconscious contains androgynous archetypes. Nothing can be securely known or fixed in the unconscious. So masculinity is rather one of a series of types of 'otherness' for the psyche of a woman.

Archetypal images* Archetypal images are the visible representations of archetypes. A single image can never account for the multifarious potential of the archetype. Consequently, archetypal images have a metaphorical connection to the archetype. Archetypal images are always creative yet provisional and partial images of a greater unrepresentable complexity. Crucially, they do draw representative material from culture as well as shaping energy from the archetype. Therefore Jungian psychic archetypal imagery is always cultural and historical as well as numinous and psychic.

Archetypes* Archetypes are inherited structuring patterns in the unconscious with potentials for meaning formation and images. They are unrepresentable in themselves and evident only in their manifest derivatives, archetypal images. Archetypes are containers of opposites and so are androgynous, equally capable of manifesting themselves as either gender or non-human forms. The archetype is psychosomatic meaning that it links body and psyche, instinct and image. Body and culture will influence the content of archetypal images but not govern them because archetypes are the structuring principles of an *autonomous* psyche*. Archetypes are not inherited ideas or images. When actually called upon to define archetypes, Jung insisted that they were not inherited contents. (See archetypal images*, unconscious*.)

Autonomous/objective psyche* Jung believed that the unconscious was largely independent of the understanding of the ego. He spoke of an 'objective' psyche, meaning that the unconscious was autonomous. It could initiate a relationship with the ego thorough the desirable process of individuation*.

Body* The Jungian notion of the body is of both a separate, unknowable entity and something that is vitally connected to the psyche. Archetypes are rooted in the body as well as having a transcendent spiritual dimension. For Jung the body cannot control signifying, but it does influence it. For example, sexuality is a bodily function that can liberate archetypal energies. A sexual act has its bodily integrity, yet it may simultaneously become a rite, entering a numinous dimension that alchemists (and Jung after them) called a sacred marriage.

Collective unconscious* The collective unconscious is the common inheritance of archetypes that all human beings share. Everybody is born with them in the same way. How the archetypes are then manifested as archetypal images will depend upon the particular culture and history of any individual.

Consciousness* Consciousness is that part of the psyche realized by the ego*. It is the known and knowable about every human person. For Jung, psychic health requires that consciousness needs to be in touch with healing unconscious powers through individuation*. One way to be in contact with the unconscious is in the enjoyment of art.

Counter-transference* (see transference*) This refers to the tendency of the unconscious contents of the analyst to get projected onto the patient in analysis. Jung was one of the first to realize the importance of this phenomenon.

Dreams* Unlike the Freudian usage, dreams to a Jungian are spontaneous expressions or communications from a superior part of the human mind. They are not derivative of ego concerns or necessarily about sexuality (unless they belong to the trivial class of dreams derived from the residue of the psychic processing of the previous day). Dream images are not secondary. They are a *primary* form of reality and must not be 'translated' into the mode of the ego, into words. Jung thought something very similar about art, that it could offer a primary mode of expression of the unconscious if it fell into the visionary* category of art in which the artist is possessed by the archetypal imagination.

Ego* The ego is the centre of consciousness concerned with the sense of a personal identity, the maintenance of personality and the sense of continuity over time. However, Jung considered the ego as something less than the whole personality, as it was constantly interacting with more significant archetypal forces in the unconscious. Jung tended to equate the ego with consciousness in his writings.

Enantiodromia* This term expresses a core Jungian insight – that in the psyche things have the habit of turning into their own opposite. The emergence of opposites in the unconscious is a frequent characteristic of individuation*.

Eros* Eros is another of Jung's concepts based upon gendered opposites. Its other is Logos*. Eros stands for psychic capacities of relatedness and feeling, with Logos as a motif of spiritual meaning and reason. Jung aligned feminine consciousness with Eros and masculine subjectivity with Logos. Since the anima* and animus* carry Eros and Logos qualities in the unconscious, this means that males tend to have underdeveloped qualities of relating; females tend to be inferior in 'thinking' and rational argument. The consequences for Jung's views on gender are profound.

Feminine principle* The feminine principle is a name Jung gave to the qualities of Eros*, feeling, relationship, connectedness, that he expected were the characteristics of women's consciousness. After Jung, some Jungians expanded this archetype of mental functioning to something even more overtly metaphysical. Masculine and feminine principles exist transcendently in the psyche, and men and women have to negotiate them in order to forge a gender identity. The feminine principle may operate *within* cultures, but also exists independently of them in the human mind.

God-image* The Jungian archetype of the self* is frequently represented by a divine or god-image in the psyche. This is because the unconscious self is the goal of individuation, the supreme desire of the person's psyche. Therefore it is likely to produce spontaneous divine images. (See self*, religious experience*, individuation*.)

Individuation* Individuation is Jung's term for the process whereby the ego is brought into a relationship with the archetypal dynamics of the unconscious. In individuation the ego is constantly made, unmade and re-made by the goal-directed forces of the unconscious. Even 'meaning' in the ego is subject to dissolution and re-constitution by the Jungian other. For Jung, the making of art or the appreciation of art was a form of individuation because it was a confrontation with the other in the imagination.

Logos* A principle of mental functioning oriented towards reason, discrimination, and spiritual authority. Jung regarded it as characteristic of masculine consciousness. Logos operates in a gendered binary opposite with Eros*. Contemporary Jungian analytic practice treats Logos and Eros as equally available to both genders.

Mythology and myth Mythology conventionally refers to a culture's stories of gods, goddesses, monsters and divine beings that have performed a religious function in various human societies. Examples would include the mythologies of ancient Greece and Rome. Christianity may be regarded as a mythology. However, to Jung, myth is a form of language that enables some participation in the unexplored, and in some sense unconquerable territories of the mind. (Jung was aware of the colonial dimension of his psychology-writing with its topos of space and landscape, which is one of his potential contributions to postcolonialism.) To Jung, myth poses a double psychic potency. It is at the same time the most authentic representation of the interplay of conscious and unconscious, and it is an active intervention shaping such inner dialogue. So myth is both a healing technique for when the unconscious threatens mental chaos and, simultaneously, a true expression of the mutuality of the two aspects of the psyche: conscious and unconscious. For Jung and Jungian literary theory true *expression* of the psyche is privileged over conceptually based claims to *know* it. The human psyche is a myth-making organ that needs to creatively engage with the 'other' through such cultural practices as fairy tales, religion or art. To Jung, finding such means of expression is very important since he regarded the making of art as therapeutic for both the individual and the wider culture. Such a belief finds realization in Jung's own texts, which are written so as to include the creativity of the psyche. So when readers complain of a struggle to 'make sense' of Jung's texts they are closer than they know to their rhetorical heart. He himself regarded his writing as a kind of myth-making aimed at healing the alienated psyche of modernity.

Persona*   The persona is the mask worn by the ego in the outer world. It is the way that the ego adapts to present a coherent personality in social situations. Overidentification with the persona means that more challenging forces from the unconscious are being ignored. Individuation* means detaching identity from the persona in order to engage with the unconscious.

Personal unconscious*   The personal unconscious is the way that Jung drew Freudian ideas into his mature thought. What was important about the unconscious to Jung was the collective unconscious of archetypes. The personal unconscious is a Freudian unconscious created by oedipal sexual repression. It is 'personal' because it is formed through the structuring of the ego and does not refer to the superior autonomous/objective psyche*.

Phallus   To Lacan, the phallus is a privileged signifier. It represents the cultural form of patriarchy, the imposition of the Law of the Father, when a person is split by entry into the symbolic. Although it is not to be equated to the fleshly penis, the phallus organizes a person's gender upon entry to language and the symbolic. The phallus is what the masculine very ambivalently 'has' and what the feminine must 'be' for the masculine. The effect of the phallus is to make the masculine the natural home of power and meaning.

Psychic reality*   To Jung all reality is psychic. I know nothing that has not already been filtered through my psychic processing or, more radically, has not been constructed as knowledge by my psyche. What the 'I' knows is *in the first place* psychic, whatever other exterior reality that it might also claim.

Psychological art   Jung divided art into psychological and visionary* categories. Psychological art consists mainly of signs*, which point to what is known or knowable. Consequently, psychological art expresses mainly the collective consciousness of a society – what the collective is consciously debating or concerned about. Jung felt that in some art, the artist has already done most of the psychic work for the audience – hence 'psychological' work. On the other hand it is worth remembering that the unconscious cannot be totally excluded from art. So even psychological works may demonstrate a symbolic or visionary core. Psychological and visionary are linked categories pushed apart to polar extremes, not different realms.

Religious experience*   Following on from psychic reality*, religious experience in Jungian theory is distinctive because to Jung all experience is mediated through the psyche and its inherited structuring principles of archetypes. Consequently, any religious feeling can be located in the psyche and is a property of the supreme governing archetype of the self. Therefore to Jung, religious experience is indistinguishable from intimations of the self. This idea of religious feeling as psychological structuring could harmonize with external religions (especially when Christ is named a self-image) but could also validate religious experience without an external transcendent God. It is not reducible to a mythologizing of bodily drives.

Self*   The self is the supreme governing archetype of the unconscious to which the ego becomes subject in individuation*. Jung frequently described self-images in dreams in circular or mandala forms. He argued that Christ functioned as a self-image in Christianity. What is crucial here is to remember that 'self' for Jung means the not-known, the unknowable in the individual person. The self is to be found in the unconscious. It does not stand for the conscious personality.

Shadow*   The shadow is the archetypal forces of blackness, reversal or undoing. Intrinsic to the idea of a compensatory relation between ego and unconscious, the shadow is that which is denied in conscious personality. Consequently the shadow could be figured as the potential evil within everyone. Jung warned that the shadow needed to be brought into a relationship with conscious personality lest repression caused it to swell in power and break out in neurosis or violence.

Signs   Jung divided images into two types of signifying, signs and symbols*. Signs point to a known or knowable meaning. They are therefore concerned primarily with the collective consciousness and are the main ingredient of psychological art*.

Sublime   The sublime exists both in Romanticism at the time of the Enlightenment and in postmodernism. In both it signifies what can be conceived but not fully represented in culture and in the mind. For example, the divine can be a concept, but many of the possible meanings of divinity are unthinkable, ineffable. Jung offers a transition from the Romantic to the postmodern sublime.

Subtle body*   The body as imaged in the psyche is a Jungian subtle body because it is formed by both bodily and archetypal ingredients. Because archetypes are of the body as well as the non-bodily psyche, mental representations of the body are both physical and psychical – the subtle body.

Symbolic, Jungian* Jungian theory also implies a symbolic, with crucial differences to that of Lacan. Because for Jung, the unconscious is not *determined* by repression, and contains autonomous androgynous principles called archetypes, Jung's symbolic does not necessarily repress the feminine. In the Jungian symbolic, feminine imagery can exist for itself. It is not doomed to function as a screen for masculine fantasy.

Symbols Jung divided images into two types of signifying, symbols and signs*. Symbols point to what is hardly known, not yet known, or unknowable. They are therefore the chief conduit for the collective unconscious in dreams and in art. Symbols make up most of the fabric of visionary* art. Archetypal images very often manifest as symbols in which the term stands for their numinous quality.

Synchronicity* Jung used this term to describe the linking of events not by cause and effect, not by time and space, but by psychological coherence. For example if a total stranger suddenly meets a person's vital need with no apparent explanation – that is synchronicity. It refers to Jung's notion that psyche, matter, time and space are all fundamentally connected.

Transcendent function* The transcendent function occurs when conflicts within the psyche spontaneously produce some powerful symbol 'transcending' the warring forces and so able to unite them. The transcendent function produces symbols that point to the unknown in the unconscious – they must not be reduced to words, which are the ego's language.

Transference* Developed first by Freud, transference is the idea that, in analysis, the patient will use the analyst as a screen for his/her fantasies. The analyst may come to embody a parent or a set of psychic conflicts for the patient. (See counter-transference*.)

Unconscious* Jung's unconscious is his key contribution to psychology and is fundamental to all developments of Jungian theory. Like Freud, the term unconscious denotes both mental contents inaccessible to the ego and a psychic arena with its own properties and functions. The Jungian unconscious is superior to the ego and exists in a compensatory relation to it. It is the locus of meaning, feeling and value in the psyche and is autonomous. It is not, however, completely separate from the body but offers a third place between that perennial duality, body and spirit. Body and culture influence unconscious contents (archetypal images), but the unconscious is not *subject* to either force. The unconscious is structured by archetypes as hypothetical inherited structuring principles.

Visionary art Jung divided art into psychological* and categories. Visionary art mainly consists of symbols*, which point to what is not yet known or unknowable in the culture. Consequently, visionary art is primarily expressive of the collective unconscious. As such it *compensates* the culture for its biases, brings to consciousness what is *ignored* or repressed, and may *predict* something of the future direction of the culture. It is worth remembering that the ego or consciousness cannot be excluded from a work of art, so nothing is one hundred percent of the unconscious. Visionary and psychological are linked categories pushed apart to polar extremes, not wholly different realms.

Index

Lightning Source UK Ltd.
Milton Keynes UK
UKHW021151160320
360414UK00008B/2122